PRENTICE-HALL FOUNDATIONS OF
MODERN PSYCHOLOGY SERIES

Richard S. Lazarus, Editor

The Psychological Development of the Child, 3rd ed., Paul Mussen

Tests and Measurements, 3rd ed., Leona E. Tyler and W. Bruce Walsh

Personality, 3rd ed., Richard S. Lazarus and Alan Monat

Clinical Psychology, 2nd ed., Julian B. Rotter

Perception, 2nd ed., Julian E. Hochberg

Learning, 2nd ed., Sarnoff A. Mednick, Howard R. Pollio, and Elizabeth F. Loftus

Social Psychology, 2nd ed., William W. Lambert and Wallace E. Lambert

Organizational Psychology, 3rd ed., Edgar H. Schein

Abnormal Psychology, Sheldon Cashdan

Humanistic Psychology, John B. P. Shaffer

School Psychology, Jack I. Bardon and Virginia C. Bennett

EDGAR H. SCHEIN

Sloan Fellows Professor of Management
Massachusetts Institute of Technology

Organizational
Psychology

3rd edition

PRENTICE-HALL, INC., Englewood Cliffs, N.J. 07632

Library of Congress Cataloging in Publication Data

Schein, Edgar H
  Organizational psychology.
  (Foundations of modern psychology series)
  Bibliography: p.
  Includes index.
  1. Psychology, Industrial. 2. Industrial
sociology. I. Title.
HF5548.8.S35 1980   158.7   79-18086
ISBN 0-13-641340-4
ISBN 0-13-641332-3 pbk.

Prentice-Hall
Foundations of Modern Psychology Series
Richard S. Lazarus, Editor

© 1980, 1970, 1965 by Prentice-Hall, Inc., Englewood Cliffs, N.J. 07632

Printed in the United States of America

10 9 8 7 6 5 4

Editorial/Production supervision by
Marina Harrison/Barbara Kelly
Interior design and cover design by
Virginia Soulé
Manufacturing buyer:
Ed Leone

Prentice-Hall International, Inc., London
Prentice-Hall of Australia Pty. Limited, Sydney
Prentice-Hall of Canada, Ltd., Toronto
Prentice-Hall of India Private Limited, New Delhi
Prentice-Hall of Japan, Inc., Tokyo
Prentice-Hall of Southeast Asia Pte. Ltd., Singapore
Whitehall Books Limited, Wellington, New Zealand

Contents

vi

ORGANIZATIONAL STRUCTURE AND DYNAMICS
183

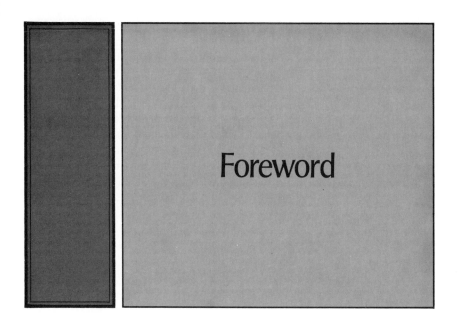

Foreword

The Foundations of Modern Psychology Series was the first and most successful in what became a trend in psychology toward groups of short texts dealing with various basic subjects, each written by an active authority. It was conceived with the idea of providing greater flexibility for instructors teaching general courses than was ordinarily available in the large, encyclopedic textbooks, and greater depth of presentation for individual topics not typically given much space in introductory textbooks.

The earliest volumes appeared in 1963, the latest in 1980 with the continuing expansion of the series into new areas of psychology. They are in widespread use as supplementary texts, or as the text, in various undergraduate courses in psychology, education, public health, sociology, and social work; and clusters of volumes have served as textbooks for undergraduate courses in general psychology. Groups of volumes have been translated into many languages including Danish, Dutch, Finnish, French, German, Hebrew, Italian, Japanese, Malaysian, Norwegian, Polish, Portuguese, Spanish, and Swedish.

With wide variation in publication date and type of content, some of the volumes have needed revision, while others have not. We have left this decision to the individual author. Some have remained unchanged, some have been modestly changed and updated, and still others completely rewritten. We have also opted for variation in length and style to reflect the different ways in which they have been used as texts.

There has never been stronger interest in good teaching in our colleges and universities than there is now; and for this the availability of high quality, well-written, and stimulating text materials highlighting the exciting and continuing search for knowledge is a prime requisite. This is especially the case in undergraduate courses where large numbers of students must have access to suitable readings. The Foundations of Modern Psychology series represents an ongoing attempt to provide college teachers with the most authoritative and flexible textbook materials we can create.

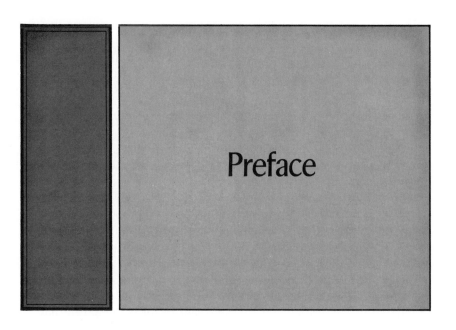

Preface

When I wrote the first edition of *Organizational Psychology* in 1965 I commented that the field was "new and in flux." In the preface to the Second Edition in 1970 I remarked that the field was "still in the process of formation." After three years of struggling with the Third Edition I can only conclude that the field has arrived. The number of textbooks on organizational behavior, managerial psychology, and industrial and organizational psychology; the number of review articles in the *Annual Review of Psychology* and the *Annual Review of Sociology*; the sheer number of research studies on all aspects of human behavior in organizations, all these things taken together can only be described as an explosion of the field. Moreover, not only is there an explosion on the academic side, with a rapidly growing number of programs in business schools aimed at various aspects of organizational "science," but there is a comparable explosion on the practitioner side, with large numbers of public and private organizations using internal and external consultants to deal with the full range of psychological and human problems in organizations.

This explosion of the field has created some real problems in structuring a Third Edition of *Organizational Psychology*. Simply revising and updating was not possible because the emphasis in the field has shifted. It has become more interdisciplinary; organization theory has advanced and made it possible to talk more constructively about organization structure and design; certain topics—such as leadership—have received so much attention that I could no longer discuss them in the context of other concepts. What I have attempted to do is to retain from the earlier editions those organizing concepts which for me still help to structure the field and make sense of it. I have added an explicitly developmental and sociological point of view to reflect the increasing interdisciplinarity of the field, even though the label "organizational *psychology*" still seems appropriate to me. Beyond that I have added a great quantity of new material, attempting to reflect the most important new concepts and research findings of the last ten years. I have also sought to keep a "story line" because I believe that the field still needs to be structured around certain key themes or concepts, including (1) managerial assumptions about human nature, (2) the psychological contract, and (3) the organization as a dynamic, open, coping, developing system.

I am also aware of leaving out a great deal, in some cases by choice, in many cases because of my sheer inability to keep up with the field. For the unwitting omissions I apologize to my colleagues at the outset. Though this edition is much larger than the first two, I am still trying to write *about* the field, not to *cover* the entire field as a full-blown textbook might.

Many people have helped my thinking and have helped to improve the manuscript by reacting to portions of it as it developed. I am especially grateful to my colleagues John Van Maanen, Lotte Bailyn, Ralph Katz, Dick Beckhard, and Jim Driscoll for providing a continuing source of stimulation and specific help with some of the chapters. I am also greatly indebted to Professor T. W. Bonham of the Virginia Polytechnic Institute, Gordon Lippitt of George Washington University, John Wakely of Michigan State University, Robert Rice of the State University of New York at Buffalo, Bill McKelvey of the University of California at Los Angeles, Matthew Arnett of Northeastern University, Steve Kerr of the University of Southern California, and John Slocum of Southern Methodist University who viewed the first draft for the publisher and provided extremely honest, detailed, and helpful feedback as well as suggestions for further work where my own reading had been too limited. The continuing support and encouragement of Richard Jursek and John Isley of Prentice-Hall must also be acknowledged because there were many times during the process of this revision when I was seriously tempted to let the project go altogether.

My wife Mary helped with editing and proofreading, my secretary Brenda Venuti managed the whole complex process of pulling the manuscript together, and Cheryl Fennessey valiantly typed and retyped the manuscript. My thanks to all of them.

Edgar H. Schein
February, 1979

The
Individual
and
the
Organization:

The Field
of
Organizational
Psychology

The first two chapters serve as an introduction to the field of organizational psychology. Chapter 1 provides an historical underpinning for a field which today encompasses a number of different perspectives, yet remains essentially psychological in its orientation. Chapter 2 presents a fairly thorough review of human (psychological) problems in organizations that, taken together, reveal a complex set of interactions between individual members of organizations and the organizations themselves.

The Field of Organizational Psychology

An area of psychology typically develops around a set of questions that involves human beings. The questions may be primarily of concern to the practitioner, for example, a teacher, parent, or manager who is trying to resolve some pressing problem; or they may be somewhat removed from practical application and represent pure scientific speculation. The field does not develop, however, until conceptual models, theories, and research methods for gathering and analyzing relevant data have been invented. When we have both a focus of interest and a way of studying it, we have the beginnings of a new "field."

Organizational psychology has undergone a considerable transformation in the last 15 to 20 years, reflecting a tremendous growth of theory and research on a variety of problems ranging from individual employee motivation, productivity, and morale to problems of how to organize large multinational corporations and how to manage interorganizational conflict such as that between businesses and government agencies. The field has become interdisciplinary, reflecting the growing interest of psychologists, sociologists, anthropologists, political scientists, systems theorists, and others in attempting to understand organizational phenomena. Although the title *Organizational Psychology* has been retained, my approach to the topics in this book will be interdisciplinary.

3

THE MULTIPLE PERSPECTIVES
OF ORGANIZATIONAL PSYCHOLOGY

The effective utilization of people in any organized effort has always been a pressing problem in society. The pharaoh building a pyramid faced problems fundamentally similar to those faced by the corporation executive or university president of today. Each must figure out (1) what he or she is basically trying to accomplish; (2) how to organize the work to achieve the goals selected; (3) how to recruit, train, allocate work to, and manage the human resources (workers and managers) available to do the work; (4) how to create work conditions and reward and punishment systems that will enable workers and managers to maintain high effectiveness *and* sufficient morale to remain effective over long periods of time; (5) how to change the organization in response to the pressures that arise from technological and social change both in the external environment and within the organization itself; and (6) how to cope with competition and other forces which derive from other organizations, from units within the organization such as unions, from regulatory agencies, and ultimately from its own "growing pains." These and many other questions which lie at the heart of any "organization" have had to be faced and resolved by politicians, managers, bureaucrats, and leaders throughout history.

Such organizational questions can be viewed from at least two major perspectives: (1) the perspective of the *individual* employee who depends upon the organization as a source of work, economic livelihood, membership, identity, social contact, and basic life routines, acknowledging the fact that most people in modern society spend the bulk of their waking hours in some form of organization; and (2) the perspective of the *manager* of the organization who is acting on behalf of the organization, creating policies and making decisions which affect the day-to-day routines of large numbers of individuals and which ultimately affect the destiny of the organization as a whole. This latter perspective is a kind of "organizational" perspective, but should not be construed to mean that the organization acts as an abstract entity; rather, it acts through the individual behavior of certain key members in crucial managerial or leadership roles.

A third perspective which does not receive much attention in this book but which is becoming increasingly important is the perspective of the *consumer* of the organization's products or services. In our role as customers, citizens, students, patients, and sometimes victims, we have a stake in understanding and influencing how

4

organizations work and how they make their decisions. Consumerism, environmentalism, civil rights with respect to employment, and so on all refer to the protection of the individual from undue exploitation by organizations of all kinds.

It is my intention in this book to provide some concepts, selected research results, and a point of view which will aid the reader in analyzing organizational problems from both the individual and the organizational perspective.

THE DEVELOPMENT OF THE FIELD

As theories and methods gradually enabled psychologists to think constructively about the problems of individuals in organizations and to test their thinking with empirical research, interest in organizational psychology grew. The first questions dealt with the assessment and selection of individual workers. Thus, the earliest successful efforts of industrial psychologists involved the testing of recruits in order to enable organizations such as the Army or a large industrial concern to improve their selection methods. Selection was made more scientific by measuring in individuals those characteristics which the organization required of its new members.

With this more scientific and systematic approach to selection, psychologists soon found themselves moving closer to organizational problems in a growing attempt to put order into the process of designing and organizing work itself. Industrial psychologists found themselves working closely with engineers to analyze the basic characteristics of work in order to give each individual worker a job which would optimize (1) his or her human capabilities and limits, (2) coordination and teamwork among employees, and (3) overall efficiency. Thus, "time-and-motion" studies were carried out to determine how competent workers actually performed a given job, and "job analyses" were carried out to standardize the work and to enable managers to better select and train workers. Physical surroundings, noise levels, fatigue, monotony, and other accompaniments of work were studied to determine their effect on the quantity and quality of work.

As psychologists studied workers, it became clear to them that the systems of rewards and punishments created by organizations have a major impact on the effectiveness of workers. Psychologists became increasingly interested in rewards such as pay or promotion and punishments such as reprimands as motivators and as conditioners of learning. The long tradition of studying human and animal learning made it possible to redefine and test within the organizational context many of the hypotheses which had been worked on in learning experiments. The kinds of incentive schemes used by management thus became still another major focus of industrial psychologists.

In delving into the motivations of workers, it was found that workers' relationships to other workers make more of a difference to production and morale than had previously been assumed. For example, how hard people work may depend more on how hard their co-workers work than on how much money they could make or how hard their boss drives them. It became increasingly clear that every organization has within it many groups which generate their own norms about the amount and type of work to be performed. In taking a second look at management, psychologists also found there groupings based on the managers' functions, ranks, or geographical locations. In some cases, groups within the organization—for example, the sales department and the production department—were competing with each other to the point of reducing their own ultimate effectiveness and that of the organization as a whole.

It was in the study of worker motivation, incentive systems, personnel policies, and intergroup relations that the organization as a total system first began to come into focus. Psychologists began to realize that for an individual member, whether worker or manager, an organization as a whole exists as a psychological entity to which he or she reacts. The quality and quantity of one's work are related to one's image of the organization as a whole, not just to the immediate characteristics of the work or the immediate monetary incentives. Furthermore, it was recognized that the individual does not stand alone in relation to the organization but is integrated into various groupings which themselves have patterns of cooperative, competitive, or indifferent relations to one another, a recognition that has led to the high degree of contemporary concern for the "quality of working life." In other words, the deeper psychologists delved into the behavior of individuals within organizations, the more evidence they found that the organization is a complex social system which must be studied as such if individual behavior is to be truly understood. It was this discovery which created organizational psychology as a discipline in its own right.

Let me repeat this point because it has been and continues to be the keynote to this entire text. Organizational psychology as a field is intimately tied to the recognition that *organizations are complex social systems*, and that almost all questions one may raise about the determinants of individual human behavior within organizations have to be viewed from the perspective of the entire social system. The difference between the industrial psychologist of the 1920s,

1930s, or 1940s, and the organizational psychologist of today is thus twofold. First, traditional questions such as those of recruitment, testing, selection, training, job analysis, incentives, work conditions, and so on are now treated by the organizational psychologist as being interrelated and intimately tied to the social system of the organization as a whole. Second, organizational psychologists have begun to concern themselves with a new series of questions which derive from the recognition of the system characterisics of organizations. These questions deal not so much with the behavior of individuals as with the behavior of groups, subsystems, and even the total organization in response to internal and external stimuli. The traditional industrial psychologist either would not have considered questions such as these or could not have dealt with them scientifically because the necessary theoretical and research tools were lacking.

Two examples will highlight the difference between the traditional concerns and the "new" questions which organizational psychology is addressing. First, given a rapidly changing technology that requires a great adaptive capacity on the part of organizations, how can internal environments be created such that members of organizations will be enabled to grow in their own unique capacities? The underlying assumption is that unless such *personal* growth takes place, the organization will not be prepared to cope effectively with an unpredictably changing external environment.

Second, how can organizations be designed to foster optimal relationships between the various subgroups that tend to develop within them? For example, how can destructive intergroup competition be converted to constructive intergroup collaboration? The underlying assumption is that intergroup collaboration will be related both to overall organizational effectiveness and to individual productivity and morale. Questions such as these recognize that the psychological forces operating on an individual are intimately bound up with what happens to the group or the total organization within which he or she is operating.

In recent years additional concepts and theories have begun to shape organizational psychology—those deriving from theories of systems dynamics and from developmental theories. Both these concepts share the idea that no system is static; rather, it changes and evolves in response to internal and external forces. From the viewpoint of individual development, it is easy to see the importance of recognizing that a worker at age 20 will face different issues from those he or she will confront at age 40. Questions about the meaning of life, complex issues of how work and family relate to each other, issues of what to aspire to and how to measure success will be dealt with differently at each age and again at the point of retirement and in old age. Much has been learned in recent years about the development of individuals throughout their total life cycle. This developmental perspective is critical if one is to understand how organizations work.

At the same time there has been increased understanding of how large systems change, grow, and develop over time, and what effects these changes have on the internal workings of organizations. For example, a newly established company managed by its founder experiences very different kinds of intraorganizational problems than a large multinational company or a government bureaucracy managed by professional administrators or politicians. Whether or not organizations progress through "stages" similar to those of the individual biological organism is not yet well understood, but organizational psychologists are examining organizations from a developmental point of view in an effort to help managers become aware of and cope with such developmental issues as may occur.

STIMULI TOWARD THE SYSTEMS AND DEVELOPMENTAL VIEW

In the above discussion we have seen how the field has evolved from an individually oriented industrial psychology to a systems and developmentally oriented organizational psychology. What are some of the forces which have stimulated and guided this evolution?

1. The penetration of sociological and anthropological conceptions into psychology and the growth of social psychology exposed psychologists to a whole range of new concepts and research methods. Although concepts like social role, status, social class, reference group, culture, and social system were developed outside of traditional psychology, they have become increasingly important in psychological analysis. Research methods such as surveys by large-scale questionnaires or interviews, the use of participant observation, and field experiments have stimulated psychologists to go beyond introspection and laboratory experiments. It is these concepts and these methods which have made it possible to tackle organizational problems, and which have shifted the focus of analysis away from the individual per se to the individual as a member of a group.

2. The development of new theories in the physical and biological sciences has made available different ways of thinking about psychological problems. Concepts of multiple causation based on a field of simultaneously acting forces have replaced mechanistic no-

tions of simple cause-effect; concepts of mutual dependency and interaction, of feedback loops and self-regulating forces have made it possible to analyze complex systems and their relationship to the external environment. Such concepts have also made it possible to begin to develop meaningful theories within organizational psychology. Most of these theories are complex "contingency theories" which recognize from the outset that the *specific* action of variable A (for example, a manager's specific behavior) is likely to have a different impact on variable B (say, a certain worker's productivity) depending on conditions such as the nature of the task, the past history of the relationship, the general "climate" of the organization, the age of the worker, and so on. In particular, the use of developmental theories makes it very clear that variables such as motives, values, and personality will themselves evolve and change throughout the lifetime of the individual, thus making it necessary to build theories which are "contingent" on the particular state, age, or stage of the person or the system being analyzed.

3. The rapid and tremendous changes in technology *and* society which have occurred within the last several decades have forced scientist and practitioner alike to recognize the interdependency of human and technological factors and the need to develop theories and concepts which can encompass such interdependencies. For example, we have seen the growth of complex man-machine systems where it no longer makes scientific or practical sense to ask where the human being leaves off and the computer or machine begins. More and more we are relying on *sociotechnical* theories which recognize that the physical organization of work affects patterns of social relationships among workers, and that these in turn affect the kind of work output which is possible.

4. Practitioners and managers have come to recognize the complex world in which they must operate and have become increasingly willing to accept help from social scientists in resolving organizational problems. As psychologists and sociologists have become more involved in higher management decisions, they have been better able to appreciate the complexities of organizations. A corollary trend has been the increasing professionalization of management. Because managers are now more aware of environmental influences and more technically qualified than ever before, they are also more willing to accept help from other professions. Thus, managers have become not only more aware of their need for help from psychologists, but have also become more willing to use this help. This development, in turn, has made organizations more accessible to researchers.

5. Finally, psychologists themselves have become more skilled

in dealing with problems of complex systems and have, therefore, been able to help organizations to a greater degree. In return, organizations have increasingly supported the efforts of those psychologists willing to tackle the more nebulous and difficult systems problems. Out of this increased interaction have come better theory, new research techniques, and new methods for (1) solving problems managers face on a day-to-day basis, (2) helping individuals to cope more effectively with their own membership in various types of organizations throughout their entire life cycle, and (3) helping individuals deal with organizations in their role as customers and citizens.

In conclusion, organizations are gradually becoming demystified, a process that should make them both more capable of acting effectively in the service of socially valued goals and more accountable to their members rather than merely to their creators or the consumers of their products and services.

THE PLAN OF THIS BOOK

This book is divided into five major parts, each consisting of several chapters. Part I spells out the basic relationship between the individual and the organization and presents a number of concepts which aid in the analysis of this relationship. Part II deals with a problem that has continued to perplex managers and psychologists alike—the problem of human nature and motivation. Why do people work? How can organizations best elicit appropriate levels of motivation? What does the individual seek from his or her job or career? Can we generalize about human nature? Do motives and needs change with age and stage of development?

Part III deals with the problem of leadership, another area that has attracted tremendous attention throughout the history of this field. What kinds of behavior on the part of managers or leaders will produce effective individual or group output, high levels of motivation, and personal growth on the part of subordinates?

Part IV deals with groups. What is a group? What functions does a group fulfill for its members, and why do groups exist within organizations? What makes a group effective in terms of its own membership and in terms of intergroup relationships? And, finally, how can intergroup relations be managed to maximize organizational effectiveness and individual fulfillment?

Part V then shifts to the perspective of the organization as a total system. We review several taxonomies and theories that attempt to spell out the relationship between the organization and its various environments and then examine the ubiquitous question of how organizations should be designed to function more effectively. The concepts of effectiveness and health are also discussed in terms of individual and organizational change. We conclude with a question that has many implications for organizational psychology and society in general: How can one conceptualize the process of "coping" with an ever-changing environment? One answer has been given by the concept of planned change and organizational development and the model of action research which underlies it. A model of the change process concludes the book.

The thrust of my efforts in this book is to help the reader develop a more diagnostic point of view toward organizational phenomena. The goal is to understand better what goes on in individuals, in groups, and in larger systems. We do not as yet have many firm principles which can guide action, but a thorough understanding of and the ability to diagnose organizational problems is, in any case, crucial as a basis for action.

Human Problems in Organizations

2

In order to understand organizational psychology, we must first understand something about organizations. What is an "organization" and how does one think about it? What kinds of human problems arise in organizations?

It is surprisingly difficult to give a simple definition of an organization. All of us have spent our lives in various organizations—schools, clubs, community groups, companies and business concerns, government agencies, hospitals, political parties, and churches. Yet is is not easy to state just what constitutes an organization. Let us examine some of the ideas proposed by sociologists and political scientists as a context for this discussion.

WHAT IS AN ORGANIZATION?[1]

Coordination

First of all, it is important to recognize that the very idea of organizing stems from the fact that the individual alone is unable to fulfill all of his or her needs and wishes. Individuals, particularly in modern society, find that they are lacking either in ability, strength, time, or endurance to fulfill their basic needs for food, shelter, and

[1] The ideas outlined in the next few pages were originally drawn from Blau and Scott (1962), Etzioni (1961), and March and Simon (1958). More recent analyses will be reviewed in Chapters 11 and 12.

safety. As several people coordinate their efforts, however, they find that together they can do more than any of them could have singly. The largest organization, society, makes it possible, through the coordination of the activities of many individuals, for all of its members to fulfill their needs. One basic idea underlying the concept of organization, then, is the idea of *coordination of effort in the service of mutual help.*

Common Goals

In order for coordination to be helpful, however, there must exist some goals to be achieved, and some agreement concerning these goals. A second important idea underlying the concept of organization, then, is the idea of achieving some *common goals* or purpose through coordination of activities.

Division of Labor

As we are all aware, organizations exist within larger organizations. The entire world consists of many cultural and linguistic groups. Within those groups there are societies and nations tied together not only by a common language and culture, but by common political and economic goals. Within each society or nation there exist economic, political, religious, and governmental organizations and institutions. Within each of these larger units, we have many smaller units—individual business concerns, political parties, churches, county seats, and cities. And within each of these units, we have smaller groupings of people which also constitute organizations—production and sales departments within a company, factions and cliques within a political party, a choir within a church, a police department within a city.

According to some theories, these progressive differentiations arise out of the fundamental notion of *division of labor*, the third property common to human organizations. Tied up with the concept of coordination and the purposeful achievement of mutually agreed-upon goals is the idea that such goals can best be achieved if different people do different things in a coordinated fashion. Human societies have found that they can best achieve their goals if they divide up among their members the various tasks that need to be accomplished. Hopefully, the division is on the basis of different innate talents or skills, but this is not necessarily so, since people can be *trained* to do different things.

The idea of division of labor is closely linked to the idea of differentiation of function. Organizations can best achieve their various goals by differentiating on the basis of types of tasks, geographical location, goals and subgoals to be achieved, talents available within the organization, or any other logical rationale. In analyzing a total society, for example, we distinguish between the *economic* system and its component organizations, and the *political* system, along with the various government organizations which comprise it. A society's economy serves the function of providing food, shelter, goods, and services for its members through organizations that at the same time provide jobs and money to enable participants to purchase goods and services. A political system, on the other hand, serves to regulate the society, to provide for the safety and protection of its members, and to coordinate the various other institutions of the society. A third vital function is served by the educational system: the maintenance and continued growth of the society through creating, conserving, and passing on knowledge to future generations. Thus each segment of society can be viewed as fulfilling a different function in the interests of total shared goals.

The same analysis can be applied to a single business organization where it is even easier to see the logic of separating into different organizational units the functions of inventing and designing products (Research and Development, Engineering), locating potential customers and selling the product to them (Marketing and Sales), manufacturing the product (Production), generating the money necessary to build the production facility and pay employees, and determining the selling price of a product based on the cost of production (Finance and Accounting), hiring and training the people who will perform each of the functions (Personnel), providing for delivering the finished product to the customer (Distribution), servicing it after it is sold (Field Service), and so on. As we will see, such simple formulas for the division of labor no longer work optimally as organizations have become more complex. Seeing the organization as a *complex set of interdependent groups* has led to a much more intricate model of differentiation. However, an *initial* analysis of any organization can be made in terms of the disparate functions performed by different members or subgroups of that organization.

Integration

The fourth and final concept needed to understand organizations is closely related to the idea of differentiation and division of labor. If different parts are doing different things, some *integrative* function is needed to ensure that all elements are working toward the commonly agreed-upon goals. The most typical, though by no means the only, form of such integration, is a *hierarchy of authority*—some system for superordinate subgroups or individuals to ensure that there is coordination among the parts through guiding, limiting, controlling, informing, and in other ways managing the activities of those parts.

The idea of coordination implies that each unit submits to some kind of authority for the sake of achieving a common goal. If each unit pursues its own self-interest and disregards the activities of other units, coordination has by definition broken down. However, the idea of submitting to some kind of authority does not necessarily imply external control. Coordination can, in principle, be achieved by voluntary self-disciplining activities such as those engaged in by two children operating a seesaw. The kind of authority implied by coordination thus can range from complete self-discipline to complete autocracy. But some kind of controlling principle to ensure integration is an essential idea underlying organization.

As we all know from daily experience, authority in most organizations is usually embodied in a complex hierarchy of positions or ranks. Ideally each position is supposed to have defined for it an area of responsibility and, theoretically, has the authority to ensure that its part of the job will be done in accordance with a more comprehensive plan. Coordination is thus implemented by the laying out of a kind of blueprint of who is responsible for what. This blueprint is usually, but not necessarily, constructed by the highest ranking members on the basis of rational criteria of job division and coordination that promote the overall goal.

A PRELIMINARY DEFINITION
OF ORGANIZATION

The basic ideas presented above can be put together into a preliminary definition of an organization. This definition is very similar to what early organization theorists used as their final definition. As we will see later, when we bring a systems and a developmental point of view to bear, the definition will have to be modified substantially to fit what we can observe in real organizations all around us.

An organization is the planned coordination of the activities of a number of people for the achievement of some common, explicit purpose or goal, through division of labor and function, and through a hierarchy of authority and responsibility.

One important point in this definition which has not yet been discussed is that the object of coordination is *activities*, not *people*. As has been pointed out by many organization theorists, notably Chester Barnard (1938), only some of the activities of any given person are relevant to the achievement of a particular goal. In fact, the same person can belong to many different organizations because in each one only some of his or her activities are relevant. From the point of view of an organization, therefore, it is sufficient to spell out the activities or roles which must be fulfilled in order to achieve the goal. In a business organization, someone must purchase the raw materials, someone must design the product, someone must build it, and someone must sell it. Which particular person fulfills the role may be quite irrelevant to the concept of organization, though it will clearly be relevant to how well the organization actually operates.

Because an organization is fundamentally a pattern of roles and a blueprint for their coordination, it exists independently of particular people and can survive in spite of 100 percent turnover of membership. If the role expectations are recorded either in documents or in the memories of managers, parents, or teachers, the organization will continue from generation to generation with new members fulfilling the roles. In principle, the organization itself will only change when the blueprint itself is changed—that is, when the roles are redefined by higher authorities or by occupants of those roles.

An organization, as we have defined it, is what sociologists term a *formal organization*, to distinguish it from two other types—a social organization and an informal organization. *Social organizations* are patterns of coordination that arise spontaneously or implicitly out of the interactions of people without involving rational coordination for the achievement of explicit, common goals. A group of friends may coordinate their activities to a high degree and have common *implicit* goals such as "having a good time," but they are not a formal organization. If they choose to make their goals explicit and formally agree to certain patterns of coordination in order to ensure having a good time, and if they establish some hierarchy to ensure proper coordination, they would become a formal organization. In society, there are many patterns of social organization, such as the family, clubs, gangs, and communities. They should be distinguished from formal organizations like business concerns, schools, hospitals, churches, unions, and prisons.

The term *informal organization* refers to those patterns of coordination that arise among members of a formal organization which are not called for by the blueprint. The organizational blueprint requires the coordination of only certain *activities*. But, for a variety of reasons, the human actors who fulfill organizational roles rarely limit themselves merely to the performance of these activities. Two workers on an assembly line are only supposed to do their particular job; yet they may wish to talk to each other, to have lunch together, to share gripes about their job and boss, and in various other ways establish relationships above and beyond the formally required ones. Such relationships tend to arise in all formal organizations. As we will see, many of the important psychological problems of organizations arise from complex interactions between formal and informal organizations.

A MODEL OF FORMAL ORGANIZATIONS

If one asks a manager for a rundown of his or her organization, the person will typically produce an "organization chart," which depicts in a two-dimensional way (1) the different hierarchical levels and (2) the different functional areas which derive from division of labor. Figure 2.1 shows a typical chart for a simple business organization.

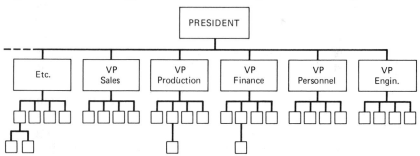

Fig. 2.1 A typical organization chart of a business.

However, if one were to interview members of the organization about how the work of the organization was actually carried out day to day, and how status and importance were defined in the organization, one would find that the organization chart gives a very incomplete and possibly inaccurate description of what actually goes on. Instead, one needs a more complex picture such as the one in Figure 2.2, which depicts three basic dimensions of an organization (Schein, 1971):

1. the *hierarchical* dimension, which reflects relative ranks in a manner similar to the organization chart
2. a *functional* dimension, which reflects the different types of work to be done depicted as the different pie-shaped sectors in the cone diagram
3. a dimension of *inclusion or centrality*, reflected in the degree to which any given person is nearer to or farther from the central core of the organization.

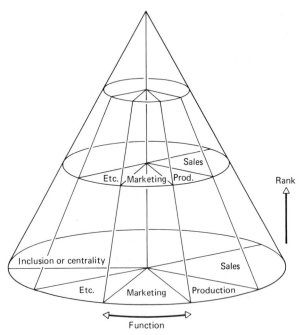

Fig. 2.2 A three-dimensional model of an organization.

It is a fact of organizational life that one not only has a certain kind of work and a certain rank or formal status, but one can also vary in the degree to which one is trusted and permitted to influence key decisions even from a position of low rank. In a classic study done in the 1950s, Melville Dalton (1959) showed that organizations not only generated informal groupings which cut across various functional and hierarchical boundaries, but that such groupings were essential to the running of the organization. High-level managers often checked out key decisions with low-level foremen or even workers whom they had come to know well over the years or with whom they shared outside activities, bypassing many levels of the organizational hierarchy. Such foremen or workers, then, can be thought of as possessing a high degree of centrality in the organization even at a low rank level.

The centrality dimension is particularly important if one takes a developmental view of organizations, because it is possible for informal groupings to arise over time which are in no way reflected in the formal organization chart. From the organizational/managerial perspective it is crucial to understand how such informal groupings arise and what role they play in the running of the organization. From the individual career perspective it is crucial to recognize that a career moves along all three of these dimensions and that a person can be leveled off in terms of rank, and can even be stuck in a given functional area, yet still move into more central influential positions in the informal system of the organization. The process of socialization into organizational roles is premised on this dimension of centrality—how much the organizational member is entrusted with organizational secrets and given access to decision making whether or not his or her formal rank warrants it.

Using the concepts and models presented thus far, let us next review what kinds of psychological or human problems arise in organizations. As we will see, many of these problems reflect the complex interaction between rank levels, functional groupings, and shifting formal and informal organizational systems. In order to fully understand human problems in organizations it is necessary to constantly remind oneself that not only do they arise from a multitude of complex interactions, but that those interactions themselves change over time as both the individuals who make up the organization and the organization itself change, grow, and develop.

HOW IS AN ORGANIZATION CREATED?

Organizations begin as ideas in the minds of people. Though it will not be the focus of attention in this book, it must be recognized that the first human problem of any organization is the process of how one or more people convert an idea into a blueprint for a set of activities to be performed by two or more other people. The inventor in the garage who decides to build his or her invention by getting together five workers in a shop; the social organizer who starts a new club or political organization on campus; the religious leader who obtains a following by preaching and eventually establishes a church; the young teacher with a vision who decides to start a school of his or her own are all creating new organizations.

If the organization is successful in accomplishing its goal of building a following or in creating demand for a new product or service, it will survive, grow, and become established. The founders or entrepreneurs who build an organization may move on or die, or be forced out by new managers who have a new vision of how the organization should operate. If the organization continues to be successful, it will survive successive generations of leadership and almost take on a life of its own. Such stability results when organizations go beyond fulfilling their original goals and take on larger functions—they become employers, they provide membership and identities for their employees, they come to play a role in the community, and they develop ideologies and myths about themselves which usually include the assumption that they should survive and grow. On the other hand, when an organization such as a business cannot maintain its basic or *primary function* of providing a product or service at a reasonable profit for the owners, it "goes bankrupt" and ceases to exist as an organization, even though the former members may "reorganize" into a new entity. Similarly, social, religious, or political organizations cease to exist when they lose too much of their following or get in the way of other more powerful organizations.

If one wants to understand the process of organizational creation, one should read the biographies of entrepreneurs and great leaders.[2] Formal research on the creation of organizations is noticeably scant, though some efforts to study entrepreneurship have been undertaken and will be reviewed in the chapter on motivation and leadership. What is important to note is that most of us encounter full-blown organizations, entities that have already developed routines, norms, ways of doing things, traditions, rules, job descriptions, a unique vocabulary, and other patterns which have to be learned by new members. Because the organization is a "given," one of its major processes is that of recruiting, training, and hiring new employees. From the point of view of the individual, this same process is one of learning how to get along, being "socialized" into the culture of the organization, or—as some sociologists have labeled the process—"breaking in" to organizations (Van Maanen, 1976).

RECRUITMENT, SELECTION, TRAINING, SOCIALIZATION, AND ALLOCATION OF PEOPLE TO JOBS

Organizations are blueprints for human activities, but they do not function until people have been recruited to fulfill the specified roles and to provide the specified activities. Therefore, the first and perhaps major human problem of any organization is how to recruit employees, how to select, train, and socialize them, and how to allocate them to jobs for most effective role performance. *Training* in this context refers to the teaching of technical skills needed to perform the job; by contrast, *socialization* refers to the process of teaching the new recruit how to get along in the organization, what

---

2 For two interesting yet contrasting examples, one could compare Chandler's (1962) analysis of several American industries and Speer's (1970) analysis of Germany under Hitler.

the key norms and rules of conduct are, and how to behave with respect to others in the organization—what is often referred to as "learning the ropes." The new recruit must learn where to be at specified times, what to wear, what to call the boss, whom to consult if he or she has a question, how carefully to do a job, and endless other things which insiders have learned over time.

The broad problem of bringing people into an organization can be broken down into two subproblems. First, it should be noted that a policy of recruitment, selection, training, socialization, and allocation designed to get the best performance out of people does not automatically ensure that the individual needs and expectations these people bring to the organization will in fact be met. Thus, one of the major dilemmas of organizational psychology arises because policies and practices that ensure organizational effectiveness may often leave individual needs unsatisfied, or worse, create problems above and beyond the ones people brought with them. Employees may become alienated, insecure, and bitter if the organization fails to fulfill minimum needs for security, maintenance of self-esteem, and opportunities to grow and develop.

The fundamental question is, then, *How can organizational policies or social practices be developed which will permit some reasonable matching of human needs and organizational demands?* Or, if these are fundamentally incompatible, psychologists must ask what other social institutions exist now or should in the future exist to ameliorate the problems created by individual-organization conflicts.

Second, the allocation and effective utilization of human resources can be pursued by two fundamentally different strategies based on entirely different assumptions (Haire, 1959). One strategy, which has come to be identified with personnel psychology, puts its emphasis on selecting the person to fit the job. The job is considered a constant while the human being is considered a variable. People can be selected and trained. From the total pool of human resources, one can attempt to find those people who already fit organizational requirements or who can at least be trained to fit them. The other approach, identified originally with engineering psychology, puts its emphasis on redesigning the job and its physical environment to fit the limitations and capacities of the human being. The person is considered a constant while the job is considered a variable. Ideally, the job would be designed in such a way that any person could perform it. Both approaches can work and have worked in the past.

How, then, should one balance the testing-selection approach with the engineering and job-redesign approach in order to maximize both the human potential available to organizations and the fulfillment of individual needs?

One of the key themes throughout this book is that it is possible to maintain *both* these perspectives—the perspective of the individual attempting to use organizations for the fulfillment of his or her needs, and the perspective of the manager attempting to use human resources optimally to fulfill organizational needs. These divergent, yet overlapping issues are further complicated by the developmental perspective, because both the needs of the organization and those of its members change over time and with experience. Therefore, solutions worked out by an organization at one point in its history may not be applicable at another point. Instead, we will see that individual-organizational interactions are in constant, dynamic flux (Schein, 1978).

UTILIZING AND MANAGING HUMAN RESOURCES

The Psychological Contract

Once people have been recruited, selected, trained, and allocated to jobs, the organization must focus on creating conditions that will facilitate a high level of performance over a long period of time, and also permit individual employees to meet some of their own most important needs through membership and work in the organization. Traditionally, this problem has been attacked by searching out and cataloging the motives and needs of workers, and relating these to the incentives and rewards offered by the organization. As studies have accumulated, it has become apparent that the problem is complex and can better be conceptualized in terms of a "psychological contract" entered into by both the individual and the organization.

The notion of a psychological contract implies that there is an unwritten set of expectations operating at all times between every member of an organization and the various managers and others in that organization.[3] This idea is implicit in the concept of organiza-

---

[3] The concept of psychological contract is an extension of all that has been written by social philosophers about social contracts. In the organizational sphere it was first discussed in detail by Argyris (1960) and by Levinson (1962). The same idea is implicit in March and Simon's (1958) "inducement-contribution" model and has been worked out in some detail by Homans (1961) in his social exchange theory of elementary social forms. Kotter (1973) has tested the idea by measuring both the employees' and supervisors' expectations and developed workshops to permit resolutions of possible mismatches in those expectations.

tional role, in that every role is basically a set of behavioral expectations (Kahn et al., 1964). The psychological contract implies further that each role player, that is, employee, also has expectations about such things as salary or pay rate, working hours, benefits and privileges that go with a job, guarantees not to be fired unexpectedly, and so on. Many of these expectations are implicit and involve the person's sense of dignity and worth. We expect organizations to treat us as human beings, to provide work and facilities which are need-fulfilling rather than demeaning, to provide opportunities for growth and further learning, to provide feedback on how we are doing, and so on. Some of the strongest feelings leading to labor unrest, strikes, and employee turnover have to do with violations of these aspects of the psychological contract, even though the *public* negotiations are often over the more explicit issues of pay, working hours, job security, and so on.

The organization also has more implicit, subtle expectations—that the employee will enhance the image of the organization, will be loyal, will keep organizational secrets, and will do his or her best on behalf of the organization (that is, will always be highly motivated and willing to make sacrifices for the organization). Some of the greatest disappointments of managers arise when a valued employee seems to have become less motivated or "unwilling to put out for the company."

Here again we find that a *developmental* perspective can provide the key to understanding these issues. The psychological contract changes over time as the organization's needs and the employee's needs change. What the employee is looking for in a job at age 25 may be completely different from what that same employee is looking for at age 50 (Hall, 1976; Schein, 1978). Similarly, what the organization expects of a person during a period of rapid growth may be completely different from what that same organization expects when it has leveled off or is experiencing economic decline.

For example, at the beginning of the career, people's needs and expectations revolve very much around "self-tests." They need to learn whether they can, in fact, contribute to an organization, whether they have the skill and strength to do certain kinds of work, whether they can make a contribution (Schein, 1964). They, therefore, expect the organization to provide them with challenges to try out their skills and are most disappointed if they are kept too long in meaningless training assignments or at tasks they regard as menial. If this happens, neither they nor the organization can learn what their talents really are.

At a later career stage, needs and expectations shift to identifying an area in which the person can experience a sense of contribution and also develop this area of specialization; in turn, the individual expects the organization to recognize his or her contribution in various ways (Dalton, Thompson, & Price, 1977). In mid-career when we are most productive we also expect the most in terms of recognition and rewards. At a later career stage, as we level off and begin to contribute less visibly, our needs for reassurance and for security may rise, and the expectations implicit in the psychological contract may shift toward being "taken care of," not being "put out to pasture" or thrown out the door. Retired people often complain that their psychological contract was violated dramatically because they had many good years of contribution left, their company was their whole life, they had really devoted themselves to it for decades, and felt that in return the company "owed" them something more than being put out of work at an age when they felt they could still contribute.

For its part, the organization needs and expects higher levels of motivation and effort when it is a young, struggling concern or in a severe competitive battle with other organizations. It expects more loyalty when it is under attack or in trouble and more "steady performance" in stable times when it feels it is offering a long-range sense of security to its employees.

Both individual employee and manager forge their expectations from their inner needs, what they have learned from others, traditions and norms which may be operating, their own past experience, and a host of other sources. As needs and external forces change, so do these expectations, making the psychological contract a *dynamic* one which must be constantly *renegotiated*. Though it remains unwritten, the psychological contract is a powerful determiner of behavior in organizations.

Power and Authority

One key element of the psychological contract is the organization's expectation that a new member will accept the authority system of that organization. Deciding to join implies acceptance of the basic rules that constitute the organization's authority system. Within defined areas the person must be willing to accept the dictates of some other person or some written rules, to accept limitations on his or her own behavior, and to curb personal inclinations if they go against rules or orders (Schein & Ott, 1962).

Authority is not the same thing as power. Pure power implies the ability to actually control others through the exercise of naked strength, the manipulation of rewards or punishments which are meaningful to others, or the manipulation of information. Power implies that others really have no choice because they are not strong enough to be self-determining or do not have access to the resources they need. It is what sociologists would call "nonlegitimate authority." Legitimate authority, on the other hand, implies the willingness on the part of subordinates to obey rules, laws, or orders because they *consent* to the system by which the rules, laws, or rank were arrived at—that is, they grant the person in authority the *right* to dictate to them. Authority is legitimate when there is consensus among the members of an organization or a society about (1) the basis on which a rule or law is to be derived, and/or (2) the system by which a person is to be put into a position of authority. In other words, a law will be obeyed only if there is consensus on the method by which laws are made, and a foreman will be obeyed by workers only if there is consensus among the workers that the promotional system by which one gets to be a foreman is fair. It is consent to the total system which permits subordinates to tolerate and take orders even from an occasional bad boss.

The organization can enforce its side of the psychological contract through the exercise of power and the use of authority. How can the employee enforce his or her side of the contract? Depending upon the total circumstances, the employee has a range of options: quitting the organization, reducing involvement in the work, going on strike, sabotage, and/or attempts to influence the situation on his or her own behalf. For employees to feel comfortable as members of the organization, they must be able to believe that they have some power to influence their own situation, to enforce their side of the contract, to ensure that if the organization does not meet their expectations in some crucial area that they have, at least, the power to be listened to, and, at most, the power to leave without severe penalty.

The actual mode of influence—whether as a free agent introducing innovations or as a member of a union—is not as important as the fundamental belief on the part of employees that they have some power to influence the situation if their side of the psychological contract is not met. The pattern of authority and influence that develops in a given society or organization will depend upon the actual basis on which the consent of the members rests. Let us turn now to an analysis of several different bases of consent.

Bases of Legitimate Authority

Many theories and conceptual schemes have been proposed to explain the different bases on which authority can rest. I have already indicated that pure power or nonlegitimate authority can rest on the possession of strength (which would include weapons) or on the control of certain rewards and punishments (giving a raise for compliance or firing someone for noncompliance) or on the control of information. However, to really understand organizations we must understand the bases of *legitimate* authority—that is, the bases on which members of organizations arrive at a consensus voluntarily to submit to authority. One of the earliest and still best analyses of such bases of authority was that of the German sociologist Max Weber (1947), who attempted through these concepts to understand the evolution of political systems.

1. *Tradition.* Most early political systems beyond those that rested on pure power derived their stability from the acceptance on the part of the governed of a belief that the ruling group had the right to rule, and this right was embodied in the traditions and norms of the society. Such traditions usually included myths about the "divine" origins of rulers and included principles of succession such as the right of the eldest son to claim the throne upon the death of the king. Authority at lower levels derived from the delegation on the part of the king or high priest to others in the society. What made the system "right" or "fair" was the belief in the traditions surrounding the idea of monarchy. Once there ceased to be consensus about such traditions, the seeds of revolution were sown. The system was only as strong as the basic consensus about it.

We can see the organizational counterpart of such a system in our own society if we examine our own attitudes about the "rights" of inheritance. In many organizations it is considered legitimate for the founder to pass on high positions of rank to members of the family, and workers will accept such authority even if they question the competence of the individual in the position. Such a system for acquiring managerial authority is not too common in the more industrialized, economically developed portions of the world, but it is still quite common in less developed countries where organizational authority functions much like parental authority, leading to a kind of unquestioned paternalism (Davis, 1971). The psychological contract is basically that the manager/parent will "take care" of his or her employees and, in return, the employees will be loyal and productive. Who gets to be a manager will be primarily a matter of the particular traditions within that culture, but typically authority is passed down along family lines.

2. *Rational-legal principles.* The replacement of traditionally based monarchies by more parliamentary democratic political systems was facilitated by the concept that the members of a society should have some voice in selecting the system by which they would be governed, and possibly even in selecting the people who would govern them. For this idea to work, the basis of legitimacy

had to shift to a rational-legal principle—that everyone would consent to a common set of laws and to the procedures set forth for obtaining such laws. Once there was consensus on how the laws were to be obtained, individual members of society would have to agree to abide by whatever laws were made. This process would maximize "rationality" in the sense of attempting to derive laws that "made sense," were in the interests of the majority, protected human rights, and provided a system for rulership based on demonstrated competence.

As we know, this principle or basis of consent does not always produce perfect laws or competent leaders. But it is a principle that is less subject to arbitrary whims on the part of whoever happens to be in a position of power. Once the members of a society have agreed to be ruled by law, there is at least a mechanism, however imperfect, of removing leaders or managers who are too incompetent or too willing to use pure power for illegitimate ends. What needs to be underlined is that the consensus on which this whole system rests is a *consensus to be ruled by a legal process.* Such a process is always vulnerable to a dictator who can establish himself or herself by the use of pure power; however, even a "benevolent" dictatorship is inherently unstable in today's world, because it does not rest on the consent of the governed and does not provide for a consensually validated means of determining succession. Consequently, most modern-day societies and organizations tend toward some kind of rational-legal system in order to avoid the arbitrariness and instability which results once a traditional system has been abandoned.

In the United States these principles are expressed through a system of legislation and the election of officials based on a rational assessment of their abilities, motives, and prior service. Applied to organizations, authority based on rational consensus is expressed in the idea of promotion based on *merit* (ability plus past performance and experience), and in the idea that authority ultimately derives from a person's expertness or competence, not family connections, money, or political power. What the boss is expert at might be quite different from what the subordinates are expert at, as when a research manager supervises ten research chemists. The boss may know less technically but presumably knows more about how to manage a research group. The acceptance by the chemists of their boss's authority ultimately rests on their perception of him or her as a better *manager,* and on their belief that the person achieved his or her position by a legitimate promotional process.

3. *Charisma.* Whereas both tradition and rational-legal principles invest a given *office* or *rank* with authority, Weber noted that many kinds of political or religious movements were based on cer-

tain compelling personal qualities of an individual leader. One can cite many instances in history of magnetic personalities being able to capture a following by virtue of mystical, magical, divine, or simply extraordinary powers attributed to them. Commonly cited examples would be Jesus Christ, Gandhi, Hitler, and, most recently, J. F. Kennedy and Martin Luther King. Such leaders elicit a strong emotional response from their followers and, like the Pied Piper, can often get their followers to do things they would not ordinarily do simply by the force of their personality.

A milder, yet similar phenomenon can be seen in organizations where certain leaders or managers elicit the loyalty of their subordinates on a very personal basis. All of us have at times obeyed orders and followed leaders simply because we trusted them completely and accepted their word as dogma, even if they had neither the expertise nor the legitimacy of an official rank. Psychologically we often follow such leaders because they set a very vivid example which enables us to identify with them, that is, to attempt to become more like them. Thus the ability of a leader to get followers to identify with him or her is one of the most powerful bases for eliciting loyalty and subordination.

One of the major problems with charisma as a basis for authority is that it does not provide as clear a principle of succession as tradition-based or rational-legal systems do. If the leader dies or loses the charismatic properties, there is no clear basis for choosing a successor. Thus, charismatically-based systems or organizations have the same problem as dictatorships—they are only stable during the lifetime of the leader. We can see examples of this instability in the power struggles that developed following the death of Lenin in the U.S.S.R. and Franco in Spain, or in several Latin American dictatorships. By contrast, both monarchies and rational-legal systems have clearly defined successions, the one based on family ties and the other on written agreements, or laws.

4. *Pure rational authority—expertness.* The ultimately rational basis on which to obey or follow someone is if that person possesses some specific information, competence, or expertness in relation to some problem we are experiencing. Such expertness is, in principle, independent of a person's personality, social origin, or official position. We accept the authority of the scholar in relation to his or her field of study, the authority of the doctor, the automobile mechanic, the television repairman, and others upon whom we are dependent when things need to be fixed. Ideally, authority would always rest on such pure competence. The problem of building an organization on this basis is that it is not always possible to judge competence or expertness, especially in relation to complex tasks. Organizations

and societies therefore develop systems of education and testing followed by apprenticeships, internships, licensing, and accreditation to ensure that those who claim to be expert are in fact expert. But it should be noted that those systems of education and accreditation must themselves be perceived as legitimate if one is to have confidence in the expert. Thus, the pure rational model also rests on a rational-legal system which reflects some consensus on how to define competence.

To illustrate how complicated the bases of authority really are from a psychological point of view, one need only pose to a group the following problem: An airliner crashes on a jungle island; the pilot is partially injured and knows nothing of survival in a jungle setting or how to build a raft. Who should be in charge—the pilot, the co-pilot, a passenger with vast experience in jungle survival, a passenger with a very strong personality who can pull the demoralized survivors together, someone who is elected by the survivors, a team of several of the above? Should issues be settled by majority rule? How should the group deal with someone who is physically very strong or possesses a gun and demands on that basis to be in charge? What the discussion typically reveals is that one cannot clearly answer the question of who should have authority until one has in the group some consensus on what the *basis* of authority should be. Until such consensus is achieved, there is a great probability of chaos and disorganization.

Psychologists have become interested in the bases on which power, or, as I have preferred to call it, authority, rests and have developed a typology similar to the sociological one (Cartwright, 1959). The two typologies are shown in Table 2.1 and can serve to summarize this discussion. What sociologists have termed nonlegitimate authority has been labeled variously by psychologists as coercive power, or the power to reward or punish; what sociologists have called rational-legal authority corresponds to the psychologists' position power; charisma has been broken down into two psychological constructs—personal power, based on the potency of the leader, and referent power, based on the ability of the leader to elicit imitation or identification in the follower; finally, pure rational authority corresponds to expert power. Tradition as a basis of authority has no clear psychological counterpart.

I have inserted this discussion of authority and its bases in order to underline the point that an organization cannot function unless its members consent to the operating authority system, and that this consent hinges upon both parties' upholding the psychological contract between them. If the organization fails to meet its

Table 2.1

Sociological Bases of Authority and Psychological Types of Power	
Nonlegitimate authority	Coercive power
	Reward-punishment power
Traditional authority	—No counterpart concept
Rational-legal authority	Position power
Charismatic authority	Personal power
	Referent power
Rational authority	Expert power

members' expectations and, at the same time, cannot coerce them to remain, they will most likely leave. Thus, the problem of motivation and organizational incentives or rewards is best thought of as a complex, continuous bargaining situation between the organization and its members. This ongoing negotiation involves the decisions of whether to join, how hard to work, and how creative to be, as well as feelings of loyalty and commitment, expectations of being taken care of and finding a sense of identity through one's organizational role, and a host of other decisions, feelings, and expectations.

COORDINATION AND INTEGRATION AMONG THE PARTS OF THE ORGANIZATION

As was pointed out earlier, division of labor is an essential aspect of organization. Such a classificatory process is often initiated by specifying the various means to accomplish a given end. Each of the means specified becomes the goal of the group of individuals to whom it has been assigned. This suborganization then generates its own means for accomplishing its goals and makes these the goals for further suborganizations. Let us take a typical business example. In order to survive and make a profit (the ultimate goal), the top level of management must create products and markets and must raise some money in order to manufacture the products and sell them (the basic means to be used to accomplish the ultimate goal). As these means are made operational through the creation of marketing, sales, engineering, finance, and manufacturing departments, the various *means* become the primary *goals* of each of these subordinate departments. That is, it becomes the goal of the finance department to raise money and the goal of the engineering department to design a good product, and so on. Each of these units may then subdivide its task in order to accomplish its goals most efficiently. For example, the marketing and sales department may choose as a means of accomplishing its task a division into different sales forces to sell to different kinds of customers. As each of these is created, what was a means for the total sales force becomes an end or goal for the subunit. Similarly, manufacturing may divide into several plants making different products, and what is a means for the total manufacturing group becomes a set of goals for each of the plants, and so on down the line.

The total organization, then, can be seen as a system of "means-ends chains" wherein the means for personnel at a higher rank in the organization's hierarchy become the ends for groups directly below them. The master blueprint of the organization often specifies only the first level of means to be employed, giving a certain amount of freedom to the next lower level to develop its own suborganization. This situation creates the possibility—in fact, the likelihood—that different parts of the organization will begin to operate at cross-purposes with one another, overlap in function, or compete for scarce resources such as "good" employees or a certain "share of the budget."

Each subunit can develop its own purposes and goals as well (McKelvey & Kilmann, 1975). In our business example, each plant may decide that for optimal performance it needs its own engineering department, which may conflict with the central engineering department's decision to have a common engineering policy implemented through a single, centrally controlled group of engineers. Or the various sales forces, in order to maximize their own sales, may promise customers certain variations of the product which are costly to manufacture—and thus may run into conflict with the decision of manufacturing to minimize costs by standardizing the product as much as possible. Competition for scarce resources could occur if each department inflates its budget in order to maximize its performance or if several departments each hoard their best people rather than making them available to other departments which may need them more. The larger the organization and the mission to be accomplished, the greater the potential lack of integration. Thus, one of the major problems organizations face is the integration of their various parts to ensure effective overall performance (Lawrence & Lorsch, 1969).

But why is this a *psychological* problem? Why should it be considered in a text on organizational psychology rather than in one on organization theory per se? Why cannot integration be ensured simply by a more careful overall organizational plan which allocates functions in such a way that duplication and competition are eliminated?

The answers to these questions all require an understanding of how informal organizations operate and how they affect the formal organization (Homans, 1950). As was pointed out above, even though organizational roles demand only certain limited activities from each person, it is the whole person who comes to work. People bring with them many attitudes, feelings, and perceptions which are not anticipated by the organization and which do not clearly fit into its plan. As they work with others, they develop relationships with them, informal agreements, and patterns of coordination, all of which go beyond those specified formally by the organization. In fact, such informal procedures often are developed precisely to cope with problems formal procedures and regulations fail to resolve.

Often, people's perceptions, feelings, and attitudes as reflected in informal procedures exhibit a strong loyalty to the subunit to which they belong and are shaped by the kind of work the subunit does. As people identify with a subunit, their self-esteem begins to be tied to its performance, and it becomes increasingly difficult for them to understand and empathize with the problems of other units or those of the organization as a whole. Increasingly, they may work for their own unit and become indifferent or hostile to other groups. The formal organization often encourages this process by rewarding competition between groups and stimulating esprit de corps within groups.

An important part of the psychological contract, possibly the part that most determines day-to-day behavior, consists of subgroup norms. Ultimately, a person's basic sense of identity derives largely from face-to-face contacts with members of a subgroup rather than from formal organizational rules. Thus it should not be surprising that many of the intergroup or interunit difficulties which arise in organizations are the product of *psychological* forces ultimately reflecting the characteristics of human beings. Such forces operate in organizations toward the establishment of informal patterns which influence and alter the formal ones. Achieving greater integration, therefore, involves not only a rational redesign of the formal organization, but also psychological procedures to improve communication and mutual understanding among the subgroups within the organization.

As we will see, one of the reasons why traditional definitions of organizations have not been very helpful in understanding what really goes on in organizations is that they have ignored the complex interplay between the formal and the informal organization, and the need to adapt both the system of differentiation and the methods of integration to the actual task to be performed and the characteristics of the people performing it (Lawrence & Lorsch, 1969). One of the most basic ideas in modern organization theory is "form follows function." That is, one cannot really design an effective organization without a careful assessment of what the task or goals of that organization are to be, and there are many ways to integrate the effort of the different parts of an organization other than the traditional hierarchy of authority. The major dilemma in the design of organizations is how to balance the gains of differentiation against the costs of potential lack of integration, and how to invent organization designs which optimize both.

ORGANIZATIONAL EFFECTIVENESS, SURVIVAL, AND GROWTH

The final set of human problems to be discussed concerns the relationship of organizations to their environments. All organizations exist in multiple environments. They exist within the culture and social structure of the larger society, and they coexist in various relations to other organizations with similar purposes, as well as disparate social organizations and groups of people who may be owners, managers, employees, customers, clients, or simply "the public at large."

In order to survive at all, an organization must fulfill some useful function. The common goals set by the architects of the organization must result in some product or service which is useful to the members of the organization or to other organizations or to the public at large. For example, Blau and Scott (1962) in their analysis of formal organizations use as the major basis for classification the criterion of *who benefits* from the existence of the organization. They define four classes of organizations:

1. Mutual-benefit associations: Those which benefit primarily the members of the organization, the rank and file (for instance, unions, clubs, political parties, religious sects, professional societies).
2. Business concerns: Those which benefit primarily the owner-managers (such as industries, stores, banks, insurance companies).
3. Service organizations: Those which benefit primarily their clients (for example, hospitals, schools, social work agencies).
4. Commonweal organizations: Those which benefit the public at large (government organizations, such as the Internal Revenue Service, Defense Department, police, fire department, and research organizations).

The survival of each type of organization ultimately depends on its ability to continue to be of use to its prime beneficiary. The survival of an organization does not involve psychological problems different from the ones already cited. To survive, the organization must continue to perform its primary task through the recruitment, proper utilization, motivation, and integration of the people in it.

When we turn to the problem of organizational growth, however, we do uncover some new psychological problems. For example, organizational growth in a business concern may well involve the development of new products and new processes for making products in order to improve the company's competitive position. New ideas for products and processes come from people. The organization, therefore, faces the problem of how to create an environment and a set of management policies which will not only get the primary task performed effectively but which will, in addition, stimulate creative thinking and innovation.

This is not a trivial problem because many of the procedures organizations develop to maximize their day-to-day effectiveness lead to a psychological climate in which innovation and creativity are actually punished. If such a climate has come into existence, how can an organization go about changing it without losing day-to-day effectiveness? Should innovation and creativity be expected of all members of the organization, or should it become the assigned task of a few members of a research and development group? If such a group is created, how should people be recruited into it, how should it be managed, and how should it relate to other parts of the organization?

Problems of growth relate closely to problems of adapting to and managing change. Today many organizations find themselves in a dynamic environment. Technological change, which is proceeding at an incredible rate, creates constant problems of obsolescence. Social and political changes occurring throughout the world create a constant demand for new services and the expansion of presently existing ones. With the advent of computers and automation, the nature of organizations themselves is changing, bringing new needs for highly educated and trained employees and managers far exceeding the present supply. Changing values in regard to the work ethic, the proper role that work and family should play in a person's life, equal employment opportunities for women and members of minority groups, all have changed the expectations of members of organizations about a reasonable and fair psychological contract. Various government agencies and public groups have begun to challenge some of the assumptions organizations have traditionally made about product safety, pollution, obligations to communities to provide employment, and what their ultimate role in society is to be.

These environmental forces not only demand creative thinking on the part of members of organizations, but they also involve a more fundamental psychological problem. This problem can be conceptualized as follows. Much of the present technological and social change is unpredictable. We cannot accurately assess what will be the environment for organizations even a decade ahead. Therefore, if organizations are to adapt to such rapid and unpredictable change, they must develop *flexibility* and the capacity to meet a variety of new problems. Such characteristics ultimately reside in the human resources of the organization. If the managers and employees are themselves flexible, the organizational blueprint can be consciously and rationally altered in the face of changing external situations, but if an organization's members are locked into a rigid pattern of responding, then altering the blueprint will be a useless exercise. The psychological problem for the organization becomes, therefore, how to develop in its personnel the kind of flexibility and adaptability that may well be needed for the organization to survive in the face of a changing environment.

For example, the employee who ten years ago had a yen for pure mathematics and was encouraged by the company to pursue this study may find himself or herself today suddenly occupying a key role in evaluating the merits of conversion to automatic data processing through electronic computers. If the organization is to make itself capable of adapting to and managing change, it may well have as one of its major psychological problems the encouragement of *diversity* of skills and the *psychological growth* of its employees. Such psychological growth may not only make management of change easier but may also ameliorate some of the other problems mentioned above, such as how to motivate employees, how to create commitment to the organization, and, most important, how to create a situation in which personal needs and organizational needs can both be satisfied.

Finally, organizational flexibility will be increased if key managers begin to develop attitudes and skills which permit them to utilize the findings of organizational psychology on behalf of the development of the organization itself. As the field of organizational psychology develops, it is becoming increasingly clear that an organization's health and effectiveness will depend ultimately upon its ability to diagnose its own problems and to develop its own solutions (Schein, 1969). The agents of planned change will necessarily be key managerial personnel, and these individuals will be required to take a systems view of organizations, to diagnose the complexities of organizational problems, to utilize outside resources where appropriate to aid in the diagnosis and intervention, and to educate others to do so within the organization. *All organizations face the problem of how to develop such attitudes and skills in their key managers.*

SUMMARY

In this chapter, we have attempted to outline the major ideas underlying the concept of formal organization and also the human problems that arise in organizations. These problems interact and overlap, but for purposes of rough classification they can be divided into the following categories: (1) problems of creating and designing the organization; (2) problems of recruiting, selecting, training, socializing, and allocating human resources; (3) problems deriving from the nature of the psychological contract between the individual and the organization; that is, how authority is delegated within the organization and how the individual can exert an influence on the organization; (4) problems of integrating the various units of a complex organization, which largely entails improving communications among the various informal organizations within the formal structure; and (5) problems stemming from the needs of the organization to be effective, to survive, and to grow and develop its capacity to adapt to and manage change in a rapidly changing world.

Motivation and Assumptions About Human Nature

Throughout history there have been many attempts to provide a comprehensive answer to the question of what really motivates people—what in the nature of human beings makes them behave in certain ways. Yet the answer continues to elude us, and the debate today about what motivates people in their work behavior continues as lively as ever.

In the next several chapters, I will attempt first to show why it is so difficult to determine the "essence" of human nature by reviewing the several perspectives that managers have historically taken on motivation. Then the implications of the various managerial assumptions for strategies of supervision will be outlined. Review of some major research findings bearing on each of the major sets of assumptions will then lead to the argument that each of the theories is partially correct, but only partially. To fully understand motivation and human behavior we must develop a complex set of assumptions about people and we must also set these assumptions in a developmental context.

The main conclusion will be that there is no one answer, no one "correct" way to manage people, no "perfect" way to organize or to design work. Instead, one must become diagnostic and flexible, sensitive to events and their subjective interpretation by the participants in a given situation, so that one can choose a course of action appropriate to that situation.

Human Nature: Why Is It Elusive?

One of the persistent problems of organizational psychology has been to develop a concept of human nature which would provide managers with clues on how to recruit, select, and manage people in order to obtain productivity for the organization and satisfaction for the employee. Typically we have looked toward theories of motivation to find such a concept—what makes people work, what ultimate needs or motives drive them, how important is money as a motivator, how similar are people in their motivation, what kinds of incentives will workers respond to if one wants to increase their productivity, why are some people highly motivated while others slack off or even turn their energy and creativity toward undermining the organization?

There are a great many competing theories of motivation which purport to explain the behavior of people in organizations, but there is relatively little clear research support for any of them. It is as if every theory that is proposed—such as the need for *security*, or the need to use one's *competencies*, or the need for *self-actualization*—is partially true in that it explains the behavior of *some* employees or *some* managers *some* of the time. But every time we attempt to generalize, we find that other, more important phenomena seem to be at work that vitiate the proposed theory. People sometimes work for money but then, to our surprise, fail to respond to a financial incentive system; people clearly want to use their competencies but then sometimes refuse a clearly more challenging job; people become demotivated and less interested in their work, yet the quality of what

39

they do remains high. How are we to explain all of these inconsistencies and how is a manager to develop sensible, rational policies for dealing with people?

THE BIOLOGICAL FALLACY

One major explanation for the variation we see in human behavior is that such behavior is only *partially* determined by whatever inner needs or motives we bring with us as members of a biological species. A far greater determinant of what we do is our learned motives and responses, which reflect our culture, our family situation, our socioeconomic background, and the actual here-and-now forces operating within any given life situation. In other words, our motives and needs are largely determined by our *perceptions* of the situation we find ourselves in, and those perceptions are themselves largely determined by prior learning.

For example, whether or not money will motivate me may depend largely upon my perception of myself as in need of more or less money, and that perception will depend in part upon how I relate my own status and condition to that of others with whom I identify, who represent my "reference group." If I have come from very humble origins and have finally achieved a reasonable subsistence level and perceive myself as "having made it" by whatever standards I assimilated in the subculture in which I grew up, I will react very differently to a monetary incentive than if I am a business school graduate starting out at the bottom of my career, aspiring to a high level in the organization and to a position of wealth which will prove to the world that I have really made it "to the top."

In other words, even though human beings may start with similar biological and genetic tendencies, they develop different patterns of needs, motives, talents, attitudes, and values that reflect the particular upbringing and sociocultural situation in which they find themselves. To give another example, a manager may have learned that one way to deal with workers is to involve them participatively in certain kinds of decisions, to build a climate of mutual trust and open communication with them. That strategy may work very well with a worker whose own parents have grown up in a middle-class business-oriented community, yet it may fail dismally with a third-generation political activist whose family helped initiate the development of unionism and has always operated from the initial assumption that managers can *never* be trusted.

So not only is it a fallacy to look for "human nature" in our biological origins, but there is overwhelming evidence that some of the strongest motivational determinants of human behavior are *situational* and *role related*. For example, an otherwise unaggressive person might fly into a rage and quit a job if he or she is insulted by a boss or treated in an undignified manner; a totally honest individual might embezzle company funds if confronted by a medical crisis at home; an indolent worker might suddenly become superenergetic if a co-worker is someone with whom he or she has always felt highly competitive; a person who was always unwilling to travel for the company might suddenly want to travel because the children have grown up and a new set of activities is needed to stimulate the relationship between the person and his or her spouse; a worker might really produce at a high level for a boss who treats him or her fairly but become a saboteur if the treatment is perceived as unfair.

Sociologists have a concept called "the definition of the situation," by which they mean that human beings are always operating in some kind of situation the meaning of which is defined by the collective perceptions of, assumptions about, and expectations one has for that situation. We never operate in a social vacuum. We are always moving from one situation to another, and how we react, what our motives will be, will depend largely on how we define or structure that situation. When we enter new situations—as when we take a new job or join a new organization—the process of *socialization* can be defined partly as being taught or learning how to define or think about a given subset of that situation—what to do in the presence of the boss, how hard to work after hours, and so forth.

If we are to understand what a person is doing in a given situation and why, we must seek to understand the person's definition of the situation. If the organization has introduced a monetary incentive system to increase production, and yet production does not increase, the answer may well be that the workers are defining the situation as one in which working a little harder may lead to disrupted friendships, loss of pleasant social contacts, and possibly a later reduction in how much they will be paid for a given piece of work. From that perspective the monetary gains are not worth the risks, and behavior will not change, not because money is unimportant in some general motivational scheme, but because in that particular situation the workers' need for money was weighed by them against other values and motives which were operating. The same workers who fail to respond to a particular monetary incentive scheme may quit their jobs to take a higher paying one somewhere else. Does that make them inconsistent? No. It simply means that motives are tied to particular situations, and we cannot assume that the same motives apply to all people at all times in all situations.

The assumption that human nature is fixed and consists of a single set of motives that operate the same way in each of us has not received much scientific support. *Yet there are consistencies in how people behave.* These consistencies probably derive from the common perspectives we adopt through our various experiences of being socialized into a culture, a family, a socioeconomic stratum, a community, and ultimately an organizational role.

THE NEED FOR A
SOCIOLOGICAL/SITUATIONAL PERSPECTIVE

Some of the most predictable human responses occur in face-to-face interactions and some of the strongest human motives derive from immediate, face-to-face encounters. Anthropologists such as Edward Hall (1959, 1966, 1977) and sociologists such as Erving Goffman (1959, 1963, 1967) have shown us very clearly how highly regularized our social behavior is and how strongly we feel about maintaining the "interactional order." For example, we all know that one of the easiest ways to induce anger in someone is to insult them, and it is easy to embarrass oneself or one's associates by making a fool of oneself (by saying or doing something stupid or out of line). Learning good manners, tact, savoir faire, how to get along with others is given tremendous emphasis by most parents, even though the exact rules of the game (what is good manners or what is tactful) will vary from subculture to subculture.

The South African psychologist Raymond Silberbauer (1968) tells of having to make white foremen in the gold-mines aware of some of the cultural rules of various tribal groups from which workers are recruited. For example, workers were being perceived as untrustworthy and "shifty-eyed" by the foremen because they never looked directly at a foreman. The foremen were unaware that it was a mark of *disrespect* to look directly into the eyes of a superior! For males to hug each other is learned as a positive sign of friendship in Latin America, yet may arouse real anxiety and suspicion of homosexuality in an American supervisor unfamiliar with such customs. In most multinational companies horror stories abound of how managers from one culture mismanaged situations because they did not know the simple rules of interaction in another culture. But the same phenomenon occurs within our own society across socioeconomic groups, geographical regions, groups of different religious origins, and so on.

Pride and dignity are powerful feelings, and the desire to maintain one's dignity or "face" may be a far more powerful motivator than any of the ones we typically find in the lists put together by personality psychologists, for example, needs for power, achievement, security, and so on. As the industrial psychologist Norman Maier (1973) points out in his text, companies will spend a good deal of money to cover a mistake made by an officer in order to protect his or her feelings, that is, not to make the person "lose face." As Goffman (1967) and other sociologists have pointed out, this motive is so important because if we cannot trust others to protect our face and dignity, the whole social order becomes unsafe. If I am to feel secure in my dealings with others, I must be able to believe that they will not unduly take advantage of me, and I must show them by behaving with tact that I also can be trusted. Once we violate these norms of interaction, the very fabric of society begins to be torn down. Violators are subject to ostracism and may be viewed as emotionally unstable and in need of psychiatric treatment. Persistent violators of basic rules of conduct may be put into psychiatric hospitals until they learn to "get along with others."

Many severe labor-management crises can only be understood from the perspective of the threats or insults perceived by workers that often go far deeper than wages or working conditions. The "joke" about employees' restrooms being a good deal shabbier than management's may be rather humorless if one takes this perspective. The important conclusion is that one cannot really understand what kinds of events will threaten someone's dignity without taking a situational and sociological perspective, without studying the norms and values of the particular people in the group being observed.

THE DEVELOPMENTAL PERSPECTIVE

The developmental perspective is simply an extension of the sociological/situational one in that it alerts us to the fact that needs, motives, values, and norms all change with the evolution of society, with the growth and development of organizations, and, most importantly, with the growth and development of the individual. What may have been a paramount need or value at one stage in a person's life may change completely at another stage (Schein, 1978; Hall, 1976). One of the great problems in studying human behavior scientifically is that one cannot easily distinguish between factors that remain stable and those amenable to change and growth. As we will see later, part of life development is a process of stabilizing one's self-image and one's values, yet there are dramatic cases of change in mid-life and old age which cannot be ignored. Managers must be alert to such changes and not predicate decisions on motivational theory assumed applicable only to those of a certain age or cultural group.

THE ORGANIZATIONAL PERSPECTIVE

One of the major situational factors that determines patterns of motivation is the *organizational context* of behavior. How the organizations we work in or belong to treat us, the kinds of norms and values that operate in them, the kinds of authority and power exercised, all will powerfully affect our actions and the kinds of motives from which we act. This argument can best be understood in an historical context by noting that organizations do change their basic pattern of power and authority. It can also be understood if we compare a wide range of types of organizations in terms of their basic psychological contracts with their members.

Etzioni (1961) has provided a very useful typology of such individual-organization relationships by classifying organizations on the basis of (1) the kind of *power* or *authority* they use to elicit compliance and (2) the kind of *involvement* they elicit from members of the organization. On the authority dimension, Etzioni has identified three basically different types of organizations in terms of whether they use pure coercive power, economic or other material incentives combined with rational-legal authority, or "normative" rewards or incentives. Organizations in this last group generally provide opportunities for their members to contribute to goals which are intrinsically valued and congruent with individual goals and also display either a charismatic or a rational leadership style. Table 3.1 shows examples of each of the pure types as well as examples of some mixed structures which involve combinations of authority types.

This typology is based on a different principle from the Blau and Scott typology shown in Chapter 2 and is more useful for our purposes in that it focuses on the internal "climate" of the organization instead of the ultimate purpose or function of different kinds of organizations in society.

Etzioni also distinguishes three types of involvement of organization members, as follows: (1) *alienative*, which means that the person is not psychologically involved but is coerced to remain as a member; (2) *calculative*, which means that the person is involved to the extent of doing a "fair day's work for a fair day's pay"; and (3) *moral*, which means that the person *intrinsically* values the mission of the organization and his or her job, and is personally involved and identified with the organization.

Table 3.1

Classification of Organizations Based on Type of Power or Authority Used

A. Predominantly *coercive*, nonlegitimate authority

    Concentration camps
    Prisons and correctional institutions
    Prisoner-of-war camps
    Custodial mental hospitals
    Coercive unions

B. Predmoninantly *utilitarian*, rational-legal authority, use of economic rewards

    Business and industry (with a few exceptions)
    Business unions
    Farmers' organizations
    Peacetime military organizations

C. Predominantly *normative*, use of membership, status, intrinsic value rewards, authority based on charisma or expertise

    Religious organizations (churches, convents, and so on)
    Ideologically based political organizations or parties
    Hospitals
    Colleges and universities
    Social unions
    Voluntary associations and mutual-benefit associations
    Professional associations
    Business organizations when they are first founded

D. *Mixed* structures

    Normative-coercive: combat units
    Utilitarian-normative: most labor unions
    Utilitarian-coercive: some early industries, some farms, company towns, ships

Source: Based on Etzioni (1961).

Table 3.2 shows the nine types of organizational relationships that could logically result from this typology. Etzioni points out, however, that the type of personal involvement possible depends to a large extent on the kind of power or authority exercised by the organization. Hence there is a tendency for organizations to cluster in certain cells of the table, primarily along the diagonal from upper left to lower right. Thus, if we look back at the examples in Table 3.1, we see that the kinds of organizations listed under coercive would typically have highly alienated members. Utilitarian organizations, on the other hand, would tend to have calculative members

Table 3.2

Types of Power-Authority Versus Types of Involvement

	COERCIVE	UTILITARIAN	NORMATIVE
Alienative	*		
Calculative		*	
Moral			*

*Represents the predominant types.
Source: Based on Etzioni (1961).

who expect primarily economic rewards for their performance but who do not feel they have to like their jobs or their employer. The kinds of organizations listed under normative tend to have members who belong because they value the goals of the organization and like to fulfill their organizational roles. That is, they consider it morally right to belong.

We can restate this point in our terms by saying that the organizational types that fall along the diagonal have workable or "fair" psychological contracts with their members. What the organizations get in the way of involvement is in line with what they give in the way of rewards and the kind of authority they use. If a utilitarian organization like a manufacturing concern expects its employees to like their work—that is, to be morally involved—it may be expecting workers to give more than they receive. Or if a normative organization such as a university wishes to maintain the moral involvement of its faculty, it must use a reward-and-authority system in line with such involvement. If university administrators withhold status or privileges such as academic freedom, for example, they will be violating their psychological contract with professors. The faculty will probably respond either by redefining its role and changing the nature of its involvement from moral to calculative—which might mean putting in minimum class and office hours based on the amount of pay received—or by becoming alienated, that is, doing the required amount of teaching and research, but without concern for quality and without enthusiasm.[1]

The above typology represents "pure" types of organizations seldom found in real-world circumstances. Most organizations are a

[1] We have seen in recent years a considerable growth in faculty unionization, typically related to feelings on the part of a faculty that members were not being fairly treated on issues such as pay, opportunities to influence university policy, and the like (Baldridge, 1971; Ladd & Lipset, 1975).

complex mixture of several types. Nevertheless, it is useful to describe the pure types and to consider the basic dimensions of type of authority-power and type of psychological involvement. Historically, there has been a shift away from pure coercive and normative types of organizations toward various combinations of utilitarian with either normative or coercive. Particularly in the development of business and industry, we have witnessed the movement from a coercive atmosphere in which labor was compelled to follow company dictates because of the scarcity of jobs and an overall low standard of living, to company concern for adequate economic rewards, job security, and many other kinds of employee benefit. The growth of unions and collective bargaining has promoted the utilitarian, rational-legal type of contractual relationship between management and labor (Harbison & Myers, 1959).

As business and industry have become more complex and more dependent on high-quality performance from both managers and workers, a trend has begun toward making the psychological contract more utilitarian-normative. By this I mean that companies are seeking to establish new kinds of relationships with their members. These new relationships to some degree abandon purely utilitarian conceptions in favor of normative ones. Members are increasingly expected to like their work, to become personally committed to organizational goals, and to become creative in the service of these goals; in exchange, they are given more influence in decision making, thus reducing the authority of management.

One way of interpreting the events on many university campuses in the late 1960s is to note that students shifted the basis of their involvement from moral (being in college because they valued education for its own sake) or calculative (being in college because education paid off in better jobs and better future income) toward alienative (being in college only because of pressure to be there and finding the educational offerings irrelevant, hypocritical, or degrading). Professors' authority, being based on their scholarly expertise in a given area of inquiry, could function only so long as students accepted this expertise as *relevant* to their own values and goals. Once students defined professors' expertise as irrelevant, those professors no longer had any rational authority. They then had to rely on utilitarian authority (hope that students would see the need of an education for their own future economic well-being) or coercive authority (threaten to flunk students who were disrespectful or failed to do the work). Much of the anger felt by students and the anxiety expressed by professors in the late 1960s was due to the breakdown of the psychological contract between them. Such a breakdown basically denotes a fundamental questioning of the relationship (based on common values or goals) between the parties. Once this happens, one can expect a breakdown of communication, a failure of mutual understanding, and increasing frustration leading to various kinds of emotional responses on both the part of professors and students (Schein, 1970).

The 1970s have witnessed a gradual return to a more calculative and moral form of student involvement, but many of the basic values of the 1960s have remained—rejection of arbitrary authority, greater concern for the relevance of education, greater concern for nature and the environment, greater individualism, and greater concern for self-expression (Yankelovich, 1974).

CONTINGENCY THEORIES

One of the resolutions to the problem of defining human nature has been to develop what have come to be called "contingency theories." Such theories emphasize that there are no simple generalizations about human behavior in organizations, but that if one can spell out enough of the prior situational conditions, enough about the human actors in the situation, and enough about the properties of the task and the environment within which the task is being carried out, one can then specify hypotheses or propositions.

Such propositions would typically be in the form of "If these and these conditions are true, then the manager should do such and so." A simple version might be: "If the manager is dealing with a group of workers from an economically disadvantaged minority with low experience and skill levels, he or she should institute a training program, tightly structured rules, good economic incentives, and a high degree of supportive activities to help the workers gain self-confidence." On the other hand, "If the manager has at his or her disposal a group of sophisticated, experienced engineers, who are to design a new piece of high-technology equipment, he or she should give the group a maximum degree of freedom, provide consultative help to them as necessary, worry more about recognition than monetary incentives, and work collaboratively with the group in setting rules rather than imposing them."

In the area of how to organize work, similar kinds of contingency theories are being developed pertaining to how to divide labor, how to integrate effort, how much to decentralize, how to control the organization, and so on. The important point to recognize about these theories is that they represent progress in understanding reality, a reality that social scientists are discovering derives from the interplay of cultural, economic, organizational, and technological forces. While it is still worthwhile to ask basic questions such as, What is human nature? or What is an organization? we must recognize that *we will not find simple answers.* We will have occasion throughout this book to refer to attempts to find such simple answers, but the thrust of my argument will be that human beings and the ways in which they interact are too complex for any "blanket" theory to explain.

SUMMARY

In this chapter we have taken a broad look at some of the parameters that help define "human nature" and the psychological contract between organizations and their members. First of all, it is necessary to remind ourselves that human behavior and motivation cannot be understood except from a sociological/situational and developmental perspective. Second, it is important to recognize that different kinds of organizations depend upon different kinds of authority and power, and this in turn limits the kind of involvement their members can have—that is, leads to certain kinds of psychological contracts. Finally, we should recognize that there has been a historical evolution in the use of authority and power from more coercive forms toward more rational-legal and normative forms. In the next chapter we will examine in more detail how these historical trends have reflected themselves in managerial assumptions about human nature and the basic motivation to work.

Managerial Assumptions About Human Nature

4

"Explain to me about motivation," said the owner. "Does the coach provide motivation by telling the team to go out and win one for Max Zaslofsky? Does he say, 'Win this game and I'll let you all stay up and watch the Johnny Carson show the next time we're in Detroit?' "

"No," the General Manager said. "Motivation is a more subtle art. The coach has to make his players feel wanted. He has to make them feel they're contributing. He has to make them feel good."

The owner thought that over.

"The last time I looked at my books," he said, "I was paying about two and a half million dollars a season in salaries. Doesn't that make them feel wanted? Doesn't that make them feel good?"

"It would me," said the General Manager. "But times have changed. All that money simply makes our players self-satisfied. Big cash ties their legs together so they can't dive for loose balls, and turns their brains into fettucini so they can't figure out when to switch and when to play their own man." (Ray Fitzgerald, *Boston Globe*, January 5, 1978.)

INTRODUCTION

Human behavior is a complex result of our *intentions*, our *perception* of the immediate situation, and our *assumptions* or *beliefs* about the situation and the people in it. These assumptions are, in turn, based upon our past experience, cultural norms, and what others have taught us to expect. In order to understand how organizations function, it is necessary first to understand how the people in those organizations, especially the managers who make organizational decisions, policies, and rules, function. In this chapter we will, therefore, focus on the kinds of assumptions managers have made about human nature and motivation, because such assumptions determine to a large extent organizational policies with regard to incentives, rewards, and other personnel matters.

For example, if an entrepreneur strongly believes that one cannot trust people to work hard on their own, he or she will build an organization with tight controls to ensure that workers come to work on time and are closely supervised. Another entrepreneur in the same business may start with the assumption that people work because they get excited about a product and identify with it and will, therefore, demonstrate a management style that encourages feelings of participative ownership of and identification with the company. This entrepreneur may distribute stock, encourage worker autonomy, and rely mainly on self-discipline rather than close supervision. Both people are operating from assumptions that may be partly or totally wrong insofar as a given worker is concerned. Nevertheless, these initial assumptions strongly influence how we initially design our incentives, rewards, and controls. How accurate or inaccurate the assumptions are, therefore, becomes a critical issue in the design of organizations.

This area of organizational psychology is closely linked to a long tradition in social psychology of studying how people perceive situations, how they attribute causality in their efforts to make situations meaningful, and how their personal attitudes and values in turn influence perceptions and attributions. For example, Wrightsman (1964, 1974, 1977) has attempted to measure six dimensions of what he calls "philosophies of human nature":

1. the degree to which we believe that people are trustworthy or untrustworthy
2. the degree to which we believe that people are altruistic or selfish
3. the degree to which we believe that people are independent and self-reliant versus being dependent and conformist to groups or authority figures
4. the degree to which we believe that people have strength of will and rationality versus being controlled by irrational internal or external forces
5. the degree to which we believe that people have differing thoughts, perceptions, values versus basically the same perceptions, values, and so on
6. the degree to which we believe that people are simple versus highly complex organisms

Different populations of college students in different geographical regions were found to vary considerably in how they viewed human nature both in terms of degree of cynicism, based on the first four dimensions, and in terms of simplicity-complexity, based on the last two dimensions. Historically, as we shall see, our thinking about human nature has proceeded along these same two dimensions, from more cynical to more idealistic and from more simple to more complex.

When we examine managerial assumptions about human nature, we can think of them in McGregor's (1960, 1967) terms as part of a manager's total life view or "cosmology." In other words, every manager has a total world view, and his or her view of why people work and how one should motivate and manage them is part of that world view. In turn, this world view will reflect the cultural theories about human nature that predominate in the given society of which she or he is a member. These broader cultural theories have themselves evolved over the last century and have tended to reflect the more basic political systems of their respective societies. In other words, the kind of psychological contract that is conceivable in an organization is ultimately a reflection of the broader kind of social contract operative in the total society. This social contract in turn reflects prevailing assumptions about the legitimate bases of authority.

In this chapter, we look at three major sets of assumptions that have had a considerable influence on managerial thinking, examine some of the research evidence, and draw out the implications of these assumptions for managerial behavior: (1) rational-economic assumptions, (2) social assumptions, and (3) self-actualization assumptions. Chapters 5 and 6 will present a different set of assumptions, one that reflects a more variable, complex model of human nature, based on research evidence that is enabling us to subsume both cynical and idealistic viewpoints into a more realistic model of human motivation and behavior.

I. RATIONAL-ECONOMIC ASSUMPTIONS

The doctrine that human nature is rational-economic derives ultimately from the philosophy of hedonism, which argued that people act to maximize their self-interest. The economic doctrines of Adam Smith, based on similar assumptions about human nature, led to the theory that relationships in the marketplace between organizations and between customers and buyers should remain unregulated because the separate pursuits of self-interest would result in a self-balancing system.

In terms of employee behavior, this general line of thought led to the following assumptions:

a. Employees are primarily motivated by economic incentives and will do whatever affords them the greatest economic gain.
b. Since economic incentives are under the control of the organization, the employee is essentially a passive agent to be manipulated, motivated, and controlled by the organization.
c. Feelings are, by definition, *irrational* and, therefore, must be prevented from interfering with a person's rational calculation of self-interest.
d. Organizations can and must be designed in such a way as to neutralize and control people's feelings and, therefore, their unpredictable traits.

Implied in these assumptions are some additional ones which were made explicit by Douglas McGregor (1960) in his analysis of organizational approaches toward people. He labeled these additional assumptions Theory X, in contrast to Theory Y which will be discussed later:

THEORY X ASSUMPTIONS

e. People are inherently lazy and must, therefore, be motivated by outside incentives.
f. People's natural goals run counter to those of the organization, hence they must be controlled by external forces to ensure that they work toward organizational goals.
g. Because of their irrational feelings, people are basically incapable of self-discipline and self-control.
h. People can, however, be divided roughly into two groups—those who fit the assumptions outlined above and those who are self-motivated, self-controlled, and less dominated by their feelings. This latter group must assume the management responsibilities for all the others.

Ultimately, then, rational-economic assumptions classified human beings into two groups—the untrustworthy, money-motivated, calculative mass, and the trustworthy, more broadly motivated, moral elite who must organize and manage the mass. In many industries workers were stereotyped as fitting Theory X assumptions. As we will see, the main problem with this theory is not that it fits no one, but rather that it grossly overgeneralizes and oversimplifies human behavior.

Implied Managerial Strategy

The kinds of assumptions managers make about the nature of people will determine their managerial strategy and their concept of what the psychological contract should be between the organization and the employee. The above assumptions, for example, imply essentially a *calculative involvement*, in Etzioni's terms. The organization is buying the services and obedience of the employee for economic rewards, and the organization assumes the obligation of protecting itself and the employee from the irrational side of his or her nature via a system of authority and controls. Authority rests essentially in designated offices or positions and the employee is expected to obey whoever occupies a position of authority regardless of the person's expertise or personality.

Primary emphasis is on efficient task performance. Management's responsibility for the feelings and morale of people is secondary unless those feelings relate directly to task performance. The managerial strategy which emerges is well summarized by Koontz and O'Donnell (1972) in their principal functions of managing: (1) planning, (2) organizing, (3) staffing, (4) directing, and (5) controlling.

If people are not producing or morale is low, the solution tends to be sought either in the redesign of jobs and organizational relationships, or in changing the incentive and control system to ensure adequate motivation and production levels. Thus, an industrial organization operating by these assumptions will seek to improve its overall effectiveness by concentrating on the organization itself— who reports to whom, who does what job, are jobs designed properly in terms of efficiency and economy, and so on? Its second alternative will be to reexamine its incentive plans, the system by which it tries to motivate and reward performance. If productivity is low, the company may well try an individual bonus scheme to reward the high producer, or it may stimulate competition among workers and give special rewards to the winners. Lastly, it will reexamine its control structure. Are supervisors putting enough pressure on employees to produce? Does the system adequately identify and punish the person who fails to produce, who shirks on the job? Are there adequate information-gathering mechanisms to enable management to identify which part of the organization is failing to carry its proper share of the load?

The burden for organizational performance falls entirely on management. Employees are expected to do no more than the incentive and control systems encourage and allow; hence, even if employees did not fit the assumptions made about them, it is unlikely that they could express alternative behavior. Consequently, the greatest danger for an organization operating by these assumptions is that they tend to be self-fulfilling. If employees are expected to be indifferent, hostile, motivated only by economic incentives, and the like, the managerial strategies used to deal with them are very likely to train them to behave in precisely this fashion.

Evidence for Rational-Economic Assumptions

That there is some validity to the rational-economic image of human nature can be seen in our own day-to-day experience and throughout the history of industry. The assumptions and the management principles which follow from them are applicable to many different kinds of situations. For example, the concept of the assembly line as an efficient way to produce has proved itself over and over again. Money and individual incentives have proved to be successful motivators of human effort in many kinds of organizations. The fact that employees' emotional needs vis-à-vis work often go unmet is irrelevant if these people have no such expectations. Yet, in spite of the dramatic success of management strategies based on the rational-economic image of human nature, there were problems and instances of failure. If pay was the only thing workers could expect from the organization, then they always wanted more of it. As the standard of living in industrial society rose, employees changed their expectations of what should be provided in the way of pay and privileges. Large industrial organizations initially found it easy to exploit workers. Such exploitation led ultimately to the development of unions, however, which gave workers a more powerful tool for influencing management if their expectations were not met.

Jobs became more complex, and competition among organizations became more severe, which meant that management had to depend increasingly on the judgment, creative capacity, and loyalty of the worker. As organizations came to expect more of employees, they also had to reexamine their assumptions about them. And as organizations came to expect more, employees came to expect more as well. In broad terms, the psychological contract has tended to shift as organizations have become more complex and more dependent on their human resources.

At the same time, industrial psychologists and industrial sociologists began to study more carefully what the motivations and behavior patterns of organizational members actually were. As results were being compiled, it became clear that workers brought with them many motives, needs, and expectations which did not fit the rational-economic assumptions, yet which influenced the quality and quantity of their work and their relationship to the organization. These studies led to another set of assumptions that put greater emphasis on social needs and motives.

II. SOCIAL ASSUMPTIONS

Two classic studies first showed the importance of social motives in organizational life. The Hawthorne studies dramatically drew attention to the fact that the need to be accepted and liked by one's fellow workers is possibly more important than the economic incentives offered by management (Roethlisberger & Dickson, 1939; Homans, 1950). They further showed that a person will often resist being put into a competitive position with other people. An individual may well handle the threat which competition implies to the losers by banding together with others to resist the threat. Something akin to this happened among the coal miners studied by Trist, a second classic piece of research in the history of organizational psychology (Trist & Bamforth, 1951; Trist, Higgin, Murray & Pollock, 1963).

The Hawthorne Studies

In the late 1920s a group of women who assembled telephone equipment in Western Electric Company's Hawthorne, Illinois, plant were the subjects of a series of studies undertaken to determine the effect on their output of such working conditions as length of the work day, number and length of rest pauses, improved lighting, free lunches, and other aspects of the "nonhuman" environment. The women, especially chosen for the study, were placed in a special room under one supervisor and were carefully observed.

As the experimenters began to vary the conditions of work, they found that with each major change there was a substantial increase in production. Being good experimenters, they decided, when all the conditions to be varied had been tested, to return the workers to their original poorly lighted work benches for a long working day without rest pauses and other amenities. To the astonishment of the researchers, output rose again, to a level higher than it had been even under the best of the experimental conditions.

At this point, the researchers were forced to look for factors beyond those which had been deliberately manipulated in the experiment. For one thing, it was quite evident that the workers developed very high morale during the experiment and became extremely motivated to work hard and well. The reasons for this high morale were found to be several: (1) The women felt special because they had been singled out for a research role; this selection showed that management thought them to be important.[1] (2) The women developed good relationships with one another and with their supervisor because they had considerable freedom to develop their own pace of work and to divide the work among themselves in a manner most comfortable for them. (3) The social contact and easy relations among the women made the work generally more pleasant. On the basis of these preliminary findings, a new kind of hypothesis was formulated, namely, that motivation to work, productivity, and quality of work all are related to the nature of the *social* relations among workers and between workers and their supervisor.

In order to investigate this hypothesis more systematically, a new work group was selected, consisting of 14 men, some of whom wired banks of equipment, which others then soldered, and which two inspectors examined before labeling them "finished." The men were put into a special room where they could be observed around the clock by a trained observer who sat in the corner of the room. At first the men were suspicious of the outsider, but as time wore on and nothing special happened as a result of his presence, they relaxed and fell into their "normal" working routines. The observer discovered a number of very interesting things about the work group in the bank-wiring room.

Result 1.   Though the group had a keen awareness of its own identity, there were nevertheless two cliques within it corresponding roughly to those in the front of the room and those at the back. The men in front felt themselves to be of higher status because the equipment they were wiring was thought to be a more difficult task than that of the back group. Each clique included most of the wiremen, soldermen, and inspectors in that part of the room, but there were some persons who did not belong to either clique. Each clique had its own special games and habits, and there was a good deal of competition and mutual ribbing between them.

Result 2.   The group as a whole had some "norms," certain ideas of what was a proper and fair way for things to be. Several of

---

1 Working extra hard because of the feeling of participating in something new and special has come to be known as the "Hawthorne effect." It has been observed in many kinds of settings that almost *any* change which is introduced and which communicates interest and concern for the workers will produce an increase in production. The observer must be careful not to erroneously attribute the positive effect to the actual change. It is also a potential problem that if one group is singled out and improves because of the attention it receives, another group may become demoralized because it was *not* chosen. Finally, the effect wears off and therefore can only be used if one is prepared to continue to introduce new levels of interest and concern.

these norms concerned the production rate of the group and could best be described by the concept of "a fair day's work for a fair day's pay." In other words, the group had established a norm of how much production was "fair"—namely, 6,000 units—a figure which satisfied management but was well below what the men could have produced had fatigue been the only limiting factor. Related to this basic norm were two others: "one must not be a rate-buster," which meant that no member should produce at a rate too high relative to that of the others in the group; and "one must not be a chiseler," which meant that one must not produce too little relative to the others. Being a deviant in either direction elicited kidding rebukes, social pressure to get back into line, and social ostracism if the person did not respond to the pressure. Actually, the men were colluding to produce at a level below their capacity, a practice that has come to be called "restriction of output."

The other key norm that affected working relationships concerned the inspectors and the supervisor of the group. In effect, the norm stated that "those in authority must not act officious or take advantage of their authority position." The men attempted to uphold the assumption by making it clear that if inspectors attempted to take advantage of their role or if they acted officious, they were violating group norms. One inspector did feel superior and showed it. The men were able to play tricks on him with the equipment, to ostracize him, and to put so much social pressure on him that he asked to be transferred to another group. The other inspector and the group supervisor were "part of the gang" and were accepted for this reason.

Result 3.   The observer discovered that the group did not follow company policy on a number of key issues. For example, it was forbidden to trade jobs because each job had been rated carefully to require a certain skill level. Nevertheless, the wiremen often asked soldermen to take over wiring while they soldered. In this way, they relieved monotony and kept up social contacts with others in the room. At the end of each day each man was required to report the amount of work he had done. Actually the supervisor was supposed to report for all the men, but he had learned that the men wished to do their own reporting and decided to let them do it. What the men actually reported was a relatively standard figure for each day, in spite of large variations in actual output. In contrast to their reported "straight-line output," the individual employee's actual output varied greatly as a function of how tired the person was, his morale on a particular day, and many other circumstances. The men did not cheat in the sense of reporting more than they had done. Rather, they would underreport on some days, thus saving up extra units to list on another day when they had actually underproduced.

Result 4.   The men varied markedly in their individual production rates. An attempt was made to account for these differences by means of dexterity tests, but the results in no way correlated with individual output. An intelligence measure was then tried with similar lack of success. What finally turned out to be the key to output rates was social membership in one of the cliques. The members of the high-status clique were uniformly higher producers than the members of the low-status clique. But the very highest and very lowest producers were social isolates who did not belong to either group. Evidently, individual output was most closely related to the social membership of the workers, not to their innate ability.

The output rates actually were one of the major bones of contention between the two cliques because of the pay system: Each man got a base rate plus a percentage of the group bonus based on total production. The high-status clique felt that the low-status group was chiseling and nagged them about it. The low-status group felt insulted to be looked down upon and realized that the best way to get back at the others was through low production. Thus, the two groups were caught in a self-defeating cycle which further depressed the production rate for the group as a whole.

Conclusion.   What this study brought home to the industrial psychologist was the importance of the social factor—the degree to which work performance depended not on the individual alone, but on the network of social relationships within which he or she operated. As more studies of organizations were carried out, it became evident that the informal associations to be found in almost every organization profoundly affect individuals' motivation to work, level of output, and quality of performance. The Hawthorne studies were one of the major forces leading to a redefinition of industrial psychology as industrial *social* psychology.

Although the Hawthorne studies clearly revealed the existence of an informal social organization and its effects on work performance, it was not clear whether these informal groups served any important functions for workers as human beings. Would it have made a difference, for example, if management had tightened up on the men, enforced the rules, and shifted them around or isolated them? Systematic attempts to change the informal organization were not part of the research at Western Electric, but did figure in studies of other organizations. A good example was provided by the Tavistock Institute studies of the effects of a technological change in the coal mining industry in Great Britain.

The Tavistock Institute Coal Mining Studies

Eric Trist and his associates did extensive studies of the effects on coal mines of a technological change involving the installation of mechanical coal-cutting equipment and conveyors. The old system involved small groups, ranging in size from two to eight men, who worked as a highly interdependent team, usually in isolation from other similar teams. The team generally consisted of one skilled worker, his mate, and several laborers who removed the coal in "tubs." Each team had a small section of the coal face and was responsible for the cutting, loading, and removal of the coal from its section (shortwall method). Teams were highly autonomous. Members were picked by the team leader on the basis of mutual compatibility. Long-term relationships were established among members, relationships which included taking care of a team member's family if he was hurt or killed. Because of the anxieties aroused by working underground and in the dark, and because of the very real dangers involved in mining, strong emotional bonds formed among team members.

Conflict and competition between teams was common and various sorts of bribery and graft were involved in getting good sections of the coal face to work and in acquiring enough "tubs" to be able to take out more coal than other teams. Although fights both underground and in the community were common, they apparently served as a useful outlet for the aggressions which resulted from the highly frustrating aspects of the work itself. Competition was accepted as part of life, however, and did not disturb the basic social system of the community and the mine.

Because of the variable thickness of the coal seams in British mines, it became desirable from an engineering point of view to install mechanical equipment for cutting and removing coal (longwall method). The kind of worker group needed for this type of operation differed sharply from what was needed for the shortwall method. The organization had to shift from small teams to large groups resembling small factory departments. These new groups consisted of 40 to 50 men under a single supervisor. Where previously the traditional groupings had been small teams and a total community, now an intermediate-size social system had to fulfill the various needs of the workers.

This intermediate-size system created great social difficulties because the men were generally spread out over a distance of 200 yards, in a tunnel two yards wide and one yard high, and they were divided into three shifts. The task required such a high degree of coordination among the shifts and among the men within a shift,

60

that an inefficiently done job anywhere along the line reduced the output of the entire group sharply. Particularly sensitive was the relationship between those men who had to prepare the face by drilling and blasting the coal loose and those men who then removed it onto the mechanical conveyor. The new small groups which emerged around common tasks were differentiated in terms of the kind of work and the kind of prestige they enjoyed in the total community. Thus, not only were communications between shifts undermined by the new method, but *the new small-group organization was also similarly undermined by the differential prestige associated with the different work.*

Besides the emotional strains that resulted from the disruption of group relationships, came other problems having to do with the amount and quality of the work itself. Because the workers were so spread out, no effective supervision was possible. Because of dangers inherent in the work situation and without opportunities to release tension in close emotional relationships, the productivity of the men tended to suffer. A norm of low productivity tended to arise as the only way to cope with the various difficulties encountered. Psychologically, the consequences were a loss of "meaning," an increasing sense of anomie (of being unrelated to others and to society), and a sense of passivity and indifference.

The important lesson in this example is that a technological change dictated by rational engineering considerations disrupted the social organization of the workers to such an extent that the new mechanical system could not work efficiently. In other words, the formal organization actually impeded the formation of meaningful informal groups that could meet the men's emotional needs. Only as the coal mining industry, with the help of social scientists, began to redesign the formal and social organization rather than only the organization of work, was it possible to begin to overcome some of the difficulties created.

The essence of this reorganization was to reintroduce with further mechanization more elements of autonomy for the work group so that cooperative rather than competitive relationships would be stimulated among the specialized worker groups. A group-based pay system, more opportunity for the group to allocate members to shifts and to work roles, permitting of job trading, and generally encouraging self-regulation made it possible for the miners to meet their social needs without losing the productivity gains made possible by higher mechanization. Trist and his colleagues also pointed out that with further trends toward automation or "machine dependence" a new kind of work culture and new kinds of managerial skills would gradually have to come into being.

The results cited in these two examples are typical of what has been found in company after company when jobs have been redesigned without explicit consideration of the possible effects on the workers' social relationships. Again and again it has been shown that the informal organization does play a key role in meeting important emotional needs of the organization member and thus cannot be ignored or "forbidden" (Balzer, 1976; Schrank, 1978).

As research results have accumulated, a gradual change has taken place in the traditional concept of job design and industrial engineering. The original assumption that the layout of the work was to be dictated largely in terms of engineering principles has gradually been replaced by a more refined concept of *human engineering* which takes the interaction and mutual influence of the person and the machine (or the person and the job) as its basic point of departure. This approach has come to be called the "sociotechnical systems" approach and will be discussed in greater detail in a later chapter.

Implications of Early Research

The recognition that workers bring to the job social needs that can only find expression in informal groupings, and that such groupings create feelings and norms which actually influence how the work is performed, productivity levels, and the quality of output, led to a new set of assumptions about human nature. These propositions, first clearly articulated by Elton Mayo and his colleagues of Hawthorne fame, still dominate a good deal of managerial thinking today (Mayo, 1945). For Mayo, the evidence of the Hawthorne studies and the subsequent data obtained in interviews with workers were convincing proof that industrial life had taken the meaning out of work and had frustrated employees' basic social needs. So many workers complained of a feeling of alienation and a loss of identity that Mayo developed a very different view of human nature, one that can be articulated in the following assumptions:

1. Social needs are the prime motivator of human behavior, and interpersonal relationships the prime shaper of a sense of identity.
2. As a result of the mechanization entailed in the Industrial Revolution, work has lost much of its intrinsic meaning, which now must be sought in social relationships on the job.
3. Employees are more responsive to the social forces of the peer group than to the incentives and controls of management.
4. Employees are responsive to management to the extent that a supervisor can meet a subordinate's needs for belonging, for acceptance, and for a sense of identity.

Implied Managerial Strategy

These assumptions have drastically different implications for management strategy. *First*, they dictate that managers should not limit their attention to the task to be performed, but should give more attention to the needs of the people who are working for them. *Second*, instead of being concerned with directing and controlling subordinates, managers should be concerned with their psychological well-being, particularly their feelings in regard to acceptance and sense of belonging and identity. *Third*, managers should accept work groups as a reality and think about group incentives rather than individual incentives. *Fourth*, and most important, the manager's role shifts from planning, organizing, and controlling to acting as an intermediary between employees and higher management, listening and attempting to understand the needs and feelings of subordinates, showing consideration and sympathy for such needs and feelings, and upholding subordinates' claims at higher levels. In terms of these assumptions, the initiative for work (the source of motivation) shifts from management to the worker. Instead of being the work giver, motivator, and controller, the manager becomes the facilitator of work and the employee's sympathetic supporter.

The kind of authority and the kind of psychological contract which these assumptions and managerial strategies imply are quite different from those predicated on a traditional view of the organization. Perhaps most important is the fact that the manager acknowledges the existence of needs other than purely economic ones, and recognizes that economic incentives may have very different consequences for different people and under different circumstances. The manager must look at the total social situation in which a given subordinate finds himself or herself, and attempt to understand the meaning that person attributes to the situation—how he or she "defines" the situation and his or her role in it.

The nature of authority in an organization based on social assumptions will still be rational-legal in origin, but much more emphasis will be placed on personal factors such as the charismatic qualities of the boss and his or her ability to get emotionally close to employees and to influence higher levels of management on their behalf.

Assumptions such as these are at the root of many kinds of systems we label "paternalistic." This pattern is rather uncommon in the U.S. today, but paternalistic managers in such countries as Japan and Mexico spend much more social time with their employees, often going out to dinner with them to get better acquainted, to find out what is going on, to learn how employees are feeling, and to provide more informal opportunities to influence without having to give direct orders. The Japanese system of lifetime employment not only provides security but gives workers an important social identity (Ouchi & Jaeger, 1978).

The psychological contract in such organizations involves a commitment on the part of the organization to care for the personal and social needs of employees, and builds up expectations that such needs will be met. In return the company expects that for their part the employees will remain loyal, well motivated, and hard working. In those countries such as Japan where the law requires a company to employ someone for life, the development of a more personal psychological contract probably becomes a necessity, since the organization and its members become much more highly dependent upon each other. If employees can expect the gratification of some important emotional needs through participation in the organization, they can to a degree become more morally involved in the organization. Such involvement in turn permits the organization to legitimately expect loyalty, commitment, and greater identification with organizational goals.

On the other hand, if management creates a situation for workers in which they feel frustrated, threatened, and alienated, they often form into groups whose norms run counter to the goals of management. If management can harness these informal group forces and get group norms working in the direction of organizational goals, a tremendous reservoir of energy and motivation becomes available.

Evidence for Social Assumptions

Beyond the classic studies of Mayo, Roethlisberger, and Trist, there are many strands of research evidence which are consistent with the assumptions outlined above.

One line of evidence comes from observational studies of different kinds of work groups in a number of organizational settings. For example, Zaleznik and his co-workers (1958) noted the following observations in a department of some 50 workers in a medium-sized manufacturing concern: (1) worker productivity and satisfaction were both unrelated to an individual's pay and job status, but were related to group membership; (2) regular group members tended to be satisfied and to conform to the group norms of productivity as well as to management's expectation; (3) deviants and isolates tended to be less satisfied and to violate group norms; (4) deviants and isolates who aspired to group membership and identified with the group tended to produce below the group's norms; (5) deviants and isolates who did not aspire to group membership tended to produce above the group's norms.

In a classic study of human relations in restaurants, Whyte (1948) found that social and group factors were significantly related to absenteeism, quality of customer service, and tendency to quit work. If a supervisor permitted informal groups to form, and the resultant group was well-knit and integrated, relations within the group and the quality of work were good. If the requirements of work upset group relations, however, a variety of troubles arose. For example, if low-status workers like waitresses were put into the position of initiating the actions of higher-status workers like cooks (by shouting orders to them, for example), conflict, resistance, and poor service resulted. When a system of writing out orders and simply depositing them within reach of the cook was instituted, service improved because cooks could now accept orders at their own pace and on their own initiative.

Seashore (1954) studied the relationship between group cohesiveness, as measured by responses to a questionnaire, and a variety of other factors in a heavy machinery company. He found that high group cohesiveness was associated with high productivity if the group members had a sense of confidence in management and with low productivity if the group members lacked confidence in management. Also, persons in high-cohesiveness groups were less likely than those in low-cohesiveness groups to feel "jumpy," nervous, or under pressure.

Studies of assembly lines and mass production have consistently shown that the major source of worker dissatisfaction is the disruption of social relations, specifically the inability to talk comfortably and at their own initiative with neighbors and to pace social contacts in terms of their own needs (Jasinski, 1956; Walker & Guest, 1952; Schrank, 1978). On the other hand, where work has been redesigned in such a way as to facilitate teamwork and social interaction, both productivity and morale have been heightened (Rice, 1958; Trist et al., 1963).

Studies of combat in World War II and in the Korean conflict further underlined the importance of social relations. Not only was it found that the major source of motivation to fight was a soldier's sense of commitment to his fellow soldiers, particularly those with whom he had formed close informal relationships, but emotional breakdown in combat also proved to result from feelings of having let down a fellow soldier. In such cases, rehabilitation could be facilitated at the front lines by talking out the soldier's problems in the small group with whom he had shared the stresses of combat. Evacuating the individual tended to increase emotional difficulties by intensifying an already great sense of guilt at having "let his buddies down" (Harris & Little, 1957).

A very important series of studies by Whyte (1955) attempted to test the assumption that money is indeed a prime motivator of productivity in industrial settings. Through observing work groups, interviewing productive and unproductive workers, and studying the backgrounds of high and low producers, Whyte arrived at the following conclusions:

1. Among production workers, the proportion of those who are primarily motivated by money is very low; perhaps as few as 10 percent of workers will respond to an individual incentive scheme and ignore group pressures to restrict output.

2. When an incentive scheme works, be it an individual or a group incentive, it often works for reasons other than purely economic ones. In some instances, workers perceive the meeting of production goals as a sort of win-lose game that presents them with an exciting challenge. In a different situation, working to attain higher quotas may mean maintaining good relations with a supervisor, or at least reducing the psychological pressure the supervisor would otherwise apply. Another explanation might simply be that working at a brisk pace is often less boring or fatiguing than an erratic or slow pace. Not all of these factors argue for the validity of social assumptions, but they do indicate the inadequacy of the rational-economic assumptions.

3. "Rate-busters," people who produce above the group norms, differ in background and personality from "restricters," who work at the level of group norms. Rate-busters are highly individualistic, come from homes in which economic individualism is greatly prized (such as a farm family), and do not seem to have strong social needs; restricters come from urban working-class homes, value cooperation and getting along with others, and have stronger social needs as evidenced by a higher rate of joining outside social groups. These studies show that at least some workers fit the social assumptions but that perhaps here also the problem is overgeneralization. Not all workers have the same social needs.

The gains to be achieved from group incentive plans that harness group efforts toward organizational goals can be seen in some companies that have adopted the Scanlon Plan (Lesieur, 1958; Frost, Wakeley, and Ruh, 1974; National Commission on Productivity and Work Quality, 1975). This plan was developed by Joseph Scanlon after many years of working in industry and observing the weaknesses of individual incentive schemes, of suggestion plans to get workers' ideas on improving production methods, and of profit-sharing plans designed to give workers a sense of identification with their company. Scanlon was intuitively sophisticated both about learning theory and about the social needs of workers. To meet these needs, he decided that suggestions for improvement of work procedures should be submitted to committees consisting of both management and workers, and that individual credit for the suggestion should be played down. If a suggestion was adopted, however, and actually reduced the costs of production, the savings should be returned to the workers as soon as possible, and as a percentage of their base pay rather than a flat bonus.

In terms of learning theory, the Scanlon Plan provided immediate feedback on workers' efforts in terms of the economic rewards they obtained as a group. By contrast, the typical profit-sharing plan rarely related workers' bonuses to specific individual or group efforts; and the usual suggestion plan often inhibits those individuals who do not wish to be singled out from their group and who recognize that ideas are usually a joint product of the efforts of many. The Scanlon Plan overcame both of these difficulties by distributing savings to the group. The evaluation committees not only provided their members with immediate gratification of social needs but also led to improved communication between management and workers and greater involvement of workers in organizational activities.[2]

Many examples in current leadership and motivation research also support these basic assumptions. Most recently the projects on "autonomous work groups" (to be discussed in detail later) and a number of anthropological/observational studies of workers reinforce the importance of social factors in the work place (Mintzberg, 1973; Strauss, 1974; Terkel, 1974; Balzer, 1976; and Schrank, 1978). There is little question that many workers in a number of situational contexts are highly motivated by social needs, and that such needs can override economic needs. But is there enough evidence that the social assumptions are *the* correct ones and can serve as the basis for designing and managing organizations? Or are these assumptions just as much an overgeneralization as the rational-economic assumptions? To provide a broader perspective on this question we need to examine another theory, namely, that *self-actualization* is the key to human motivation and the principle on which to build organizations and through which to manage people.

2 The success of the Scanlon Plan in raising productivity and reducing costs has been variable. I do not mention it here as valid evidence for social assumptions theories, but as an ingenious application to management of these assumptions (Pigors & Meyers, 1977).

III. SELF-ACTUALIZATION ASSUMPTIONS

One of the major consequences of the social assumptions was the "human relations movement," an effort to train supervisors to be more aware of employees' (social) needs. While such training often improved workers' morale, the results in terms of increased productivity were not clear. At the same time, a growing number of students of organization who agreed with Mayo's basic proposition that work had become meaningless directed their attention to the nature of the work itself. Thus McGregor (1960), Argyris (1957; 1964), and Maslow (1954) among others argued that workers were alienated because the work they were asked to do did not permit them to use capacities and skills in a mature and productive way. They showed evidence that many jobs in modern industry have become so fragmented and specialized that they neither permit workers to use their capacities nor enable them to see the relationship between what they are doing and the total organizational mission. A new and more complex set of assumptions about human nature began to be formulated, best expressed in terms of what McGregor came to call Theory Y.

THEORY Y ASSUMPTIONS

a. Human motives fall into a hierarchy of categories. Beginning with the most basic, they are (1) basic physiological needs; (2) needs for survival, safety, and security; (3) social and affiliative needs; (4) ego-satisfaction and self-esteem needs; (5) needs for self-actualization, that is, making maximum use of all one's talents and resources. As the most basic needs (for food, drink, sleep) are satisfied, they release energy for satisfaction of the higher level needs. Even someone we might consider "untalented" seeks a sense of meaning and accomplishment in his or her work if other needs are more or less fulfilled (Maslow, 1954; Hughes, 1958).

b. The individual seeks to be mature on the job and is capable of being so, in the sense of exercising of a certain amount of autonomy and independence, adopting a long-range time perspective, developing special capacities and skills, and exercising greater flexibility in adapting to circumstances (Argyris, 1964).

c. People are primarily self-motivated and self-controlled; externally imposed incentives and controls are likely to be threatening and to reduce the person to a less mature adjustment (Argyris, 1964).

d. There is no *inherent* conflict between self-actualization and more effective organizational performance. If given a chance, employees will voluntarily integrate their own goals with those of the organization (McGregor, 1960).

68

Whereas Theory X was essentially a cynical view of human nature, Theory Y is clearly a more idealistic view.

Implied Managerial Strategy

If managers hold assumptions such as these, they will worry less about being considerate to employees and more about *how to make work intrinsically more challenging and meaningful.* The issue is not whether the employee can fulfill social needs; the issue is whether the employee can find meaning in work which gives him or her a sense of pride and self-esteem.

Consequently, managers may find themselves in the role of interviewers, attempting to determine what will challenge a particular worker. They will more often be a catalyst and facilitator rather than a motivator, director, or controller. Above all, they will delegate more, in the sense of giving their subordinates just as much responsibility as they feel they can handle.

The implications for authority and the psychological contract which derive from these assumptions are profound. First of all, authority no longer resides in a particular person or even in a given role but in the *task itself.* The challenge of working a problem through—in a sense, controlling and developing oneself—is the heart of self-actualization. The manager actually assumes a secondary role, that of communicating the task requirements. Thus, the whole basis of motivation shifts from being *extrinsic*, implying that the organization must do something to arouse motivation, to being *intrinsic*, implying that *the organization provides an opportunity for the employee's existing motivation to be harnessed to organizational goals.*

In both the rational-economic and social theories, the psychological contract involves an exchange of extrinsic rewards (economic ones or social ones) for performance. In self-actualization theory, the contract involves the exchange of opportunities to obtain intrinsic rewards (satisfaction from accomplishment and the use of one's capacities) for high-quality performance and creativity. This, by definition, creates a *moral* rather than a calculative involvement, and thus releases a greater potential for commitment to organizational goals and creative effort in the pursuit of those goals.

Employees have much greater influence if they are granted a certain amount of autonomy in doing their job, which means that managers must give up certain of their traditional prerogatives, particularly in the area of control. Therefore, an organization that operates according to Theory Y assumptions will tend toward a much broader power base—what Leavitt (1963) has called "power equalization"—and will value the participation of employees in organizational decision making.

The whole concept of "participative management," the idea that employees should be involved in those decisions which directly affect them, flows most clearly from the assumptions that employees want to be morally involved in their work organizations, want to influence decisions, and want to be able to use their capacities in the service of organizational goals.[3] According to Argyris (1964), only if managers adopt these assumptions will organizations and management systems be designed to elicit from employees responsible adult behavior. If organizations are built on either of the other two sets of assumptions, they will end up treating employees as children, expecting them to behave in a dependent, submissive fashion more characteristic of childhood. Managers under those systems should not be surprised, then, if those same employees act like children— rebellious, emotional, and uninvolved in organizational goals.

Evidence for Self-actualization Assumptions

The original interviews with employees of the Hawthorne plant and of other companies studied in the 1920s and 1930s were actually as much evidence for employees' needs to find challenge and meaning in their work as they were evidence for social needs. Argyris in his studies of various kinds of manufacturing organizations found again and again that if the job itself thwarted employees by being too limiting or meaningless, they would create meaning and challenge in outwitting management or in banding together with others in groups. Fantastic creativity has been observed over and over again among production workers when they develop fancy rigs to make their work a little easier or develop complex schemes to enable them to avoid working. The interesting feature of these activities is that they often involve greater expenditure of energy than doing the job set by management. The willingness to expend energy to find something meaningful, even if it is only a poor joke on management, testifies to the strength of the need for meaning. Assembly lines and mass production systems destroy social relations, but even more importantly, they often take meaning and challenge out of work.

It is not clear whether all people expect their work situation to provide challenge and meaning or whether for some, notably workers from lower socioeconomic levels in society, work is *not* a "cen-

---

3 As we will see in subsequent chapters, the idea of participative management has been implemented in a number of ways in recent years, including in some European countries worker participation as members of boards of directors.

tral life interest" in the first place (Dubin, 1956, 1976). For some workers it may be enough to establish an essentially calculative-utilitarian psychological contract with their employer—"a fair day's work for a fair day's pay." If work affords economic security, then meaning and challenge can be sought elsewhere—in family activities, hobbies, or community involvement. However, lower levels of work involvement are not evidence per se against human needs for self-actualization; McGregor, for example, hypothesizes that workers have learned not to expect challenge and meaning in their work and have, therefore, adapted to these lowered expectations. In fact, as was pointed out previously, one of the great dangers of holding rational-economic assumptions is that they can be a self-fulfilling prophecy.

At the same time, Argyris and others have argued that to settle for lower levels of motivation is a potential waste of human resources which many organizations can ill afford. In an increasingly complex and competitive world it may be essential for organizations to fully involve all their employees in order to maximize productivity and creativity over the long range.

The clearest evidence for self-actualization assumptions comes from studies of professionals, managers, and technical employees who tend to be highly work involved and for whom challenge and meaningful work are central values (Pelz & Andrews, 1962; Bailyn & Schein, 1979). In his studies of accountants and engineers Herzberg (1968; Herzberg, Mausner, & Snyderman, 1959) clearly showed that what motivated them most was job challenge and accomplishment. Factors such as the nature of supervision, pay, and working conditions could reduce morale if they were considered inadequate, but remedying these conditions could not increase motivation per se. As the number of well-educated and semiprofessional employees in organizations has increased, the importance of intrinsic motivators has increased because of the high cost of having an upper-level employee be unproductive. Looking back at other findings from this perspective suggests the possibility that the early industrial studies did not discover genuine motivators because lower order needs in Maslow's hierarchy were insufficiently satisfied. As long as workers felt threatened, insecure, underpaid, and poorly supervised, they had to cope with these factors. Perhaps only as such needs have been laid to rest has it been possible to discover that the important motivators lie above and beyond job conditions—they concern the basic nature of the job itself.

Looking again at companies that have used the Scanlon Plan, it is also clear that once employees do become committed to organizational goals, they are capable not only of greater production but also of innovations which reduce costs often beyond the best efforts of the industrial engineers.

The concept of self-actualization stresses higher order needs for autonomy, challenge, growth, and full use of one's capacities and talents. It is assumed that all people have this innate tendency, but that it first makes itself felt as lower order security and social needs come to be satisfied. There is clear evidence that the drive toward self-actualization is an important—perhaps crucial—aspect of managerial and professional behavior. It is not clear, however, how relevant this motive is to the lower level employee, although many of the problems originally interpreted as examples of thwarted social needs could as easily be reinterpreted as instances of thwarted needs for challenge and meaning at *all* levels of the organization.

We can only conclude that workers who are not actively seeking challenge or self-actualization at the place of work either lack this need or they have not been given an opportunity to express it. This may occur because lower order needs have not yet been fulfilled or because the organization has "trained" workers not to expect meaning in their work as part of the psychological contract.

SUMMARY

We have reviewed in broad terms the three major competing sets of assumptions that have emerged historically to explain human nature, and have derived the implied managerial strategies for organizations based on each set of assumptions. Each perspective on human nature is to some degree correct, and each, therefore, provides some important insights into how organizations work and how they should be managed. But, as is so often the case in an emerging field, each theory is an oversimplification and an overgeneralization. The more we study human behavior, the more we discover its complexities, and the more we find ourselves having to adopt a combined sociological, developmental, and situational perspective toward human behavior in organizations. In the next two chapters I will outline a more complex view of human nature—a set of assertions, assumptions, empirical findings, and hypotheses that do not as yet constitute a unified theory, but which help us to understand more fully how people behave in the complex organizational world.

A Developmental and Situational View of Motivation

5

INTRODUCTION

In Chapter 4 we traced the major trends in management theory via its assumptions about human nature. One of the major missing ingredients in all these earlier theories was the notion of human *development*—that motives, needs, abilities, attitudes, and values change and develop, not only during childhood but throughout the adult life cycle. This chapter will, therefore, summarize some of the major theories and research findings about human development, particularly as they impinge on organizational membership and the psychological contract.

One reason for the contradictory evidence about what motivates people is that some theorists are talking about *biologically derived* needs, drives, or instincts. Other theorists are talking about *motives learned in childhood*, patterns that are probably not only culture specific but also vary from subculture to subculture. Still other theorists examine the more *immediate values and goals* people have in relation to their work, values that may or may not be ultimately connected to their biological or socially learned needs, but which certainly vary tremendously among individuals and also with the age or developmental stage of the person.

Finally, a number of newer theories have bypassed the attempt to list particular needs or motives, and have instead argued for universal *process models* of motivation. Such theories, variously labeled "path-goal" theories or "expectancy" theories, essentially postulate that employee behavior will be a function of how much a worker values a given outcome (for example, money, responsibility, accomplishment) and what kind of behavior the person expects to lead to that outcome, such as working harder or improving the quality of work.[1] What we have to recognize at the outset is that these various theories are *not* competing with each other so much as they are attempting to explain different things at different "levels of analysis."

THE BIOLOGICAL ORIGINS OF HUMAN NATURE

The basic controversy still rages as to whether human nature is rooted in biologically and genetically determined "instincts" operative in all human beings, or whether it is essentially a set of learned needs which derive from the basic socialization processes in the culture in which the person grows up. Cultural anthropologists have provided overwhelming evidence of the plasticity of human nature. Some cultures consider aggression and competitiveness completely natural and instinctive, while others view cooperation and altruism as completely natural and instinctive.

On the other hand, the recent work of ethologists and sociobiologists points toward the influence of biologically derived instincts on behavior (Barash, 1977; Lorenz & Leyhausen, 1973). This evidence supports Freud's basic theory that every human being has both a set of *life instincts* which lead to the constructive drives of growth, love, personality expansion, and the integration of the person with the surrounding world, and a set of *death instincts* which lead to the destructive drives of aggression, hate, contraction of the personality, alienation from the surrounding world, and ultimately death. It is likely that all humans are *both* aggressive and loving, altruistic and selfish, social and isolated, and that these broad sets of "instincts" can be molded and channeled into many kinds of specific motives by a given culture and set of life experiences.

Furthermore, it may well turn out that the best way to understand the human personality is to see it as a perpetual, life-long effort on the part of each person to reconcile not only conflicting inner forces which derive from instinctive biological forces (what

---

1 I will not review these theories in detail here. For examples the reader should consult Vroom (1964) and House (1971).

Freud called the *id*), but also to reconcile these "instinctual" impulses with opportunities and constraints that derive from the external world, first through parents and later through the various social institutions, organizations, and interpersonal relationships in which people find themselves.[2]

What the biological model teaches us, if anything, is that the *content* of what motivates people is not as relevant to understanding human nature as is the *process* of conflict resolution, of coping, of developing defenses against both inner impulses and outer constraints and pressures. The process of conflict resolution is what life is all about and molds our individual personalities. Thus a worker might want to work harder to gain some more money but recognize that harder work might put him or her into conflict with fellow workers if norms have developed that one should not be a "rate-buster." The important question, then, is not which is more important—money or belonging to the group—but rather, how does a person resolve conflict situations of this sort and/or how can managers and leaders create situations which might minimize such conflicts in the first place?

THE IMPACT OF SOCIALIZATION AND EARLY DEVELOPMENT

All theories agree that the person as a biological organism could not survive and become "human" without being nurtured in some kind of human group. The learning of language is one of our most basic capacities and skills, and it is largely through language that we learn how to organize our experience, how to perceive what is going on around us, how to label external events and internal feelings, in short, how to think.[3]

It is through language that we learn values, what we should and should not aspire to, how to interpret our experience and give it meaning, how to relate to other human beings, and so on. One of the most basic ways in which cultures and societies thus pass on their basic perspectives is through teaching new members the language of that culture.

The process of socialization makes its first imprint on the per-

2 An excellent short summary of psychoanalytic theory can be found in Levinson's (1968) book *The Exceptional Executive*.

3 There is some evidence that the great apes and perhaps dolphins can "think" in terms that are at a rudimentary level similar to how humans think. It is significant that both these groups are social animals with some rudimentary capacity for language.

sonality during childhood, but it recurs in adolescence and again in adulthood whenever one moves from one role to another or one organization to another (Van Maanen & Schein, 1978). One of the basic ways of understanding what actual motives or values a person will have is to examine the kinds of socialization experiences that person has undergone at various stages of life.

From a Freudian or psychoanalytic perspective, the process of socialization involves the *ego*, the rational, calculating, decision-making capacity that gradually develops as the person seeks to control inner impulses and to channel inner drives so as to minimize external punishment and to maximize external reward. In this process the child "borrows" the strength of the parent by identifying with the parent and thereby internalizes some of the rules, values, and perspectives of the parent (or parent surrogate). We have all observed small children saying to themselves "No, you must not do that" in the process of trying to curb some impulse they know has been disapproved of or punished in the past. The internalization of rules, of values, of an idealized model of what one wishes to become is what makes up our conscience or what Freud termed the *super-ego*. It is that part of ourselves which sits in judgment on us and induces *shame* or *guilt* if we have violated some external or internal rule, and *pride* if we have lived up to our values or ego ideal.[4]

This same process viewed from a sociological perspective is a process of learning to see ourselves as others see us. Because of the capacity of the human brain to abstract and become conscious of itself, it is possible for a young child to perceive not only trans-actions of the outside world as they apply to others but also to extrapolate such behavior to his or her own situation—to imagine how a specific behavior appears to important others. The process of developing a social self is one of gradual generalization. In other words, each person develops a self-concept based on the sum total of others' perceptions of him or her combined with his or her own perceptions of self (Cooley, 1922; Mead, 1930).

Sociologists argue that because the self-concept is basically derived from interactions with others, human beings are truly social animals. If there were no others in a child's environment, he or she would have no referents by which to establish a self-concept. The integration of thousands of messages from others—"you are a good boy," "how tall you are getting to be," "girls should not play with trucks," "what a pretty girl you are," "you should not have hit your little brother, that is not what nice boys do"—combined with the

---

4 The book *I'm OK; You're OK* by Harris (1967) gives a good popularized account of the persistence of the child's way of thinking and responding in each of us.

person's self-perceptions based on internal conflict resolution, initiates the process of self-formation, which continues throughout life.

A young person may have many conflicting impulses—aggressive feelings, fears, desires, and so on—that important adults in the subculture disapprove of, which nonetheless continue to occupy the person's thoughts. If the conflict is severe enough, the individual may repress these negative impulses and become unconscious of them. Yet their continued presence is testified to by a constant set of defensive maneuvers—denying that one is angry, projecting anger onto others, provoking others into aggressive acts which then justify one's own aggressive responses, and so forth. Hopefully, the person will find socially acceptable ways of releasing these feelings such as in competitive sports or in a high-pressure occupation that requires a good deal of aggressiveness.

In extreme cases, an individual may become very mild-mannered, build his or her entire self-concept on the denial of aggression, and learn to use positive motivation to be a loving, cooperative person as a way of controlling a strong opposite impulse (what psychoanalysts have called reaction-formation or overcompensation). The existence of defense mechanisms such as overcompensation in some people does not mean that one can infer that every mild-mannered person is defending against strong inner aggressive impulses; what it does mean is that the formation of the personality is a complex conflict resolution process, that much of the conflict is unobservable, and that surface motives or values are not always consistent with underlying needs and drives.

Part of the emerging self is what Freud and others called the *ego ideal*, that set of goals and values toward which we aspire and that set of criteria we use to measure how we are doing in life. The ego ideal is a learned part of the self that reflects the values in the broader culture, the norms of the subculture or socioeconomic group, the community, and, most importantly, the values within the family itself. Much of the variation in human motivation can be understood only if we realize the multiplicity of forces which act on every child in the process of growing up, and the complexity in each human being of the ego ideal. The occupations we enter, the kinds of intimate relations we seek, the sort of family we build for ourselves, the kinds of organizations we want to join and work in can all be viewed as a process of working out our self-concept and moving toward some conception of self which we value.

The *ultimate motivator* for human adults, therefore, can be thought of as *the need to maintain and develop one's self-concept and one's self-esteem*. We do things which are consistent with how we see ourselves; we avoid things which are inconsistent with how we see ourselves; we strive to feel good about ourselves, and we avoid situations which make us feel bad about ourselves.

This process of searching for the self is a life-long one. We keep finding not only new external challenges to test our self-concept, but also new feelings and impulses that arise from within and may or may not fit our self-concept. These new perceptions must then be integrated, denied, or in some other way dealt with. Such new challenges and feelings arise when we enter new relationships, when we take on new occupational or social roles, when we move geographically to new communities, and when we experience bodily changes because of illness, or biochemical changes related to aging.

At such times the human being experiences a new cycle in the socialization process and finds himself or herself coping to develop new integrations of the self (Schein, 1978; Van Maanen & Schein, 1977). Such times can be constructive and growth producing or constrictive and limiting, depending upon the person's ability to cope and upon the environment's ability to provide growth opportunities. Thus, the lesson for the leader or manager is that each subordinate is a complex human being capable of a broad range of responses who is constantly trying to structure situations to make subjective sense. Subjective restructuring always has as its goal the integration of the new experience with prior experiences and thus the affirmation of the evolving self-concept.

OCCUPATIONAL CHOICE AND CAREER DEVELOPMENT

An area of psychology which bears importantly on these motivational questions yet which has been almost totally ignored in organizational psychology is the study of occupational choice and career development (Hall, 1976; Schein, 1978; Osipow, 1973; Holland, 1973; Roe, 1956; Super & Bohn, 1970). In a society such as ours a person's occupation, the daily work that satisfies basic economic needs, has been shown to be a central aspect of the person's self-concept and source of self-esteem. For example, some of the internal conflicts housewives have in mid-life when their central role as mother takes on less importance have been attributed to the fact that they have not had a chance to develop an equivalent identity or self-concept to that of the fully employed husband whose work career continues while the wife's "family career" may undergo sharp changes. Many of the problems of retirement stem from the sudden loss of identity which accompanies formal termination of employment. In other words, our occupational self-image is an important part of our total self-image, and for many people, it is the most important part.

Theories of *occupational choice* have attempted to link such choice to more basic human motives or needs but have encountered the same difficulties in supporting their hypotheses as other motivation theories. For example, Roe (1956) has theorized that occupational choice will reflect basic personal orientations which derive from childrearing practices. She hypothesized that parents who are very *attentive*—in the sense of being either very loving and/or overprotective, or highly demanding—tend to develop a "people orientation" in their children, which the children then try to express through choosing professions in the area of service, some aspects of business, entertainment, and the arts. Less attentive parents, who are casual, rejecting, or neglectful of their children, tend to develop a "nonpeople orientation" in their children which should lead to occupations such as science, engineering, or isolated outdoor occupations such as forestry.

It has been very difficult to confirm or disconfirm Roe's developmental theory, partly because of the difficulties of obtaining the relevant data on parental behavior, but adults *can* be measured and classified as being more or less people oriented (Osipow, 1973). Whatever the origin of the orientation, there are variations among occupations in the degree to which the person will value "working with other people," and this orientation will fit better with some occupational roles than others. For example, engineering permits the person to work primarily alone, while management as an occupation inherently requires working with other people.

The kinds of orientations people develop in the course of their work lives, and which may have caused them to choose certain occupations, are reflected in numerous contexts. For example, in a recent study of the occupations and work values of MIT alumni surveyed roughly 15 years after graduation, Bailyn and Schein (1972, 1976, 1979) found a patterning of occupational types which reflected both background factors and current values. Three basic career patterns could be identified.

1. *Engineering-based careers.* This basic pattern was defined by a combination of (a) majoring in *engineering*; (b) *average* performance in school; (c) leaving school after a *bachelor's* or *master's* degree; and (d) a *first job in a staff engineering* role. The alumni in this pattern either remained in staff engineering or were found 15 years later in occupations such as business staff, engineering management, functional management, general management, entrepreneurial activity, or consulting. The alumni in this group shared a

common set of values around the need for a challenging job, the need for opportunities to advance, opportunities to exercise leadership roles, opportunities for high earnings, and opportunities to contribute to the welfare of the organization in which they were working. People in this group need organizations to express their basic orientations and values.

2. *Scientific/professionally based careers.* This basic pattern was defined by a combination of (a) majoring in some field of *science*; (b) *above-average* performance in school; (c) continuing graduate education through the *doctorate*; and (d) a *starting job other than engineering* staff. The alumni in this pattern ended up in one of four occupations: professors of science, professors of engineering, managers of scientific projects or laboratories, or science staff. Their value system differed from the engineering-based career types in being relatively more oriented toward the intrinsic challenges of a task, opportunities to be creative and to feel a sense of accomplishment in one's work, and opportunities for further education. In this group there was relatively little concern about leadership, earnings, or contribution to the success of the employing organization.

3. *Pure professional careers.* This basic pattern was defined by majoring in a narrowly defined professional field and entering that field immediately after graduation. In the MIT sample only architecture fitted this model, but medicine, law, social work, and the ministry are other probable examples. We did not have enough cases to characterize the value system of this group, but they tend to show some combination of the values of the autonomous professional (such as the professors in the scientific/professional pattern) with the organizational syndrome of the alumni in the engineering-based pattern. Though it is difficult to unscramble cause and effect, Bailyn and Schein found evidence in all three groups that both a person's prior orientation and his or her subsequent occupational socialization affect the values which are evident 15 years after graduation.

As part of the effort to understand the patterns of job satisfaction in this group of alumni, Bailyn derived an index of "work involvement" based on several items reflecting (a) the relative degree of satisfaction obtained from work/career versus other areas of life, and (b) the importance of work to the alumnus. People in managerial, entrepreneurial, consulting, and academic roles were clearly more work involved than people in engineering, science, or business staff roles, and within the engineering staff group (the group that showed the lowest amount of work involvement) it was the engineers who were "people oriented" who showed the lowest work involvement and job satisfaction. Engineers who remained technically oriented at mid-life were more likely to remain work involved.

The implications for management are clear—even within a fairly homogeneous occupation like engineering one will find many motivational patterns and degrees of work involvement, requiring different managerial strategies to optimize the organization's need for a productive employee and the employee's need for a career to satisfy his/her predominant needs.

Holland's Career Theory

A general theory which attempts to relate personal orientations more directly to occupational environments has been developed and tested by Holland (1966, 1973). Both orientations and environments can be described in terms of the following six dimensions:

1. *Realistic:* The realistic *person* is one who copes with life by seeking objective, concrete goals and tasks, who likes to manipulate things, tools, machines, people, animals, and so on. Such persons are best matched with *environments* that confront them with explicit physical, concrete tasks, suggesting *occupations* such as skilled or unskilled labor, agriculture, engineering, outdoor conservation work, and the like.
2. *Intellectual:* The intellectual *person* is one who copes with life through the use of intelligence, the manipulation of ideas, words, and symbols. Such persons are best matched with *environments* that confront them with tasks which require abstract and creative abilities, suggesting *occupations* such as science, teaching of various sorts, or writing.
3. *Social:* The social *person* is one who copes with life by selecting tasks that demand the use of interpersonal skills and interest in other people. Such persons are best matched with *environments* that require them to interpret and modify human behavior, suggesting *occupations* such as social work, counseling, the ministry, some kinds of teaching, and work which requires organizing others.
4. *Conventional:* The conventional *person* is one who copes with life by selecting goals and tasks which are sanctioned by custom and society. Such persons are best matched with *environments* that require systematic, routine processing of various kinds of information, suggesting *occupations* such as accounting, various types of office work, and administration.
5. *Enterprising:* The enterprising *person* is one who copes with life by selecting goals and tasks that permit the expression of high energy, enthusiasm, adventuresomeness, dominance, and impulsiveness. Such persons are best matched with *environments* that place a premium on verbal facility used to direct and persuade other people, suggesting *occupations* such as sales, entrepreneurship, management, politics, foreign service, and the like.

6. *Artistic:* The artistic *person* is one who uses feelings, intuitions, emotions, and imagination to create art forms or products. Such persons are best matched with *environments* that require the interpretation or creation of artistic forms through taste, feeling, and imagination, suggesting *occupations* such as writing, the fine arts, and the performing arts.

Obviously people are complex and their orientations can reflect various combinations of the basic six identified. The strength of the theory lies in identifying specific measurable traits that will allow vocational counselors to improve the occupational choice process. This kind of model builds on decades of work by E. K. Strong (1943) and others who showed that different occupations reflect different interest patterns. By focusing on a person's interests, one can bypass the motivational issue by simply acknowledging the here-and-now demonstration of interest. By the time a person has reached adolescence, there has formed an identifiable pattern of interests and preferences which can be diagnosed and used as a basis for vocational guidance.

Super's Developmental Theory

The work on occupational choice is necessarily limited in scope because it ignores the developmental issues that arise continuously before, during, and after such choice. People make educational choices in order to get into an occupation and then discover some new interests or skills. Their first jobs often reveal mismatches between their expectations and the realities of the work situation. People discover in the early career years some talents and values which they were not aware of, and which require new adaptations or changes. The most extensive model dealing with this life-long process has been that of Super and Bohn (1970) who postulate that career development is essentially a process of synthesis of the person's self-concept with the realities of the external environment. A basic underlying motive driving this process is the *implementation of the self-concept.* All people attempt to work out in their occupational (and other) roles their concept of themselves during six major stages:

1. *Exploration:* Childhood and adolescent development of the self-concept.
2. *Reality testing:* The transition from school to work and early work experiences.
3. *Trial and experimentation:* Attempts to implement the self-concept by staking out a career(s).

4. *Establishment:* Implementing and modifying the self-concept in the middle career years.
5. *Maintenance:* Preserving and continuing to implement the self-concept.
6. *Decline:* New adjustments of the self-concept following termination of one's occupational role.

One of the implications of developmental theory is that the pattern of needs, motives, and values a person brings from childhood and adolescence serves as an *initial* set of goals and constraints on the process of choice. Thereafter, the person is always in a dynamic process of attempting to integrate inner forces and impulses with outer opportunities and constraints in order to implement the self-concept, which is itself changing and growing as a result of new experiences.

Career Anchors

Support for a developmental type of theory is provided by a longitudinal study of 44 male graduates of the MIT Sloan School of Management (Schein, 1975, 1978). These men were studied intensively by means of interviews and attitude surveys before they graduated in the early 1960s and again in 1973 when they were 10 to 12 years into their careers. The motives and values which they expressed before graduation were *not* reliable predictors of subsequent careers, largely because the subjects made discoveries early in their careers about matches and mismatches between their own needs, values, and talents, on the one hand, and the requirements of the organizational environments in which they were working, on the other hand. Especially *talents* could not be clearly assessed until actual jobs were experienced, yet one's perceptions of one's own talents is one of the most important parts of one's self-concept. Many of the alumni in the study were unaware of certain needs, values, and talents until they had been in an occupational environment for several years, and some of them did not achieve a clear self-image until they had been through several different jobs, organizations, or even occupations.

The gradual clarification of the self-image around (1) *needs and motives*, (2) *talents*, and (3) *values* was conceptualized as a process of finding a "career anchor," which began to function as a constraint on and guiding force to the career (Schein, 1978). A career anchor is thus different from a motive because it includes a self-perception of talents and values as well, and is based on actual occupational experience. It was found that the 44 cases could be clustered into five career anchor groups, where *the anchor is that set of needs, values, and talents which the person is least willing to give up if forced to make a choice:*

1. *Technical/functional competence:* The entire career is organized around a particular set of technical or functional skills which the person is good at and values, leading to a self-concept of remaining in an occupation that would continue to provide challenging work around those particular skills wherever they were. Alumni in this group were in various jobs ranging from technical staff roles to functional management.

2. *Managerial competence:* The entire career is organized around climbing an organizational ladder to achieve a position of responsibility in general management in which decisions and their consequences could be clearly related by the individual to his own efforts in analyzing problems, dealing with people, and making difficult decisions in uncertain conditions. Alumni in this group were clearly striving for general management positions such as president and executive vice-president.

3. *Creativity:* The entire career is organized around some kind of entrepreneurial effort which would permit the individual to create a new service or product, to invent something, or to build his or her own business. Some alumni in this group already had formed businesses which were successful while others were still struggling and searching.

4. *Security or stability:* The entire career is organized around the location of an organizational niche that would guarantee continued employment, a stable future, and the ability to provide comfortably for the family through achieving a measure of financial independence.

5. *Autonomy:* The entire career is organized around finding an occupation such as teaching, consulting, writing, running a store, or something equivalent which permits the individual to determine his own hours, lifestyle, and working patterns. This group of people was most likely to drop out of conventional business organizations, though their consulting or teaching activities continued to be related to business and management.

Obviously one can imagine other kinds of career anchors, such as service to others, working for ideological, political or religious causes, variety, or power, but the fact is that the five groups described above were sufficient to encompass all 44 cases in the panel study. Attempts to apply these anchors to other occupations have also proved productive in that, for example, Van Maanen (Van Maanen & Schein, 1977) was able to classify urban policemen on the basis of whether they were primarily oriented to and anchored in the technical work of policing, climbing the departmental ladder, creatively using police work to build other kinds of businesses (for example, making deals with organized crime), using policing as a safe, civil service type of occupation, or being the "loner" autonomous detective. Similarly, one could take an occupation like medicine or law and analyze the different career anchors of various doctors or lawyers. Instead of trying to find *the* single set of motives or values which determine occupational *choice*, it may be more productive to realize that any given occupation can meet a variety of needs and use a variety of talents.

In summary, the value of such concepts as career anchors is that they are explicitly developmental and attempt to reflect the search of every human for a clear and workable self-concept, a search that may continue throughout life.

BASIC NEED THEORIES REVISITED

Having provided some developmental perspectives, we can now re-examine and summarize the often quoted classifications of Maslow, Alderfer, Herzberg, and McClelland and indicate their strengths and weaknesses. Table 5.1 shows the basic needs or motives postulated by these theorists in juxtaposition to each other and illustrates thereby the considerable similarity of their approaches.

Maslow (1954) felt that the basic human needs were arranged in hierarchical order, and argued that higher order needs would not become active until lower order needs could be satisfied. The strength of the theory lies in drawing attention to the variety of needs and motives which operate, but the evidence for the hierarchical notion is weak and the need categories tend to be very general. For example, self-actualization can be achieved in many different ways, and the meaning of self-actualization may change with developmental stages, so it may not be very helpful to know that everyone is concerned about achieving it.

Alderfer (1972) takes the Maslow needs and groups them into three more basic categories—needs for existence, needs to relate to others, and needs for personal growth. This set of categories has been most useful in a context that attempts to measure how much of each need a given adult has at a given point in time. This approach acknowledges the possibility that not everyone has an equal amount of each of the basic needs, as Maslow's theory tends to imply.

McClelland's (1961, 1976) theory of basic needs is probably most applicable to understanding the organizational careers of entrepreneurs and managers. McClelland identifies three basic needs—need for *achievement*, need for *power*, and need for *affiliation*. Each of us sometimes acts out of a need for affiliation, or for power or

Table 5.1

A Comparison of Basic Motivational Categories Proposed by Maslow, Alderfer, McClelland, and Herzberg

MASLOW CATEGORIES (Hierarchy)	ALDERFER CATEGORIES	McCLELLAND NEEDS		HERZBERG FACTORS (Implied Hierarchy)
1. Physiological needs	Existence needs			Working conditions
2. Safety needs (material)			H Y G I E N E	Salary & benefits
Safety needs (interpersonal)		Power		Supervision
3. Affiliation, love, social needs	Relatedness needs	Affiliation		Fellow workers
4. Self-esteem needs (feedback from others)			M O T I V A T O R S	Recognition
				Advancement
Self-esteem (self-confirming activities)	Growth needs	Achievement		Responsibility
5. Self-actualization				Job Challenge

achievement, and the intensity of our need (and behavior) will vary according to the situation. On the average, however, we are likely to have some bias toward either achievement, power, or affiliation. Studies of different occupations have revealed that entrepreneurs, as contrasted with teachers or lawyers, tend to be higher than average in achievement motivation and lower than average in affiliation motivation. They are most concerned, as might be expected, with successful task accomplishment.

By contrast, high-level general managers who have worked their way up tend to have high needs for power relative to other occupations and to display this power in what McClelland and Burnham (1976) call a "socialized" way by trying to influence others toward the accomplishment of valid and accepted organizational goals, not for personal self-aggrandizement. A high overall level of motivation, the tendency to want to do things on behalf of the organization, and the need to influence others through becoming "interpersonally competent" has been shown by a number of researchers as relevant to success in management (Ghiselli, 1971; Harrell & Harrell, 1973; Schein, 1978).

McClelland has argued that the economic health of a society depends upon entrepreneurial activity and has shown that such activity has historically been closely associated with strong achievement motivation among its members. To put this theory to the test, he designed training programs to increase achievement motivation in managers of developing countries. It has been extremely difficult to evaluate the success of these efforts, but enough positive correlation has been demonstrated to encourage this program of research and action to continue. For our purposes, the important point to note is that here we have a theory of motivation which explicitly postulates that motivation is changeable even in adulthood.

Herzberg's (1966) hygiene and motivational factors are shown in the far right column of the table. As can be seen these "needs" are more specifically job related and reflect some of the concrete things people want from their work. The problems of validating this theory have been considerable, however, because of the tendency of people to want different things at different times and to attach different meanings to given job values, as we will see in the next section.

In summary, what can be said of the various need theories is that they have provided a useful set of categories for analyzing human motivation and have drawn attention to the fact that human needs may be hierarchically organized, though the hierarchy itself may vary from person to person. However, such theories have not adequately dealt with individual differences, have not been sufficiently linked to models of adult development, and have usually been stated at a level of generality that makes them difficult to use in practice.

JOB VALUES AND JOB DIMENSIONS

Many organizational researchers have bypassed the above arguments about *basic* human motives and have attempted instead to relate what people value in their work to job satisfaction and work motivation. From the Herzberg model we get a basic distinction between those factors which are "intrinsic"—that is, relate to the immediate interaction between the worker and the job—and those which are "extrinsic," such as the pay, benefits, working conditions, and other aspects of the job situation. In a recent analysis of job factors that were important to 3,000 employees in various state and urban governments, Katz and Van Maanen (1977) identified three clusters of factors which they called "loci of work satisfaction:"

1. *The job itself*—corresponding to intrinsic factors
2. *The interaction context*—corresponding to those contextual factors which have to do with co-workers, supervisors, and other people in the job environment
3. *Organizational policies*—corresponding to those contextual factors which have to do with pay, promotional policies, working conditions, and other issues less immediately under the control of the employee or the supervisor

Each of these three areas was related to job satisfaction to some degree.

To begin to understand how the job itself can contribute to satisfaction and motivation, Hackman and his colleagues (Hackman & Lawler, 1971; Hackman & Oldham, 1975, 1979) developed a more refined set of job factors by analyzing a large number of jobs and identifying the basic dimensions which could apply to *any* job. These dimensions and their relationship to more important underlying psychological states and relevant outcomes are shown in Table 5.2.

Table 5.2

Basic Dimensions of Jobs and their Relationship to Psychological States and Work Outcomes

CORE JOB DIMENSIONS	CRITICAL PSYCHOLOGICAL STATES	OUTCOMES
Skill variety		High internal work motivation
Task identity	Experienced meaningfulness of the work	
Task significance		High quality work performance
		High satisfaction with work
Autonomy	Experienced responsibility for work outcomes	
		Low absenteeism and turnover
Feedback	Knowledge of the actual results of work activities	

MODERATORS
Ability and skill
Strength of employee's growth need
Context satisfaction

The basic theory underlying the model is that desirable outcomes both for the person, in terms of internal satisfaction and motivation, and for the organization, in terms of high quality performance and low absenteeism and turnover, will result only if the worker can achieve three *critical psychological states*:

1. The work must be experienced as *meaningful*, worthwhile, or important.
2. The worker must experience that he or she is personally *responsible* for the work outcome, that is, accountable for the product of his or her efforts.
3. The worker must be able to determine in some regular and reliable way how his or her efforts are coming out, *what results are achieved*, and whether or not they are satisfactory.

The *core job dimensions* are then derived by observing what kinds of job characteristics are more or less likely to lead to the desired psychological states:

1. *Skill variety:* The degree to which a job requires the workers to perform activities that challenge a variety of skills and abilities.
2. *Task identity:* The degree to which a job requires completion of a whole and identifiable piece of work—doing a job from beginning to end with a visible outcome.
3. *Task significance:* The degree to which the job has a substantial and perceivable impact on the lives of other people either within the immediate organization or in the world at large.

The above three dimensions together create the degree to which the worker experiences the job as "meaningful."

4. *Autonomy:* The degree to which the job gives the worker freedom, independence, and discretion in scheduling work and determining how the work will be carried out.

This dimension is directly related to giving workers a sense of personal responsibility, the second critical psychological state.

5. *Feedback:* The degree to which the worker gets information about the effectiveness of his or her efforts, either directly from the work itself (such as when a quality test is run by the worker on the work) or from supervisors, co-workers, quality-control inspectors, or others in the work flow.

This dimension is directly related to knowledge of results, the third critical psychological state.

Any given job can be analyzed, in terms of these five dimensions, for its "motivating potential" (MPS) using a job diagnostic survey and aggregating the scores on the job dimensions. The degree to which the relationship between job dimensions, critical psychological states, and outcomes will hold true will, according to the theory, be moderated by three additional factors—the degree to which the worker has the necessary skills to do the job (if he or she does not, then obviously changing the job on any of the dimensions is irrelevant); the degree to which the worker is motivated by the need to grow and sees work as growth producing (if he or she is not work involved, then a more enriched job is not going to be more motivating); and the degree to which the worker is satisfied with the contextual factors comprising the formal and informal organizations (if social and work conditions or pay are not satisfactory, then an enriched job will probably not be motivating to the worker).

If one decides that job enrichment can succeed, one can influence the job dimensions by creating more natural work groups; by optimally combining tasks; by involving the worker more with the clients or consumers of the product; by "vertical loading," which means giving workers more say in planning, producing materials, and controlling their work flow; and by opening up additional feedback channels as needed. One of the real advantages of this kind of theory is that it leads to practical redesign of work based on an immediate diagnosis of what is bothering workers without getting into debates about ultimate motives or the reasons why people work in the first place.

Job Longevity

Job enrichment is not a cure-all for motivational problems, however, as Hackman and others have frequently cautioned. To illustrate the complexity and highlight once again the developmental perspective, we need to examine the concept of job longevity recently developed by Katz (1978). In the employee survey previously referred to, it was possible to determine how long a given employee had been on a particular job—the operational definition of job longevity. It was also possible to measure the degree to which each of the Hackman job characteristics was present in a given job, and to relate the degree of presence or absence of that factor to job satisfaction. When this set of correlations was run for the entire sample, all of the job factors related about equally to job satisfaction at a fairly low positive level. When the sample was divided into groups varying in job longevity, however, it was found that different factors were important at different times, as shown in Figure 5.1. For example, when an employee was new to the job, variety was uncorrelated

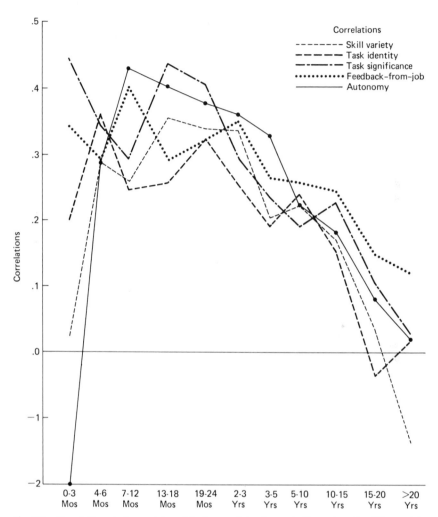

Fig. 5.1 Correlations between job satisfaction and the five task dimensions for different job longevity periods. *Katz, 1978.*

and autonomy was *negatively* correlated with job satisfaction, while task significance and feedback were positively correlated. In the period from roughly six months to five years, all of the factors were highly correlated, but after five years all of them began to drop off to the point where, after 15 to 20 years, none of them correlated with job satisfaction to any substantial degree. Contextual factors such as pay, benefits, co-workers, and compatibility with supervisor were equally important in all job longevity groups, which means that their *relative* importance became greater as job longevity increased.

Though the study is not longitudinal, it clearly confirms that

91

what is important to a person on a job *will change* as a function of how long the person has had that job. Katz suggests that in every job we go through three periods: (1) *socialization*, when only task significance and feedback are important; (2) *innovation*, when all job features are important; and (3) *adaptation*, when contextual factors become relatively more important. For adapted workers job redesign may be less motivating than better pay or working conditions.

SUMMARY

This chapter has reviewed biologically based psychoanalytic theory, socialization theory, and vocational development theory to broaden our concept of human nature and human motivation. One of the more productive ways of dealing with these issues has been to focus specifically on *work* motivation and to identify specific features of the work itself and the context of work, as these relate to job satisfaction and motivation. This approach permits a testing of many of the developmental hypotheses and facilitates the measurement of individual differences in what motivates people at work.

The Complexity
of Human
Nature

Organization and management theory has tended toward simplified and generalized conceptions of human motivation. Empirical research has consistently found some support for the simple generalized conception, but only some. Consequently, the major impact of many decades of research has been to vastly complicate our models of human nature and how to manage people. Not only do people have many needs and potentials, but the patterning of those needs changes with age and stage of development, with changes in roles, with situation, and with changes in interpersonal relationships. What assumptions can be stated which do justice to this complexity?

COMPLEX ASSUMPTIONS

1. Human needs fall into many categories and vary according to stage of development and total life situation. These needs and motives will assume varying degrees of importance to each person, creating some sort of hierarchy, but this hierarchy is itself variable from person to person, from situation to situation, and from one time to another.

b. Because needs and motives interact and combine into complex motive patterns, values, and goals, one must decide at what level one wants to understand human motivation. For example, money can satisfy many different needs, even the need for self-actualization for some people; on the other hand, social motives or self-actualization needs can be met in a wide variety of ways and in different ways at different stages of development.

c. Employees are capable of learning new motives through organizational experiences. This implies that the overall pattern of motives and goals at a given career or life stage (as reflected in the person's psychological contract with the organization) is the result of a complex sequence of interactions between initial needs and organizational experiences.

d. A given person may display different needs in different organizations or in different subparts of the same organization; the person who is alienated in the formal organization may find fulfillment of his or her social and self-actualization needs in the union or in an informal work group. If the job itself consists of a variety of skills, numerous motives may be operative at different times and for different tasks.

e. People can become productively involved with organizations on the basis of many different kinds of motives. Ultimate satisfaction for the individual and ultimate effectiveness for the organization depend only in part on the nature of such motivation. The nature of the task to be performed, the worker's abilities and experience, and the atmosphere created by one's co-workers all interact to produce a certain pattern of work and feelings. For example, a highly skilled but poorly motivated worker may be as effective and satisfied as a very unskilled but highly motivated worker.

f. Employees can respond to many different kinds of managerial strategies, depending on their own motives and abilities and the nature of the task; in other words, there is no one correct managerial strategy that will work for all people at all times.

IMPLICATIONS FOR MANAGEMENT— CONTINGENCY THEORIES

If assumptions such as those just listed come closest to empirical reality, what are the implications for managerial strategy?

Perhaps the most important implication is that *managers should be good diagnosticians and should value a spirit of inquiry.* If the abilities and motives of the people under them are so variable, managers should have the sensitivity and diagnostic ability to be able to sense and appreciate the differences. Rather than regarding the existence of individual differences as a painful truth to be wished away, *managers should learn to value differences* and to value the diagnostic process which reveals differences. To take advantage of diagnostic insights, *managers should be flexible enough and have the interpersonal skills necessary to vary their own behavior.* If the needs and motives of subordinates are different, they should be treated differently.

It is important to recognize that these points do not contradict any of the managerial strategies previously cited. I am not saying that adhering to rational-economic, social, or self-actualization assumptions about subordinates is totally wrong. What I am saying is that any of these assumptions may be wrong in some situations and with some people. Where we have erred is in oversimplifying and overgeneralizing. If managers adopt a more scientific attitude toward human behavior, they will test their assumptions and seek a better diagnosis, and if they do that they will act more appropriately to whatever the demands of the situation turn out to be. They may decide to be highly directive at one time and with one employee but totally nondirective at another time with another employee. They may use pure engineering criteria in the design of some jobs, but let workers structure another set of jobs themselves. In other words, they will be flexible, and will be prepared to accept a variety of interpersonal relationships, patterns of authority, and psychological contracts.

Variable or flexible behavior based on situational realities has come to be called a "contingency theory," signaling the fact that what is a correct way to organize, manage, or lead in any given situation is contingent upon a large number of factors.[1] Contingency theories have become very popular in this field in recent years because of the recognition of the inherent complexity of human nature, tasks, situations, and the leadership/management process itself (Lawrence & Lorsch, 1967; Fiedler, 1976; Vroom & Yetton, 1973; Luthans, 1976).

EVIDENCE FOR COMPLEX ASSUMPTIONS

In a sense, all of the researches previously cited support the assumptions stated in this chapter, but it will be helpful to cite a few additional studies which highlight human complexity and human differences. For example, both Whyte and Zaleznik in the studies previously cited showed that the background and pattern of motivation of rate-busters differed from that of underproducers. Both types were group deviants, but the reasons why one group was indifferent

---

[1] Theorists like Argyris, Bennis, and McGregor have argued for more diagnostic ability and skill-flexibility in managers. My argument here summarizes theirs and attempts to make it more explicit and general. A similar analysis and generalization has also been made by Bennis in his "Revisionist Theory of Leadership" (1961).

to group sanctions while the other group aspired to membership and was rejected were found in their different personal and social backgrounds.

Different responses to a similar environment were found in a study of prisons (Grusky, 1962). Because the prison is a coercive organization which forces its inmates to be totally dependent and submissive, it should create primarily an alienative involvement in inmates. But Grusky found that those prisoners who had submissive and dependent kinds of personalities were relatively less alienated, more cooperative, and more positive about prison life. Both Pearlin (1962) and Argyris (1964) in studying the alienation of workers in industrial organizations found cases of workers who were not alienated because their personal needs and predispositions made them comfortable in a highly authoritarian situation which demanded little of them, either because they did not seek challenge and autonomy or because they genuinely respected authority and status.

In a classic study of four types of industrial workers, Blauner (1964) found evidence for very different patterns of alienation depending on the nature of the technology involved in the work situation. He defined *alienation* as being the resultant of four different psychological states which are, in principle, independent of each other: (1) sense of powerlessness or inability to influence the work situation; (2) loss of meaning in the work; (3) sense of social isolation, lack of feeling of belonging to an organization, work group, or occupational group; and (4) self-estrangement, a lack of any self-involvement with work, a sense that work is merely a means to an end.

Automobile workers on assembly lines were found to be alienated in terms of all four criteria. At the other extreme, members of the printing trades felt a sense of influence, meaning, integration into the occupational group, and deep involvement in their work. Textile workers resembled automobile workers but were highly integrated into communities in which traditional values taught them not to expect a sense of influence or meaning. These values in combination with paternalistic management practices made them feel reasonably content with their lot in spite of strong forces toward alienation. The fourth group, chemical workers, presented still another pattern. Because the continuous processes in chemical plants tend to be highly automated, chemical workers had a great deal of responsibility for controlling the process, considerable autonomy and freedom, a close sense of integration with others on their shift and in the plant, and high involvement in the work because of the high responsibility. The variation in these four types of workers illustrates the danger of generalizing about alienation among factory workers and the utility of more refined concepts of alienation and technology such as Blauner has developed.

In discussing varieties of motives, Gellerman (1963) has pointed out that even economic rewards can and do have vastly different meanings to different people. For some people, money represents basic security and love; for others, it represents power; for still others, it is a measure of their achievement in society; and for still others, it represents merely the means to the end of comfortable and sumptuous living. Thus it is difficult to judge, even in the case of a given reward, what all of its symbolic meanings are to the person and how it connects to other motives.

Lawler (1971, 1975) reviewed much of the research literature on monetary incentives and reached the conclusion that pay systems must ultimately be "individualized" in the sense of being fitted to the particular needs of the organization and the people within that organization. No generalizations about the "right" way to use money as an incentive have yet been found.

Another line of evidence comes from studies of *changes* in motivation as a result of organization experience. It has been difficult to determine, for example, whether alienated workers lacked motives toward achievement and self-actualization when they first joined an organization, or whether they became that way as a result of chronically frustrating work experiences. This point is critical, because if motives are not capable of being elicited or stimulated, more emphasis should be placed on selecting those workers who initially display the patterns of motivation required by the organization; if, on the other hand, by changing organizational arrangements and managerial strategies, it is possible to arouse the kinds of motives desired, more emphasis should be given to helping organizations change.

For example, in companies adopting the Scanlon Plan, workers who for years took an apathetic attitude toward organizational goals were able, with an organizational change, to become highly motivated and committed to such goals (Pigors & Myers, 1977). In a field study concerned with motivational changes, Lieberman (1956) attempted to determine what attitude changes would occur as a result of shifting a worker's role from union steward to foreman. Those stewards who were promoted to foremen showed consistent attitude changes—from prounion to promanagement—within a few months of the promotion. Because of economic reverses, the company subsequently had to demote some of these foremen. When a second attitude survey was conducted, it was found that the demoted foremen had once again adopted prounion attitudes. Clearly, motives and attitudes can change but we do not as yet know enough about the conditions or limitations of such changes.

CONCLUSION: MOTIVATION AND THE PSYCHOLOGICAL CONTRACT IN PERSPECTIVE

In the last several chapters we have examined the relationship of the individual and the organization from various points of view. First, with Etzioni's typology, we viewed the basic types of power or authority used by organizations and the basic kinds of involvement people have in organizations. Then we examined the process of management in terms of some of the major sets of assumptions that have been made about human behavior in organizations. Finally, we spelled out the implications of these assumptions for the nature of superior-subordinate authority, the kind of psychological contract which was implied, and the actual managerial strategy which would be most appropriate. Insofar as possible, we then reviewed the empirical evidence for the rational-economic assumptions, social assumptions, and self-actualizing assumptions. The last two chapters in this section have concentrated on presenting a more balanced view of the *complexity* of human nature.

The emphasis so far has been on *motivation*, particularly the motivation of the employee; but motivation is, of course, not the only determinant of effective performance. The ability of the person, the nature of the work setting, the tools and materials available to do the work, the nature of the job itself, and the ability of management to coordinate employee, group, and departmental efforts—all enter into organizational effectiveness. The reason for our focus on motivation and our extensive exploration of it rests on the fact that in the motivational area there have been too many myths and misconceptions. It has been particularly difficult to resist the temptation to infer motives from observed organizational behavior. Thus management has often accepted organizational circumstances as a given and has explained behavioral variations as a function of different motives: The good worker could be assumed to have a high achievement need while the poor worker or alienated worker could be assumed to lack ambition. In some cases, this assumption might have been correct, but in other situations it would have been more correct to see the good worker as having a boss who provided challenging work while the poor worker had a boss who provided a fragmented and intrinsically meaningless assignment, or in some other way was insensitive to the worker's needs, goals, interests, career anchors, job values, or degree of job involvement.

By way of conclusion, I would like to underline the importance of the *psychological contract* as a major variable of analysis. It is my central hypothesis that whether people work effectively, whether they generate commitment, loyalty, and enthusiasm for the organization and its goals, and whether they obtain satisfaction from their work depends to a large measure on two conditions:

1. The degree to which their own *expectations* of what the organization will provide to them and what they owe the organization in return matches what the organization's expectations are of what it will give and get in return.
2. The nature of *what is actually to be exchanged* (assuming there is some agreement)—money in exchange for time at work; social need satisfaction and security in exchange for hard work and loyalty; opportunities for self-actualization and challenging work in exchange for high productivity, high quality work, and creative effort in the service of organizational goals; or various combinations of these and other things.

Ultimately the relationship between the individual and the organization is interactive, unfolding through mutual influence and mutual bargaining to establish and reestablish a workable psychological contract. We cannot understand the psychological dynamics if we look only to the individual's motivations or only to organizational conditions and practices. The two interact in a complex fashion that demands a systems approach capable of handling interdependent phenomena.

Furthermore, our concepts must reflect the fact that the psychological contract is constantly renegotiated throughout the organizational career. Both the individual's and the organization's needs change over time, requiring repeated episodes of *organizational socialization* as organizational norms change (Schein, 1968; 1971). Some of these norms can be thought of as *pivotal*, in the sense that adherence to them is a requirement of continued membership in the organization. For example, American managers are socialized to believe in the validity of the free enterprise system; professors must accept the canons of research and scholarship; engineers must believe in product safety. Other organizational norms are *peripheral*, in the sense that it is desirable but not essential for members to adhere to them. For example, it may be desirable from the point of view of the organization that managers be men, have certain political views, wear the right kind of clothes, buy only company brands, and so on. For professors, it may be desirable that they like to teach, be willing to help in the administration of the university, spend most of their time on campus rather than on consulting trips, and so on. Violation of these norms does not cause loss of membership, however, if the pivotal norms continue to be adhered to.

The adjustment of the individual to the organization can then be conceived of in terms of acceptance or rejection of pivotal and/or peripheral norms, as shown in Table 6.1. Acceptance of both pivotal and peripheral norms can be thought of as "conformity," the tendency to try to fit in completely and to take a custodial orientation toward how things have been done in the past—becoming the loyal but uncreative "organization man." Acceptance of peripheral norms combined with rejection of pivotal ones is "subversive rebellion" in that, by rejecting the organization's basic premises but adhering to its peripheral norms, the person is concealing his or her rebellion. In contrast, rejecting both sets of norms is open rebellion or revolutionary behavior, usually leading to voluntary or involuntary loss of membership.

Table 6.1

		PIVOTAL NORMS	
		Accept	*Reject*
	Accept	Conformity	Subversive Rebellion
PERIPHERAL NORMS			
	Reject	Creative Individualism	Open Revolution

Individual Adjustment to the Organization

If an organization is concerned about its own capacity to grow and innovate in the face of a complex and changing environment, the ideal individual response might be what I have termed "creative individualism," which is based on accepting pivotal norms but rejecting peripheral ones. The creative individualist is strongly concerned both about basic organizational goals and about retaining his or her sense of identity, and is willing to exercise creativity to help the organization achieve its basic goals.

Creativity on behalf of the organization can be thought of in two way. One can focus one's energies on creating new products or services, the kind of creativity traditionally identified in most organizations as research and development. Or creativity can be conceived of as "role innovation," the development of new ways of doing a job or fulfilling a role to make the organization more effective, efficient, or adaptable (Schein, 1970; Van Maanen & Schein, 1979). A manager can invent a new product (content innovation) or can focus his or her creative energies on new ways of integrating the efforts of two departments, new ways of establishing effective financial controls, new ways of supervising people to maximize their productivity, and so on (role innovation). A professor can derive a new scientific law or publish a new theory (content innovation), or can invent new ways of teaching more effectively, making better use of others' skills, or involving them in social causes (role innovation).

One might hypothesize that people's needs to be conformist, rebellious, or innovative are tied in complex ways to their underlying motive system, and also that such needs change over the course of their career. For example, at the beginning of their career, as apprentices, people are probably most conformist. Upon obtaining organizational "tenure" and reasonable security, they embark on a period of maximum creativity, sometimes involving rebellion. Later stages of the career probably produce more of a tendency to become either role innovative or conformist depending upon the degree to which the individual remains work involved. How the organization manages people's transitions from one organizational segment to another across functional, hierarchical, or inclusionary boundaries probably strongly affects whether the person will become more custodial and conformist or more innovative (Van Maanen & Schein, 1979).

For individuals, for organization managers, and for members of social institutions who are concerned about social policy, the most important conclusion to be drawn from this entire discussion is that human motivation and career development are highly complex and not yet fully understood. Therefore, a continued spirit of inquiry and a commitment to diagnosing situations before leaping into action appears to be the only safe course. It is not clear whether the "best" kind of psychological contract is one that maximizes creative individualism, for it is easy to imagine conditions under which both the individual and the organization would be happier with a conformist response. However, one must diagnose the potential consequences of whatever course one embarks on, using whatever analytical tools are available. And one must be aware that personal assumptions and biases can operate as powerful filters to make the world look simpler than it actually is.

Leadership
and
Participation

Few topics in organizational psychology have received as much attention as leadership. As the previous several chapters have demonstrated, any analysis of human nature and motivation inevitably leads to a discussion of how leaders and/or managers should handle followers. Thus leadership is in a sense the reverse side of motivation. Whereas the analysis of motivation and human nature focused us more on followers, the next chapters will focus explicitly on leaders. After examining in some detail why it has been so difficult to identify just how an effective leader should behave, we go on to review some major theories of leadership. Not all leadership theories will be discussed. We shall focus on those of Fiedler, Vroom, Hersey and Blanchard, and Argyris because this cross section illustrates some of the most important contrasts in approaches to the leadership problem. From these theories also come some of the most carefully thought out practical programs of training.

In Chapter 8 we will look at leadership as a set of functions and attempt to put the various issues of leadership into perspective, particularly the desirability of participative leadership—that is, how much leaders should share power and decision making with their followers. Worker participation is a hotly debated issue in organizational psychology, more so because in many countries it is actually being *legislated.* It becomes critical to understand the implications of participation so that we can understand the conditions under which it will or will not lead to greater effectiveness for organizations and satisfaction for employees.

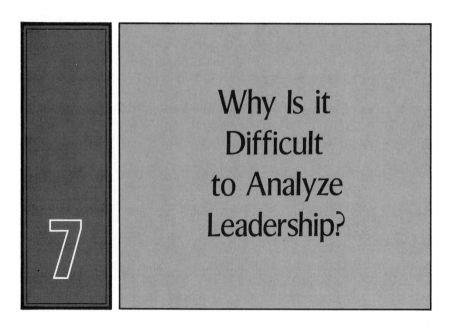

Why Is it Difficult to Analyze Leadership?

7

In this chapter we will attempt to unravel the problem of leadership so as to become aware of which factors contribute to its complexity. Similar to the difficulties we encountered in trying to devise a simple model of human nature, we will see that a simple model of good leadership is impossible to find. Several definitional and analytical problems have to be recognized at the outset.

PROBLEM 1: IDENTIFYING WHO IS A "LEADER"

When we set out to analyze leadership behavior, what is our point of reference for the term *leader* or *manager*? Consider an organization like a professional football team, consisting of: (1) owners; (2) a general manager hired by the owners; (3) one or more levels of managers below the general manager who deal with the basic business aspects of running the team; (4) a head coach; (5) a number of assistant coaches dealing with various specialties such as offense, defense, kicking; (6) one or more team captains elected by the players or appointed by the coach or both; (7) the quarterback who calls the plays; (8) player representatives if the players are unionized; and, finally (9) the various "informal leaders" among the players themselves.

If we decide to analyze "leadership style" in relation to team performance, *whose* style do we analyze? Who is the leader on whom we should focus? Some will say we should look at the informal leaders—the quarterback or the defensive captain who have the most immediate inspirational effect on the players out on the field; others will say that the key leader is the head coach, while still others will say it is the general manager who, after all, decides what kind of head coach to hire. Some may even relate the team's performance to the owners who decide how much money to invest in the recruitment of high-level talent and whose compensation schedule may or may not be considered "fair" and therefore elicit higher or lower levels of morale or performance.

Obviously, the organization as a whole will not perform well unless the leadership *at every level* reaches some minimum standard of effectiveness. The most brilliant coach cannot produce a winning team if there is no talent on the team. And we have all witnessed the problems of a brilliant quarterback who does not have good enough protection from his offensive line to permit him to throw accurate passes.

But minimum performance at every level is only a partial answer, because many organizations reach such a minimum at every level and then still perform more or less effectively as a function of more brilliant performance by one or more leaders somewhere in the organization. And the search for "leadership" is, in a sense, a search for those traits or those behaviors which define this brilliance, which produce some kind of extra effort on the part of subordinates. So we often resolve the dilemma of "who is the leader" by saying that we want *everyone* in the organization to approximate more closely some ideal model of good leadership. And we often make the assumption that such an ideal exists, that there are universal leadership traits or behaviors which would make every level of management more effective, an assumption which, as we will see, is highly questionable.

PROBLEM 2: WHAT IS THE SCOPE OF "LEADERSHIP"?

A second dilemma of definition illustrated by the football team and by every other organization is the *scope of a leader's influence*. Does leadership refer to the *face-to-face influence* of a supervisor over his or her immediate subordinates, or do we mean the ability to influence by some means or other *all of the levels* that are under a given leader or manager, whether or not he or she deals with them directly? Should chief executives be measured by how they lead their vice-presidents, or should they be measured by the overall performance of their organization? This is not a trivial question because one key skill of higher level managers may be the *selection* of effective managers below themselves, not their own actual skill in managing those subordinates. If a political or religious "leader" is effective in communicating a message to large numbers of followers on an impersonal basis, we consider this good "leadership" even though there is no face-to-face interaction whatsoever. So we must be careful in looking for the key to leadership to state clearly what degree and kind of influence we are really talking about.

PROBLEM 3: WHAT IS THE CULTURAL CONTEXT?

A third dilemma is that any definition of "good leadership" usually reflects the historical, social, or cultural context in which the analysis is conducted. What we consider "good" leadership not only reflects our concepts of human nature as outlined in the previous chapters but is likely to be heavily colored by the political ideology and the socioeconomic circumstances in which the behavior takes place. Table 7.1 illustrates this issue by taking Etzioni's basic types of organizations, along with their corresponding forms of involvement and bases of authority, and expanding the analysis by adding the various leadership roles associated with each system. Etzioni's types can be applied to both political systems and to organizations within the broader society.

In the *coercive* type of system based on the control of rewards and punishments, or on traditional bases of legitimacy, such terms as *emperor, king, queen, dictator, autocrat, tyrant,* and *boss* come immediately to mind. Depending upon how benign the leaders are, the basic feelings of subordinates are likely to be either (a) submission, dependence, and resignation, or (b) anger, resentment, and counter-dependence, or (c) loyalty and commitment to the leaders.

How such coercive organizations will perform typically depends solely on the ability of the dictator or autocrat to correctly analyze what needs to be done, and his or her ability to elicit from a basically passive set of subordinates some reasonable level of performance through the manipulation of rewards and punishments. In many so-called "developing" countries, it is argued that only a strong autocratic kind of leadership can work because only a small elite group really knows what the country needs, and only strong centralized control can ensure the coordination necessary to meet those needs. If such leaders can persuade the citizens or members of their organizations that what is being done is ultimately in their own best interests, they can elicit fairly high levels of motivation as we

Table 7.1

Concepts of Leadership in Different Types of Systems

	BASIC ORGANIZATIONAL TYPE*		
	Coercive	*Utilitarian*	*Normative*
Basic form of involvement	Alienative	Calculative	Moral
Basis for authority	Nonlegitimate Control of rewards and punishments	Ration-legal: Authority of position	Charismatic Rational authority based on expertise
	Traditional		
Leader terms or concepts	King or queen Emperor or empress Dictator Tyrant Autocrat Benevolent autocrat Boss	Supervisor Manager Executive Bureaucrat Representative Senator	True leader Messiah Savior Entrepreneur Manager Executive
Subordinate feelings	Dependence Submission Resignation or Anger Resentment Counterdependence or Loyalty Identification with leader Commitment	Caution Suspicion Independence Concern with equity Self-protective Uninvolved	Involvement Commitment Dedication High motivation Sense of shared goals Interdependent
Basic leadership dilemma	How to ensure correct goals and how to sell them	How to create involvement	How to maintain involvement How to manage succession

*The types can apply either to total political systems or to organizations within a given system.

have frequently witnessed in countries whose dictators are admired and supported.

The situation is quite different in utilitarian systems whose basic assumption is that the proper relationship between subordinates and their leaders should be based on rational-legal principles. Unless the leader can meet some of the subordinates' needs, the contract specifies that they can vote him or her out of office or get him or her fired. In this kind of system such terms as *supervisor, manager,* bureaucrat, executive, representative, and *senator* all imply to some degree that the leader's authority basically resides in the *office* or *position* granted to the person, and that some minimum amount of expertise to perform the duties of the position is ultimately required to retain the position. It is nice if we have a boss who really "turns us on" or inspires us, but in the typical utilitarian system, we do not really expect it. All we ultimately expect is equity and fair treatment in terms of whatever the contractual arrangements are.

In this kind of system subordinates typically feel caution, suspicion, some need for self-protection as would be provided by unions or citizen-consumer groups, a sense of independence, and somewhat limited involvement with the organization. It is noteworthy that this kind of organization typically elicits the greatest concern with how to be an effective leader, because the basic psychological contract between the employee and the organization does not guarantee any initial commitment, loyalty, or motivation. Somehow the individual leader or manager must gain the confidence of group members and overcome their suspicion and caution. Because utilitarian organizations are typically found in free enterprise systems, and because such organizations are in competition with each other, it becomes especially important to solve the riddle of what leaders or managers have to do to get that extra effort to make their organization more productive and effective than the competitor's.

The leadership problem is least troubling in *normative* systems, those types of organizations which are tied together by common causes and mutual goals, by high levels of moral involvement and a belief that what is being worked on is important and exciting. Authority in such organizations typically rests on the *personal* qualities of the leader, his or her charisma or basic expertise in solving some important shared problems. The leadership terms one typically associates with such systems are *entrepreneur, leader, messiah, savior,* but the terms *supervisor, manager,* or *executive* could fit this concept equally well if the subordinates saw their bosses as "real leaders."

The fact that a limited number of people do have the particular personal qualities (charisma) to elicit strong emotional support from their subordinates at a given time and place further complicates the problem of analyzing leadership. It is all too easy to assume that all we need to do is to find more such charismatic individuals or to teach people how to become more charismatic. We forget that many kinds of organizations do not involve tasks or missions that could elicit high levels of involvement in the first place, and that the presence of a charismatic leader (even if we could get one) would not change a fundamentally utilitarian organization such as a company manufacturing textiles or a government bureaucracy into a normative one. Leadership, then, is partly a cultural phenomenon and must be analyzed within a given cultural, political, and socio-economic context.

PROBLEM 4: WHAT IS THE TASK?

The fourth dilemma of defining leadership is that within a given system the nature of the task may change, the situation surrounding the task may change, or the subordinates themselves may change, any of which may require an adaptive change from the leader. As we will see later, leadership is ultimately a matter of matching up the personal characteristics of the leader, the personal characteristics of the subordinates, the nature of the task, and the situation surrounding the task—such as time constraints, historical circumstances, and so on. Thus, even if we can pin down one setting in which to analyze leadership, we will have to take into account how that setting may change over time and thus find ourselves once again relying on the leader's diagnostic ability and flexibility. For example, an engineering manager working with a design group may initially decide to be a participative leader. Later, however, the pressure of time which may result from a competitor's entry into the market may force that same manager to exercise a more autocratic style in order to save time and get a product out fast. The subordinates may be quite willing, under these circumstances, to accept a more autocratic role from their manager, and may be quite effective in spite of having less say in every decision if they understand that the change in style is based on a rational decision.

PROBLEM 5: WHAT IS THE DEVELOPMENTAL STAGE BETWEEN LEADER AND FOLLOWERS?

The fifth and final problem in defining leadership derives from the common observation that what is appropriate and effective leadership behavior will vary as a function of the degree to which a leader and a given group of followers have learned to work together. The stage of development of the group being led as well as the "maturity" of the leader-follower relationship will impose limitations and opportunities on leader behavior. For example, a new group with a new leader facing a new task may require much more guidance and autocratic behavior from the leader than a team which has worked together for a long time and could almost make its own decisions without the leader even being present. On the other hand, certain kinds of autocratic behavior might not be tolerated by a new group which is testing its leaders, yet be completely accepted by a mature team which trusts its leader. Therefore, when we analyze a leadership situation, we must consider how long subordinates have worked with each other, the climate which has developed within the group, the length of time the leader has been in his or her job, and the kind of relationship he or she has been able to develop with subordinates.

The same issue can be addressed in broader terms within a business context. A young entrepreneurially oriented organization needs leadership behavior fundamentally different from a mature second- or third-generation organization run by professional managers. Organizations that have entered turbulent environments and must revitalize their mission or goals require different leadership behavior, especially at the top of the organization, from those which have clear goals and exist in stable environments. Organizations in decline or "ill health" in terms of quality of performance need different leadership from those which are growing and thriving. In each case, the key will be *the basic nature of the task*, as this derives from the organization's developmental stage, and the *form of involvement that is needed from subordinates*.

To summarize, before we can really analyze leadership behavior we must take into account (1) which level of the organization we are referring to; (2) whether or not we mean face-to-face influence or some broader concept of task accomplishment which may cut across many organizational levels; (3) what kind of cultural, political, or socioeconomic concepts underlie the organization or situation being analyzed; (4) the nature of the task, the subordinates, and the situational constraints that may be operating; and (5) the stage of development of the subordinate group and the leader-subordinate relationship. As we will see, different theorists focus on different aspects of the leadership issue.

A DIAGNOSTIC FRAMEWORK FOR ANALYZING LEADERSHIP

In order to deal with the complexity inherent in the analysis of leadership, we need to break it down into a number of components that can serve as guidelines for reviewing leadership research and theories (see Figure 7.1). The center of the figure (Box A) represents an objective picture of the leader as viewed by an outsider in terms of his or her inherent characterisics, traits, personality predispositions, skills, and other measurable properties presumed to be more or less stable in the person. On the left side are shown the subordinate characteristics as they might be observed by an outsider (Box B), and on the right side are the task/situational characteristics from this same vantage point (Box C).

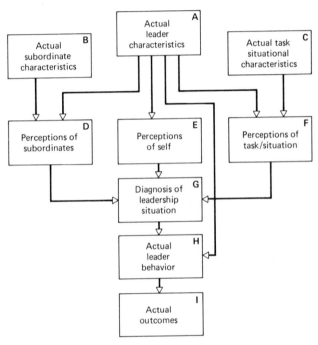

Fig. 7.1 The components of a leadership situation.

Next is shown a series of leader perceptions—how the leader perceives subordinates, the task and situation, and himself or herself in relation to the subordinates and the task (Boxes D, E, F). These perceptions will be a *joint* function of the actual characteristics as they might be observed by an outsider and the leader's own predispositions, biases, defense mechanisms, and personality.

The sum total of such perceptions will be the leader's "diagnosis" of his or her total situation, and it is from such a diagnosis, whether consciously arrived at or not, that the leader will choose an intended course of action (Box G). Such a diagnosis can be highly intuitive and reflect leader perceptions and predispositions, or it can be very systematically arrived at by conscious checking out of various factors.

The leader's actual behavior (Box H) is then a *joint* result of the diagnosis and the actual predispositions of the leader, alerting us to the commonly observed fact that what the leader intends to do and what he or she is actually observed doing may be quite different. The actual behavior will then lead to various outcomes (Box I) which will influence subordinate, task, and leader characteristics in future situations.

Much of the early research on leadership was focused on the leader's "traits" (Box A) in an attempt to identify those characteristics which would clearly distinguish successful from unsuccessful leaders, for example, intelligence, aggressiveness, judgment, and so on. Literally hundreds of studies were conducted, but traits that correlated with success in one situation often failed to hold up in another situation, or a trait that seemed to work for one leader failed to work for another. It was the failure of these early efforts which ultimately resulted in a redefinition of leadership as a *relationship* between the leader, the followers, and the task/situational characteristics (Gibb, 1969). Nevertheless, some researchers and theorists continue to place important emphasis on basic leader characteristics.

The next chapter will review several approaches to the study of leadership which represent different ways of focusing on leadership issues. What we must remember is that although each theory refers to most of the components shown in Figure 7.1, it typically focuses research and theoretical attention on only one or two of those components.

Theories of Leadership and Participation

FOCUS ON THE LEADER: FIEDLER'S LEADER-MATCH THEORY

One of the oldest and still most controversial theories and research programs on leaders of task-oriented groups is Fiedler's (1967, 1971) leader-match theory. Working primarily with groups whose leaders could be clearly identified and whose output could be precisely measured (basketball teams, bomber crews aiming at practice targets, open-hearth steel shops, and small cooperatives, for example), Fiedler first developed a measure of the leader's basic orientation called LPC (least preferred co-worker). The leader is asked to think of all the people with whom he or she has ever worked and then think of the person with whom he or she "could work least well." The leader is then asked to describe that person on 18 bipolar dimensions such as "pleasant—unpleasant," "trustworthy—untrustworthy." The adjectives are scored in terms of the degree to which the leader sees the least preferred co-workers (LPC) as exhibiting negative, or at the other extreme, positive, characteristics. A *low LPC* leader (mainly negative ratings) is seen as primarily *task* oriented, and a *high LPC* leader (mainly positive ratings) is seen as primarily *relationship* oriented.

Fiedler considers low LPC leaders to be very concerned about task performance because they perceive anyone who contributes to poor performance in very negative terms; by contrast, high LPC

114

leaders are considered to be relationship oriented because even their least preferred co-worker is seen as a worthwhile person. Note that LPC as a measure of leader orientation belongs in Box A of Figure 7.1 in that it focuses on a basic leader characteristic. It should also be noted, however, that actual leader behavior was not explicitly studied or correlated with LPC scores in Fiedler's research.

In his early studies Fiedler attempted to show that absolute LPC scores correlated with team performance, but the correlations tended to be very low. Gradually Fiedler, like so many other leadership researchers, found that the relationship between the leader and subordinates as well as the nature of the task influenced the correlations, leading to the current version of his contingency theory:

1. If (a) the leader has *good relationships* with group members, as measured by their degree of acceptance of the leader, and (b) the leader's *position power is high* such that he or she can clearly reward or punish members, and (c) the *task is highly structured* in that there are clear goals, few correct solutions, few ways of accomplishing the task, and clear criteria of success, *then* the leader is said to be in a *highly favorable* situation. Under these conditions Fiedler found consistently negative correlations between LPC and performance. In other words, *situations highly favorable to the leader produce the best outcomes with low LPC (highly task-oriented) leaders.*

2. If the situation is only *moderately favorable* to the leader because the acceptance by members is lower, or position power is lower, or the task is less structured, then the correlation between performance and LPC tends to be consistently positive, suggesting that *situations moderately favorable to the leader produce the best outcome if the leader is high LPC (relationship oriented).*

3. If the situation is *unfavorable* to the leader because acceptance is low, position power is low, and the task is unstructured, the correlations again tended to be negative, suggesting that *situations unfavorable to the leader produce the best outcomes with low LPC (task-oriented) leaders.*

Why should the relationships exhibit such a curvilinear shape? First of all, it should be noted that Fiedler's LPC construct is a leader trait, an orientation or value which is fairly stable, and which produces consistent biases in the way the leader behaves. As Fiedler argues but has not proven, the high LPC or relationship-oriented leader attempts to accomplish tasks by means of building and maintaining good interpersonal relationships among group members. In situations *very favorable* to the leader marked by high control, this person tends not to worry about relationships and may spend a good deal of time trying to please his or her supervisor, often taking subordinates for granted. By contrast, the task-oriented leader in this same favorable situation feels very relaxed because things are under control and clear, permitting him or her to set clear targets and to comfortably monitor group progress.

In situations which are *unfavorable*, where the leader has low control, the high LPC, relationship-oriented leader becomes unwilling to put any task pressure on subordinates in order to avoid alienating or angering them. The high LPC leader may then become so involved in attempting to build up relationships that the task suffers. By contrast, the low LPC, task-oriented leader is again in his or her element. Becoming impatient, this person quickly structures the situation, ignores resistance, and produces successful outcomes by helping to reduce ambiguity for the group.

In situations that are *moderately favorable*, and thus require the building of relationships and innovative solutions to relatively less structured problems, the high LPC, relationship-oriented leader is at his/her best. In such situations low LPC leaders feel out of their element, pay too little attention to interpersonal problems in the group, retreat too much to the task, and as a result do not produce as good outcomes.

Inasmuch as LPC is an orientation that is supposed to be relatively stable, the implications of this kind of theory are that leaders should discover their own orientation and then seek a situation optimally matched to this style. Low LPC leaders should seek highly favorable or highly unfavorable situations, or should work to change situations into the degree of favorableness which produces the best results for them. Similarly, high LPC, relationship-oriented leaders should seek moderately favorable situations or develop them.

Fiedler, Chemers, and Mahar (1976) have developed a self-administered training booklet which permits the reader to test and score himself or herself on LPC. The booklet first asks the person to diagnose situational favorableness by analyzing leader-member relations, task structure, and position power, and then invites a diagnosis of how well matched the person is to the situation. If the match is poor the program offers guidelines on how to create a more favorable situation.

The *strength* of this model is that it gives explicit attention to each of the necessary components—the leader, the subordinates, and the task. It helps the leader to make an explicit diagnosis based on analysis of self, task, and leader-member relationships, and it acknowledges from the outset that the leader's behavior is *not* that flexible. Rather, the leader's problem is how to find a good match between his or her own strengths and what the situation requires.

The *weaknesses* of the model are, *first*, that the diagnostic categories are complex and often difficult to assess—how good the leader-member relations are, how structured the task is, and how much position power the leader has may be difficult to determine in practice. *Second*, Fiedler devotes little attention to a diagnosis of subordinate characteristics. *Third*, no attention is given to the actual technical competence of the leader or the subordinates. The theory assumes adequate technical competence both in the leader and in the followers. *Fourth*, the correlational evidence for the matching concept is relatively weak. The correlations are generally in the right direction on the average, but they are often low and statistically nonsignificant. *Finally*, the concept of LPC itself is vague and the characteristics of high and low LPC people are only gradually beginning to be understood. In a recent review of research bearing on Fiedler's theory, Hosking and Schriesheim (1978) seriously challenge even the basic premises of the theory by noting that LPC is neither stable nor well understood and that the basic correlations between LPC and situational outcomes are too weak to warrant the *practical* claims made for the theory.

None of these are fatal weaknesses, but they have kept Fiedler's theory from becoming a universal solution to the leadership problem.

FOCUS ON THE TASK/SITUATION: VROOM'S CONTINGENCY THEORY

Whereas Fiedler's theory began with a measurement of leaders (LPC), Vroom has always been more concerned about tasks and subordinates (Boxes B and E in Figure 7.1). In a recent statement of his theory Vroom (1975) starts with a quote from Stogdill's 1948 summary of 25 years of leadership research:

> The pattern of personal characteristics of the leader must bear some relevant relationship to the characteristics, activities, and goals of the followers. . . . It becomes clear that an adequate analysis of leadership involves not only a study of leaders, but also of situations. (Stogdill, 1948, pp. 64–65)

Some of Vroom's early research (1960) showed that subordinates with certain kinds of personalities and working on certain kinds of tasks preferred *autocratic* leaders, a finding that challenged the normative emphasis on democratic and participative leadership styles of the Michigan group (Likert, 1961; 1967). Building on this idea, Vroom asserted that leaders have the ability to vary their behavior (Box H) along a scale from highly autocratic to highly participative, so the leadership problem can actually be restated as developing diagnostic criteria that would help leaders decide in which situations to use which kind of behavior (Boxes F and G). Vroom distinguishes five basic points along this dimension, each of which reflects a behavioral option for the leader (Vroom & Yetton, 1973):

TYPES OF MANAGEMENT DECISION STYLES

AI.   You solve the problem or make the decision yourself, using informa-
      tion available to you at that time.
AII. You obtain the necessary information from your subordinate(s), then
      decide on the solution to the problem yourself. You may or may not
      tell your subordinates what the problem is in getting the information
      from them. The role played by your subordinates in making the
      decision is clearly one of providing the necessary information to you,
      rather then generating or evaluating alternatives solutions.
CI.   You share the problem with relevant subordinates individually, get-
      ting their ideas and suggestions without bringing them together as a
      group. Then *you* make the decision, which may or may not reflect
      your subordinates' influence.
CII. You share the problem with your subordinates as a group, collec-
      tively obtaining their ideas and suggestions. Then *you* make the
      decision, which may or may not reflect your subordinates' influence.
GII. You share the problem with your subordinates as a group. Together
      you generate and evaluate alternatives and attempt to reach agree-
      ment (consensus) on a solution. Your role is much like that of
      chairperson. You do not try to influence the group to adopt "your"
      solution and you are willing to accept and implement any solution
      which has the support of the entire group.[1]

This decision dimension closely parallels the continuum of leadership behavior first proposed by Tannenbaum and Schmidt (1958), but goes beyond it in suggesting a specific way of analyzing problems by means of eight ordered criterion questions which the leader can ask himself or herself and a set of decision rules put in the form of a decision tree which leads to the most desirable option to be employed (see Figure 8.1).

The seven questions are arranged so that a leader can analyze his or her immediate problem situation and, by answering yes or no to each question, arrive at feasible decision alternatives. For many paths through the decision tree, the answer generated may still reflect a viable choice between an essentially autocratic or essentially participative alternative. In that case the leader can assess whether

---

[1] It should be noted that other options exist such as delegating the problem to a subordinate or the group and letting them make the decision by themselves.

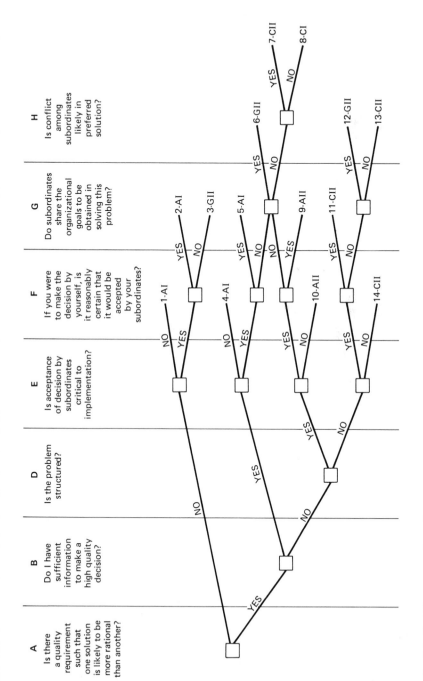

Fig. 8.1 Decision process flow chart.

A
Is there a quality requirement such that one solution is likely to be more rational than another?

B
Do I have sufficient information to make a high quality decision?

C
Is the problem structured?

E
Is acceptance of decision by subordinates critical to implementation?

F
If you were to make the decision by yourself, is it reasonably certain that it would be accepted by your subordinates?

G
Do subordinates share the organizational goals to be obtained in solving this problem?

H
Is conflict among subordinates likely in preferred solution?

1-AI
2-AI
3-GII
4-AI
5-AI
6-GII
7-CII
8-CI
9-AII
10-AII
11-CII
12-GII
13-CII
14-CII

he or she wants to use a short-run model to maximize short-term efficiency (through use of the more autocratic solution) or a long-run developmental model that maximizes the ability of subordinates to learn how to solve problems themselves. The underlying decision rules that lead to the feasible alternatives are listed below.

Rules Designed to Protect the Quality of the Decision

1. *The information rule.* If the quality of the decision is important and if the leader does not possess enough information or expertise to solve the problem alone, AI is eliminated from the feasible set. Its use risks a low-quality decision.

2. *The trust rule.* If the quality of the decision is important and if the subordinates cannot be trusted to base their efforts to solve the problem on organizational goals, GII is eliminated from the feasible set. Alternatives which eliminate the leader's final control over the decision reached may jeopardize the quality of the decision.

3. *The unstructured problem rule.* In situations in which the quality of the decision is important, if the leader lacks the necessary information or expertise to solve the problem alone, and if the problem is unstructured (that is, he or she does not know exactly what information is needed and where it is located), the method used must provide not only for him or her to collect the information but to do so in an efficient and effective manner. Methods that involve interaction among all subordinates with full knowledge of the problem are likely to be both more efficient and more likely to generate a high-quality solution to the problem. Under these conditions, AI, AII, and CI are eliminated from the feasible set. AI does not provide for the leader to collect the necessary information, and AII and CI represent more cumbersome, less effective, and less efficient means of bringing the necessary information to bear on the solution of the problem than methods which encourage such interaction.

Rules Designed to Protect the Acceptance of the Decision

4. *The acceptance rule.* If the acceptance of the decision by subordinates is critical to effective implementation and if it is not certain that an autocratic decision made by the leader would receive that acceptance, AI and AII are eliminated from the feasible set.

Neither provides an opportunity for subordinates to participate in the decision and both risk the necessary acceptance.

5. *The conflict rule.* If the acceptance of the decision is critical, and an autocratic decision is not certain to be accepted, and subordinates are likely to be in conflict or disagreement over the appropriate solution, AI, AII, and CI are eliminated from the feasible set. The method used in solving the problem should enable those in disagreement to resolve their differences with full knowledge of the problem. Accordingly, under these conditions, AI, AII, and CI, which involve no opportunity for those in conflict to resolve their differences, are eliminated from the feasible set. Their use runs the risk of leaving some of the subordinates with less than the necessary commitment to the final decision.

6. *The fairness rule.* If the quality of the decision is unimportant, but acceptance is critical and not certain to result from an autocratic decision, AI, AII, CI, and CII are eliminated from the feasible set. The method used should maximize the probability of acceptance, as this is the only relevant consideration in determining the effectiveness of the decision. Under these circumstances AI, AII, CI, and CII, which generate less acceptance or commitment than GII, are eliminated from the feasible set. To use them is to run the risk of getting less than the required acceptance of the decision.

7. *The acceptance priority rule.* If acceptance is critical, but not assured by an autocratic decision, and if subordinates can be trusted, AI, AII, CI and CII are eliminated from the feasible set. Methods which provide equal partnership in the decision-making process can provide greater acceptance without risking decision quality. Use of any methods other than GII results in an unnecessary risk that the decision will not be fully accepted or receive the necessary commitment on the part of subordinates.

By means of these sets of rules and his decision tree, Vroom has provided a logical and clear basis for diagnosing task situations. However, a critical reseach question that has not yet been satisfactorily resolved is whether or not leaders do in *fact* have the flexibility to vary their behavior across the feasible set of alternatives. Vroom cites two kinds of evidence: (1) what 500 managers from 11 different countries *said* they did (that is, self-reports) in response to a recent decision-making situation; and (2) what managers say they *would* do on standardized problems developed by Vroom (1976) for training purposes. Based on these kinds of data, Vroom finds that managers claim to be highly flexible and to vary their style according to the circumstances. The difference *between* managers in the degree to which they used certain decision types more than others was less than the variation *within* a given manager across problem types. As Vroom himself notes, however, these data are based on what people say they will do in leadership situations not on actually observed behavior, so the question of actual flexibility in real decision situations remains unanswered.

Vroom's training program asks groups of managers to work through a set of standardized problems and to select their own decision alternatives. These are fed into computers so that each trainee can obtain fairly rapid feedback on (a) the correct solution via the theory; (b) the pattern of solutions selected by other trainees; and (c) an analysis of the trainee's own pattern of answers that reveals characteristic biases and decision rule violations. These feedback sheets then are discussed in groups that have been working together on cases and have built up a joint understanding of the theory and of each other's observed leader behavior. The discussion in the small groups is crucial for correcting the biases people have about their own behavior.

Vroom's and Fiedler's models are, at the present time, the most thoroughly worked out programs of leadership training. How do they compare? We do not yet have much comparative research evidence but some obvious conceptual differences can be identified. Fiedler's model has been built on a broad range of leadership situations in which a hard criterion of group effectiveness was invoked. While Vroom's earlier research focused on similar kinds of situations, his present model is limited to managers in organizations describing their own behavior in the context of specific decision problems. Fiedler's research base of leader behavior is, therefore, much broader and his results are potentially more widely applicable, but, as we have noted, the concepts are also more general and vague, especially in the criteria for judging situations. Vroom, by contrast, is highly specific in his criteria and described leader behavior and offers a much broader range of specific behavioral options to the leader. Fiedler, as we have already stated, focuses on a basic leader orientation—task versus relationship orientation (Box A), while Vroom focuses on the specific requirements for leader behavior demanded by a particular task (Box C).[2] One would guess that Fiedler's self-analysis training program is not as powerful as Vroom's, which is based on small-group work and specific feedback to trainees on their diagnostic abilities. On the other hand, Vroom's tendency to treat decisions as discrete may not match many situational realities which require the leader to display a certain style or set a tone which is not reducible to specific discrete decision alternatives.

---

[2] Vroom and Yetton (1973) report that the correlation between LPC and their measure of participativeness is nonsignificant and near zero.

FOCUS ON THE SUBORDINATES: HERSEY
AND BLANCHARD'S SITUATIONAL
LEADERSHIP THEORY

Another major leadership research program marks its beginning in the 1940s at Ohio State University, where researchers sought to define precisely what kind of behavior is actually exhibited by leaders (Hemphill, 1950; Stogdill & Coons, 1957). Thousands of behavioral descriptions were eventually reduced to two independent dimensions called *initiating structure* (essentially a task orientation) and *consideration* (essentially a relationship orientation). Leaders high in initiating structure would assign tasks to group members, emphasize the meeting of deadlines, expect workers to follow routines closely, stress being ahead of the competition, let group members know what was expected of them, and the like. Leaders high in consideration, by contrast, would find time to listen to group members, be friendly and approachable, help subordinates with personal problems, stand up for subordinates, and the like.

This dimension is similar to Fiedler's high and low LPC, and to the Michigan distinction between production-centered and employee-centered managerial behavior (Katz, Maccoby & Morse, 1950). It should be noted, however, that both Fiedler's and the Michigan dimension are single dimensions with task and employee orientation as opposite ends of a single continuum. The Ohio State studies deliberately built the scales to be independent of each other on the theoretical assumption that a leader could be high or low on both dimensions. Furthermore, the Ohio State studies focused heavily on leader *behavior* (Box H) rather than internal attitude or orientation (Box A). It may turn out that attitudinally one cannot be equally high in task and people orientation, but that one can control one's behavior to reflect equal attention to both issues.[3]

Group dynamics research on the emergence of leadership in small groups (Cartwright & Zander, 1960; Bales, 1958) had also shown that for groups to work effectively they had to be concerned both with task accomplishment and the building and maintaining of the group. Bales called these "task" and "socioemotional" dimensions and found that sometimes different members tended to emerge as leaders in each role. Thus it is clearly possible to establish the need for both kinds of behavior, but it remains questionable whether a single individual can comfortably exhibit both kinds of behavior and whether it is possible to be equally concerned about both.

---

3 Blake and Mouton in a widely used managerial training program called *The Managerial Grid* (1964) argue for these same two dimensions and assert that the ideal position is to be both production and people centered, but they do not provide clear evidence of whether or not this is psychologically possible.

123

Hersey and Blanchard (1977) start their analysis by rejecting the idea that there is one ideal managerial style, because all of the research on these various dimensions shows that productive and satisfied groups can be found under virtually any kind of leadership behavior (Fleishman, 1973; Larson, Hunt, & Osborn, 1975). Their basic proposition is:

> The more managers adapt their style of leader behavior to meet the particular situation and the needs of their followers, the more effective they will be in reaching personal and organizational goals. (p. 101)

Hersey and Blanchard's focus on subordinate needs (Box B) contrasts sharply with Fiedler's assertion that leaders must locate situations that fit their *own style*, and Vroom's assertion that leaders must adapt their style to the nature of the *task*.

Hersey and Blanchard define four basic leadership styles as shown in Figure 8.2 and give them the shorthand labels of *telling*

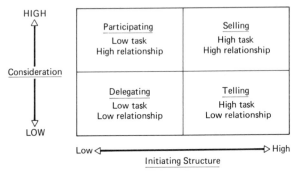

Fig. 8.2 Basic leadership behavior styles.

(high-task and low-relationship behavior), *selling* (high-task and high-relationship behavior), *participating* (low-task and high-relationship behavior), and *delegating* (low-task and low-relationship behavior). Effective leadership behavior is defined as behavior which is appropriate to a given situation within the larger environment. So far Hersey and Blanchard do not differ appreciably from the other contingency theorists. Now, however, they introduce another variable, a key dimension of the environment—the *maturity* of the subordinates, or their *readiness to tackle the task facing the group*. Maturity, defined only in reference to a specific task confronting a group, is:

> . . . the capacity to set high but attainable goals (achievement motivation), willingness and ability to take responsibility, and education and/or experience of an individual or a group. (p. 161)

It should be noted that this definition of subordinate characteristics emphasizes both motivation and competence, and refers both to job maturity—the ability and technical knowledge to do the job—and to psychological maturity—the feeling of self-confidence and self-respect that makes high goal setting and the assumption of responsibility possible. The basic theory can now be stated as follows:

1. If maturity is low, the leader should be high in task and low in relationship behavior to help the group to achieve some success and begin to learn.
2. As the level of maturity of followers increases, the leader should begin to reduce task behavior and increase relationship behavior to help the group grow in its own competence.
3. As the level of maturity continues to increase the leader should begin to reduce both task and relationship behavior, because the group is developing self-confidence and the ability to work on its own.
4. As the group achieves maturity the leader can continue to reduce both task and relationship behavior, and essentially delegate tasks to the group and expect them to be accomplished.

This sequence is illustrated in Figure 8.3. As maturity increases from right to left the appropriate leader behavior moves along the bell-shaped curve through the quadrants shown. The emphasis on the growth of maturity in subordinates, which should ultimately lead to minimal task and relationship behavior on the part of the leader, makes this theory quite different from most others that either ignore talent and ability altogether (for example, Fiedler) or assume it to be a static property. Hersey and Blanchard's developmental sequence argues that appropriate leader behavior is not only a function of subordinate characteristics in general, but also a specific function of the stage of the group's development. If the leader wants to develop maturity among subordinates, the model suggests reducing task behavior by delegating more to subordinates but being ready to in-

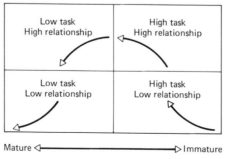

Fig. 8.3 What a leader's behavior should be in terms of degree of subordinate maturity.

crease relationship behavior as a positive reinforcer of the group's success.

In order to help train leaders, Hersey and Blanchard designed a questionnaire (LEAD) which involves 12 situations depicting different levels of subordinate maturity. For each situation the respondent is to pick one of four responses, reflecting the four basic behavior types. As in the Fiedler program there is self-scoring and analysis, but the group training program is not as computerized or structured as the Vroom program.

The strengths of this theory are conceptual rather than empirical. The model is intended to reflect what previous research has shown about leadership, but little independent research has as yet been done on the model itself. The analysis of subordinate skill and self-confidence levels is an important addition to leadership theory inasmuch as other theories tend to pay only lip service to this variable. The theory also has a dynamic, developmental aspect lacking in other models.

On the other hand, the four behavior styles of the leader—telling, selling, participating, and delegating—are somewhat oversimplified and not much attention is given to the problem of behavioral flexibility. Can managers vary their behavior as the theory prescribes? It will be important to see whether the use of the LEAD questionnaire will increase our understanding of the leader-follower relationships, and whether future research on the model will bear out its basic propositions.

A crucial weakness in the theory is that there is as yet no systematic measurement or diagnostic device developed to measure *actual* follower "maturity." Given the central importance of that concept in the model, one would have thought that its proponents would have developed and validated an instrument to help measure this variable. There is no lack of evidence that subordinate characteristics can and do influence leader behavior (Farris, 1969; Lowin & Craig, 1968), but we still lack a clearly defined and measurable set of variables to systematically analyze those subordinate characteristics (Box B).

FOCUS ON LEADER BEHAVIOR:
ARGYRIS'S MODEL I AND MODEL II

Argyris has always been concerned with improving the level of psychological functioning in organizations on the assumption that if both managers and subordinates could act in a more psychologically mature fashion, the organization as well as the people within it would benefit. In his early research, Argyris (1957, 1964) found evidence that the values by which most organizations operated (pyramidal values) tended either to assume or to produce a level of psychological *immaturity* in employees by treating them as dependent and irresponsible. Argyris believes that leaders tend knowingly or unwittingly to reinforce such values and assumptions, which makes it hard for either the leader or the organization as a whole to develop greater psychological maturity.

Argyris notes that most managers and leaders whom he has observed operate from two different "theories": (a) an *espoused* theory, consisting of the goals, assumptions, and values that the person *says* guide his or her behavior; and (b) a *theory-in-use*, consisting of the implicit assumptions that actually guide overt behavior (Argyris & Schon, 1974; Argyris, 1976). Espoused theories vary widely from autocratic to participative, but when leaders are actually observed in groups, it turns out that their theories-in-use almost uniformly reflect what Argyris has called Model I. This model of behavior is built on four basic assumptions, what he terms "governing variables": (1) that one must achieve one's own goals as one sees them; (2) that one must win rather than lose; (3) that one must minimize eliciting negative feelings in relationships; and (4) that one must be rational and minimize any emotionality.

These governing variables, Argyris claims, lead to behavior which is controlling of others, which maximizes one's own safety, and which leads to minimal confrontation of any emotionally charged issues. If one is confronted by others, it leads to defensiveness. The net result is what he calls a "self-sealing" process, or single-loop learning in which one sets up the situation to confirm one's own premises, but never learns whether or not those premises themselves are valid. If one starts with the assumption that confronting people is bad because it will elicit defensive emotional behavior, one will most likely confirm this expectation and learn how to be less confrontive, rather than learning how to deal with one's own and others' defensiveness. In the end, the basic assumptions upon which the model is based will never be tested publicly, thus preventing the leader from learning potentially more effective behavior.

Argyris and Schon have studied leaders' "espoused" and "in use" theories through analysis of tape-recorded scenarios in which both overt verbal behavior and the private thoughts which accompany the overt behavior are elicited and categorized. The striking thing in these protocols is the degree to which the overt behavior is not only nonconfrontive but also in direct contrast to the person's inner feelings. Since subordinates can often sense the incongruity but are playing by the same rules, real feelings are rarely confronted, forcing both leaders and subordinates to engage in guessing at the others' feelings and then manipulating the situation to accomplish their intentions.

It is this circular process which accounts for the frequent reports that leaders can go to training programs and learn new methods such as how to be more participative, yet find that their subordinates do not respond to their new approaches. The fact is that the leader may have changed only his or her espoused theory, not the actual, contextual behavior. If this finding is generally correct, and if Model I behavior is on the autocratic end of the leadership behavior scale, Argyris is, in effect, saying that leaders are culturally *unable* to behave participatively in any real sense of this term, even if they believe in and espouse participation as their preferred style. Participation requires a degree of openness to one's own and others' feelings, and it is precisely such openness which is difficult for leaders in organizational contexts to achieve.

Argyris proposes that organizations would be better off if leaders could learn how to behave according to Model II, which is governed by a different set of premises: (1) that action should be based on valid information; (2) that action should be based on free and informed choice; and (3) that action should be based on internal commitment to the choice and constant monitoring of efforts to implement one's choices. Here, the theory builds on the basic "learning how to learn" assumptions which underlie such group dynamics training as is exemplified in encounter groups, sensitivity training groups, and the like (Bradford, Gibb, & Benne, 1964; Schein & Bennis, 1965).

The training program Argyris proposes to help people reach Model II behavior is a direct extension of the kinds of mutual exploration and feedback common to sensitivity training groups. Trainees (administrators, company presidents, managers, and so on) must first discuss artificial scenarios from the point of view of what they would do and what their inner feelings are in order to learn how their own Model I assumptions enter into their thinking. Such training occurs in groups and is aided by professional staff members who help trainees become aware of the pervasiveness of Model I assumptions. Trainees are then invited to invent new solutions to the scenarios and to become consultants to each other on their progress in applying the collaborative, confrontive, open assumptions of Model II.

During this gradual learning process of several days, trainees begin to consider how best to experiment with the new assumptions in their real settings. The anticipation of negative responses from subordinates often rekindles the anxieties common to Model I thinking, namely, that being more confrontive will just produce more defensiveness. It is then necessary to combat this potential setback by working through these anxieties and developing a more experimental attitude toward one's own behavior. Group support is crucial at this stage because group members at least share the new set of assumptions and have learned how to be more open and confrontive with each other. Because this method permits leaders to get at their basic assumptions and to change them if needed, Argyris and Schon have termed it "double-loop learning."

The concept of double-loop learning is not new. It is derived from Bateson's (1972) concept of "deutero-learning," first used in the analysis of the double binds schizophrenics perceive as a result of conflicting parental messages, for example, "I love you, but because you have been bad I must punish you." The double bind is that if the child confronts the parent with the inconsistency by complaining, the parent can accuse the child of being bad, thus leading to another cycle of punishment and professed love. An organizational counterpart might be, "I like you and accept you, but I can't get closer to you because you trigger some negative feelings in me. However, I can't tell you what those negative feelings are because that would hurt you and I am trying to avoid hurting you because I like you." Learning how to learn means the establishment of a relationship that permits more openness, the sharing of feelings, perceptions, and assumptions, and the development of subsequent actions based on more accurate and valid information.

Most consultants who work from behavioral science principles accept this model as fundamental and attempt to change their clients' basic assumptions through various kinds of diagnostic and intervention activities (Beckhard, 1969; Schein, 1969; Blake & Mouton, 1976; Bennis, 1966, 1976; Dyer, 1972). Argyris and Schon admit that the model may be somewhat utopian and will require great effort on the part of leaders, but they argue it is a necessary step if human potentials are to be fully utilized in organizations.

If we compare the Argyris model of leader behavior with those of Fiedler, Vroom, and Hersey and Blanchard, we see that the other three models are much more static in their orientation and assume that leadership behavior can be improved simply by properly diagnosing one's own style and the characteristics of one's task and subordinates. If Argyris is correct, these models will not really change behavior, only the espoused theories of the leader. To really change leader behavior requires getting at the underlying assumptions and emotions that support such behavior, and this requires a much more intensive process of the sort Argyris describes.

In effect, Argyris is attempting to change some of the cultural values from which assumptions about competition, rationality, and nonconfrontation of negative emotions are ultimately derived. He is asserting that unless such basic cultural values change, organizations will continue to be only marginally effective, and, worse, will be incapable of learning how to become fundamentally more effective. The validity of these assertions has not been demonstrated by any broad-scale research program, although individual cases of successful organizational change have apparently hinged on the key leaders moving from Model I to Model II assumptions (Argyris & Schon, 1978).

Argyris and Schon also come to grips with specific, real changes that must be made in becoming a more participative leader. Vroom, Hersey and Blanchard, Blake and Mouton, and others seem to assume that if one can *convince* leaders or managers to be more participative and show them how, it will automatically happen. The analysis of Model I and Model II behavior highlights the strong emotional bases of theories-in-use and alerts us to the real difficulties which may be involved in asking a manager to change his or her style. The implication of this line of thinking may well be that the development of interpersonal competence and the ability to behave in terms of Model II assumptions is a kind of precondition for the flexibility demanded by contingency theories. If Argyris is right that Model I assumptions dominate most leaders' thinking, then their ability to behave in a contingent way is limited even if they reach a correct diagnosis of the situation.

On the other hand, Argyris' initial assertion that virtually everyone operates according to Model I is poorly documented. Considering the critical nature of this assertion in the theory, more research should be done to test whether it is indeed true, and if so, why. Also, Argyris does not seem to allow for the possibility that Model I behavior may be valid and effective in some situations.

SUMMARY ISSUE 1: TASK VERSUS PEOPLE ORIENTATION

Virtually every major research program on leadership, including the above four, has recognized the distinction between task and people orientation.

RESEARCH GROUP	TASK	PEOPLE
Ohio State	Initiating structure	Consideration
Hersey and Blanchard	Task behavior	Relationship behavior
Michigan (Likert)	Production centered	Employee centered
Fiedler	Low LPC (Task)	High LPC (Relationship)
Blake and Mouton	Concern for production	Concern for people
Bales	Task leader	Socioemotional leader
Benne and Sheats (1948)	Task functions	Group building and maintenance functions

Researchers continue to differ in two crucial and as yet unresolved ways, however: (1) whether task concern and people concern are two ends of a single continuum or two independent dimensions such that one could be high or low on both; and (2) whether the dimensions refers to inner attitudes and values or only to overt behavior. My own clinical observations of many leaders and managers leads me to the following general hypothesis about this issue:

The higher the level in the organization, the more important it is to be oriented attitudinally toward people and to be interpersonally competent, and the less important it is to be oriented to task problems and to be task competent, provided task orientation and competence remain at some reasonably high level.

Lower level leaders and managers have to be task oriented and technically competent but can get by with a minimal amount of interpersonal competence. For middle-level managerial jobs, technical competence and task orientation are still important but people orientation and competence becomes more so. At higher general management levels people orientation becomes crucial but task orientation must remain high. One of the problems in locating effective *general* managers may be that this ability to be both task and people oriented cannot easily be trained, and that it exists in only a limited number of people.

The above assertions are partially supported by the way in which managers who are climbing the organizational ladder talk about their own learning process (Schein, 1978). In the MIT panel study, those alumni who were clearly motivated toward becoming general managers described their own development at the 10 to 12 year mark in their careers in terms of their own "discovery" that they had three kinds of relevant competence:

1. *analytical competence*—the ability to identify, analyze, and solve problems (task competence)
2. *interpersonal competence*—the ability to work under, with, and through other people and in groups

3. *emotional competence*—the ability to make tough decisions either in the task or interpersonal area

Only if *all three abilities* were present did the panelists feel confident they could continue to aspire to higher level managerial jobs. In other words, the degree to which the leader needs to be task or people oriented and competent may depend very much on the particular job and the organizational level being considered.

SUMMARY ISSUE 2: AUTOCRACY, CONSULTATION, PARTICIPATION, OR DELEGATION

Virtually every major researcher or theorist including the four we have studied has wrestled with the question of how much a leader should share power with subordinates in decision making. The following tabulation shows the various degrees along this dimension and the labels selected theorists have given them.

RESEARCH GROUP	PARTICIPATION LEVEL			
Lewin et al.	Autocratic	Democratic		Laissez-Faire
Harbison and Myers	Autocratic	Paternalistic	Consultative	Participative
Bass (1965)	Directing	Manipulating Consulting	Participating	Delegating
Likert (1967)	System 1	System 2	System 3	System 4
Tannenbaum and Schmidt	Leader control	Shared control		Group control
Hersey and Blanchard	Telling	Selling	Participating	Delegating
Vroom	Leader decides	Consults	Shares	Delegates
Argyris and Schon	Model 1		Model 2	

Researchers and theoreticians continue to differ sharply, however, in what they advocate as the "correct" leadership style, and current theories are almost all moving toward contingency models, which in effect say that it depends upon the task, the nature of the subordinates, and other historical or environmental factors. One clear conclusion can be stated:

There is no consistent evidence that any given position on this dimension of leadership style is the best one.

The debate about whether it is better to be autocratic or participative is fruitless unless one specifies the nature of the task, subordinates, and surrounding conditions.

On this dimension as on the previous one, it is also not clear whether we have an attitudinal property, which would suggest that any given person is inherently more or less "participative," or whether we have a purely behavioral dimension, which would suggest that any given person can vary his or her behavior from auto-cratic to delegative. Argyris has clearly pointed out that *congruence* between underlying attitude and overt behavior is itself an issue. If a basically autocratic person learns how to behave participatively (but without changing underlying attitudes) will subordinates respond positively to such behavior or will they sense the incongruence and react even more negatively than they might to the "honest" autocrat? If flexibility of response is important to a leader, it clearly argues for a realistic approach to the learning of such flexibility.

LEADERSHIP AS A DISTRIBUTED SET OF FUNCTIONS

No one theory has made this point its central focus, but many observers have been struck by the fact that leadership behavior can fulfill a wide range of different functions for the group or organiza-tion. Thus, it may be more productive to focus on the functions rather than on a given individual who is defined as a "leader." Such functions may include stating basic values, setting and announcing goals, organizing resources (human and nonhuman), planning, sup-plying information, monitoring, giving feedback on progress, sup-porting, clarifying, summarizing, testing consensus, deciding, rewarding and punishing, and so on.

Once we identify such a broad range of functions, it becomes clear that *any* member of a given group can perform them and that there is no *necessary* connection between the functions and a given appointed or informal leader. In fact, one can think of an effective group as one in which the functions are optimally distributed among all the members of the group according to who has the particular talents needed to perform that function (Benne & Sheats, 1948).

At the same time, appointed leaders and managers do exist in organizations, and we can ask the question whether there are indeed some functions which are uniquely associated with leadership roles, which *only* the leader can perform. If we think of leaders as being the linking pins between organizational levels, it becomes clear that one unique and critical function of leaders becomes *the translation of directives from higher levels into goals and targets for the next lower level.* If the leader is at the very top of the organization, his or her function is to translate the opportunities, demands, and con-straints of the environment into strategies, goals and targets for the organization. How the goals are achieved may be highly variable, reflecting different styles, tasks, subordinate characteristics, and so on, but the leader remains primarily accountable for ultimate goal selection and achievement.

If the leader is accountable for goal achievement, then *monitoring progress toward the goal* becomes a second unique function of the leader. Monitoring progress will reveal what is needed to accomplish the task, thus creating as a third key leadership function *the supplying of whatever functions are missing* if goals are to be achieved.

One cannot predict a priori what missing functions will arise. The group might need key items of information, or it might need clarification of its goals. Perhaps members need feedback on how they are doing or need to be motivated through rewards, threats, or punishments. Whatever is observed to be missing, it is the leader's role to ensure its accomplishment, even if this requires personal intervention. In order to supply missing functions, the leader must be very skilled at observing group problem-solving processes and intervening in such processes effectively (Schein, 1969).

So far we have talked about goal accomplishment. Another critical function in all organizations is the growth and maintenance of interpersonal relationships within the group. In this area also the appointed leader must ensure group development and maintenance, monitor progress, and supply missing functions such as encouraging, supporting, training and developing people, resolving conflict, going to bat for the group, and so on. The issue is not whether to be task oriented or relationship oriented, so much as to *ensure that the missing functions are fulfilled in both areas.*

For example, if the task is challenging and complex, subordinates can get satisfaction from the task itself and do not need a considerate, relationship-oriented leader. In fact, such a group thrives under a leader who is task oriented and facilitates task performance. On the other hand, if the task is dull or frustrating, subordinates will need a relationship-oriented, considerate leader to help them to deal with the frustration of the task (House, 1971). Similarly, Katz (1977) has shown that if a group is experiencing conflict around task issues, it pefers a task-oriented leader; if it is experiencing interpersonal conflict, it prefers a relationship-oriented leader. Yet even under conditions of interpersonal conflict, a task-oriented leader often proved more successful, which suggests that what a conflict-ridden group may need most is to be able to focus on a task and have some task success.

In summary, one could argue that leadership functions can be widely distributed among members but that the leader's *critical functions* are (1) to determine, articulate, or transmit the basic goals or tasks to be accomplished; (2) to monitor progress toward task or goal accomplishment; (3) to ensure that the group of subordinates is built and maintained for effective task performance; and (4) to supply whatever is needed or missing for task accomplishment and group maintenance.

Nothing is implied in this formulation about *how* the leader should go about performing these functions, how autocratic or participative the leader ought to be. All that is implied is that it is inherent in the concept of leadership that the leader is accountable ultimately for the fulfillment of these particular functions.

DECISION AREAS: THE WORK ITSELF, THE INTERACTION CONTEXT, AND/OR ORGANIZATIONAL POLICIES

If leadership orientation (task versus relationship) and leadership style (autocratic, participative, delegative) are both contingent on the type of task or decision area which is involved, we need a dimension along which to classify decision types. One basis for such a dimension is the classification proposed by students of job satisfaction—whether the decision is *immediately work related*, whether the decision involves the interaction *context* in which the work is being done (which might also include the means to be used in accomplishing the job), or whether the decision involves *organizational policies*, ranging from basic decisions about organizational mission and design to policies about the role of employees in the governance of the organization—that is, personnel policies, pay, benefits, promotions, career development, and so on (Katz & Van Maanen, 1977). This dimension is by no means the only one that can be used to analyze decision types. Vroom's criteria include (1) who has what information, (2) how critical is implementation, and (3) how likely are subordinates to share organizational goals and, therefore, to be motivated to implement the decision. Fiedler and others use the criterion of how structured the decision is. Hersey and Blanchard use the criterion of how capable the subordinates are in solving the problem and how motivated they are to solve it. All of these are relevant, but they need to be supplemented by the more fundamental dimension being suggested here—degree of job/work relatedness.

Figure 8.4 shows this decision dimension in relation to degrees of participativeness as defined in the previous section. The purpose of this grid is to aid the leader or manager in diagnosing the various decisions required during the normal course of operations and in deciding *how much involvement on the part of subordinates is appropriate for that decision area*. Additional criteria, such as how structured the decision is and who possesses how much information, can be applied subsequently.

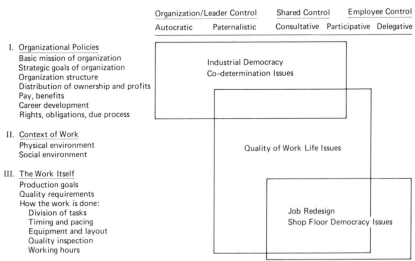

AREAS OF PARTICIPATION

DEGREE OF PARTICIPATION

	Organization/Leader Control		Shared Control	Employee Control	
	Autocratic	Paternalistic	Consultative	Participative	Delegative

I. Organizational Policies
   Basic mission of organization
   Strategic goals of organization
   Organization structure
   Distribution of ownership and profits
   Pay, benefits
   Career development
   Rights, obligations, due process

   Industrial Democracy
   Co-determination Issues

II. Context of Work
   Physical environment
   Social environment

   Quality of Work Life Issues

III. The Work Itself
   Production goals
   Quality requirements
   How the work is done:
     Division of tasks
     Timing and pacing
     Equipment and layout
     Quality inspection
     Working hours

   Job Redesign
   Shop Floor Democracy Issues

Fig. 8.4 The dimension of job relevance as it relates to degree of participation.

For example, decisions in the upper left-hand quadrant typically tend to be made autocratically because (1) owners and senior managers of organizations usually have the right and obligation to define the mission and goals of the enterprise and how the work should basically be organized, and (2) the owners and senior managers tend to have the most relevant information and expertise on such problems. On the other hand, many of the decision problems in this policy area tend to be more or less unstructured and one may run into major implementation problems, suggesting a more participative approach. Historically, of course, organizational practices have sometimes been so exploitative of employees that unions and prolabor legislation was required to restrict the owners' license to do as they pleased. Thus where strong unions exist, many of the employee relations policies must now be jointly negotiated rather than unilaterally decided by the leadership of the organization.

Furthermore, in an increasing number of countries the basic mission of the organization is itself being redefined to include the welfare of employees, and legislation has been passed to ensure that many categories of policy decisions are "codetermined" by workers and managers/owners. An extreme form of such a policy has been adopted in Sweden, where *every* managerial policy decision must now be put before workers' councils before it can be implemented.

Worker representatives on boards of directors and governments dominated by labor parties doing centralized planning are an even more extreme form of such forced participation, resulting, in some cases, in complete control of policy by the workers through their elected or appointed representatives. In other words, in the final analysis the degree to which organizational policies are handled participatively depends largely on the economic and political system within which the organization exists and what its basic mission is defined to be. When one encounters terms like *industrial democracy* or *codetermination* it is this area of participation that is usually involved.

The middle of the figure shows that set of decision areas which have to do with the physical layout of the work and such environmental conditions as noise, light, quality of the equipment, and safety conditions. The context of the work also includes social factors such as the predominant kind of co-worker relationships, the "climate" of the organization, the degree to which the work facilitates or undermines desired social contacts, and so on. Much of the debate about the "quality of work life" has to do with this decision area, and much of the tension about participation has to do with assumptions about who has the right and obligation to define how these areas are structured—the industrial engineering expert, the finance manager, or the employee who has to live and work in the environment.

The Hawthorne studies, the coal mining studies, and many others since then have reinforced the insight that basic production levels and the quality of production will be affected by how people feel about their environment, yet organizations have a hard time legitimizing a higher degree of participation in the design of such environments. For example, many organizations do not permit employees (even high-level managers) to decorate their immediate work area with personal effects or art of their own choice. Yet here is an area that clearly could be virtually abdicated by the leader with potentially no ill effects. Safety programs based on employee commitment clearly work better when employees are involved in the design and acceptance of the program rather than having it unilaterally imposed on them. Even the basic *layout* of a factory can be jointly negotiated among industrial engineers, managers, and future employees in the facility, since each group has relevant information to bring to the design task and a stake in the final decisions.

The third decisional area is the most sensitive and perhaps the most controversial. How much should employees participate in decisions about the design of their own work, the setting of work goals, the defining of realistic quality standards, the timing and pacing of the work, the division of labor among them, the placement and maintenance of their own equipment, and the inspection of their own work? Here is an area where the subordinate, after having learned the job, typically has as much or more information about how to get it done than the manager/leader, but the leader is often not prepared to be more participative, because of suspicions about the motivation and commitment of the subordinate.

Most leadership research, notably the Michigan studies (Likert, 1967), has clearly shown that in the long run both production and morale benefit from "less close" supervision, by which is meant that the supervisor sets targets and reviews performance against those targets, but then allows the employee considerable latitude on how he or she actually does the work. The whole philosophy of management by objectives which was first formulated by Drucker (1954), and the whole point of McGregor's Theory Y (1960) was to get managers to give more latitude to their subordinates, to delegate more of the day-to-day routine, and to measure only final results rather than every step of every task. In other words, it may be worthwhile to determine work goals and quality standards jointly, but the actual means of accomplishing the work can be delegated completely if, in Hersey and Blanchard's sense, employees are "mature" in having both the necessary skills and the motivation to perform the work.

The notion of employee readiness for different areas and levels of participation can also be viewed in light of the developmental perspective. Not only will employees differ in their basic needs to be involved in different decisions, and not only will such needs to be involved vary with their skill level and sense of responsibility, but the area of involvement that they will care about will vary as a function of their job longevity (Katz, 1978). If the employee is in a "learner" stage, involvement in job design is not very important, but job significance and feedback are important, which argues for involvement of the employee in when and how to receive feedback from boss and peers. During the "responsive" stage when the employee is fully involved in work issues, participation in the design of work will be of maximum importance. If the employee stays in the same job until the "adapted" or "unresponsive" stage is reached, involvement in work issues will decline, but involvement and needs to participate in contextual and organizational policy issues will remain high or even become higher. Thus, the less employees come to care about the actual work they do, the more they will come to care about the work environment, their pay and benefits, and their long-range situation in the organization.

CONCLUSION

We can see that the degree of participation that is appropriate for a given decision area at a particular time depends not only upon how structured the problem is and who has what information, but also upon the socioeconomic and political circumstances which define the basic nature of the organization, whether we are talking about organizational policies, the work environment, or the work itself, and whether the past history of the organization has led to formal mechanisms of joint decision making such as unions, worker councils, or labor-management committees such as those found in Scanlon Plan companies. Thus, while it is important and necessary to think through the leadership issue in individual leader terms, it is ultimately necessary to answer the question of what kind of leadership behavior is appropriate in much more general terms, considering the decision area and the environmental context as equally relevant criteria. What this ultimately highlights is the previous conclusions about the motivational complexity of human nature—that above all the leader/manager must increase his or her diagnostic skills and personal flexibility in order to fulfill whatever leadership functions are most needed in any given situation.

Groups
in
Organizations

Groups within organizations are the subject of much mythology and the target for strong feelings. Though the group is a nearly universal phenomenon, some managers who have little faith in teamwork and committees pride themselves on running an operation in which tasks are primarily accomplished by individuals, not by groups. Elsewhere, one finds managers saying with equal pride that they make all their major decisions in groups and rely heavily on teamwork. People differ greatly in their stereotypes of what a group is, what a group can and cannot do, and how effective a group can be. A classic joke told by those who are against the use of groups is that "a camel is a horse put together by a committee."

What, then, is the "truth" about groups? Why do they exist? What functions do groups fulfill for the organization and for their members? How does one judge the goodness or effectiveness of a group? What kinds of things can groups do and what can they not do? What impact do groups have on their members, on each other, and on the organization within which they exist? What are the pros and cons of intergroup cooperation and intergroup competition? How does one manage and influence groups? These are some of the questions we will discuss in the next two chapters.

Our major reason for devoting a good deal of attention to groups is the fact that they *do* have a major impact on their members, on other groups, and on the host organization. Group formation ultimately receives its impetus from the very activity of organizing.

As we saw in Chapter 2, an organization divides up its ultimate task into subtasks which are assigned to various subunits. These subunits in turn may divide the task and pass it down further, until a level is reached where several people take a subgoal and divide it among themselves as individuals, but no longer create formal units. At this level of formal organization, we have the basis for group formation along functional lines. The sales department or some part thereof may come to be a psychological group; the production department may be a single group or become a set of groups; and so on. What basically breaks an organization down into groups, therefore, is division of labor. The organization itself generates forces toward the formation of various smaller functional task groups within itself.

Recently much attention has been devoted to the deliberate use of groups as organizational building blocks (Leavitt, 1975). Instead of assigning work to individuals, rewarding or punishing individuals, and holding individuals responsible for output, it is possible to conceive of organizations in which an entire group is assigned a task, made responsible for it, and paid as a group. In some industries it has been discovered that both higher productivity and better quality can be achieved by delegating clusters of tasks to an entire work group. Such *autonomous work groups* are then made responsible for producing an entire product such as a radio, an engine, or some total component of a large machine. Such autonomous work groups first made their appearance many years ago in industries such as mining, electronics, and aircraft production. Their recent rediscovery by the automobile industry has been highly publicized in the well-known experiments in the Swedish factories of the Volvo company (Lindholm & Norstedt, 1975).

In earlier chapters, several examples from the Hawthorne studies and the Tavistock coal mining studies were cited to show how groups affect production methods, output, and quality. These researches also showed how dependent people are on groups and how important groups can become as an outlet for important psychological needs, as anxiety reducers, and as sources of strength in dealing with other groups. These findings will be reemphasized in Part IV.

The Structure
and Functions
of Groups

DEFINITION OF A GROUP

What is a "group"? How big can a group be? What differentiates a group from a crowd? Since we are focusing primarily on psychological problems in organizations, it would appear most appropriate to define a group in *psychological* terms:

A *psychological* group is any number of people who (1) interact with one another, (2) are psychologically aware of one another, and (3) perceive themselves to be a group.

The size of a group is thus limited by the possibilities of mutual interaction and mutual awareness. Mere aggregates of people do not fit this definition because they do not interact and do not perceive themselves to be a group even if they are aware of each other as, for instance, a crowd on a street corner watching some event. A total department, a union, or a whole organization would not be a group in spite of thinking of themselves as "we," because they generally do not all interact and are not all aware of each other. However, work teams, committees, subparts of departments, cliques, and various other informal associations among organizational members would fit this definition of a group.

Having defined a group, and having indicated that the basic force toward group formation arises out of the organizational process itself, let us now examine the kinds of groups actually found in organizations.

145

TYPES OF GROUPS IN ORGANIZATIONS

Formal Groups

Formal groups are those groups which are deliberately created by managers in order to fulfill specific tasks clearly related to the total organizational mission. Formal groups can be of two types, based on their duration: (1) *Permanent* formal groups are bodies such as the top management team, work units in the various departments of the organization, staff groups providing specialized services to the work organization, permanent committees, and so on. (2) *Temporary* formal groups are committees or task forces created for a particular mission. Thus, an organization may create a committee or study group to review salary policies, to study the relationship between the organization and the community, to come up with proposals for improving union-management relations, to think of new products and services, and so on. Temporary formal groups may exist for a long time. What makes them temporary is that they are defined as such by the organization and that the members feel themselves to be a part of a group which may at any time go out of existence.

Informal Groups

As has already been pointed out, members of organizations are formally called upon to provide only certain activities in order to fulfill their organizational role. But, because the whole person actually reports for work or joins the organization, and because people have needs beyond the minimum ones of doing their job, they will seek fulfillment of some of these needs through developing a variety of relationships with other members of the organization. If the ecology of the work area and the time schedule of the work permit, these informal relationships will develop into informal groups. In other words, the *tendency* toward informal groups can almost always be assumed to exist because we all have needs to relate to other people. How this tendency works itself out in the actual creation of groups, however, depends very much on the physical location of people, the nature of their work, their time schedules, and so on. Informal groups, therefore, arise out of the particular combination of "formal" factors and human needs.

Some examples may help to clarify this important point. In the bank-wiring room of the Hawthorne studies, the two major informal cliques were the "group in the front" and the "group in the back." This pattern arose out of actual job-related interactions as well as

146

slight differences in the work performed in the two parts of the room. The men in front considered themselves to be superior because they believed they were doing more difficult work, though the pay scale did not reflect any distinction. Thus, informal groups tend to arise partly out of the formal features of the organization (Homans, 1950).

It has also been found in a number of studies of friendship and informal association that these relationships are often based simply on the probability of one person's meeting another in the course of daily activities. In a housing project, for example, probability of friendship was largely determined by the actual location and direction of doorways (Festinger, Schachter, & Back, 1950).

Striking results illustrative of this same "proximity" phenomenon were observed in a number of R & D laboratories of various industrial and private organizations. Allen (1977) found that the frequency of communication on technical matters which occurred between various engineers and scientists in the laboratory was directly related to the physical distance between the employees' desks or offices. Once this distance exceeded 40 meters, the probability of communication between people dropped to near zero. Being across the street or down the hall was not much different from being in another town.

Since the quality of an engineering department's technical solutions depends on the exchange of information among its members, it becomes important to design physical facilities in such a way as to maximize the probability of interaction by minimizing the physical distance between people. Or, if such a physical solution is not possible, other compensatory mechanisms must be found to stimulate communication. Allen found that some people in the laboratory remained especially well informed and functioned as "technological gatekeepers" for others because they were well-connected sociometrically, thereby helping the laboratory to be more effective. A well-informed engineer who was a social isolate could not function as a gatekeeper, by definition (Allen, 1977).

Informal groups almost always arise if the opportunities exist. Often such groups come to serve a "counterorganizational function" in that they attempt to counteract any coercive tendencies of the organization. Such groups can become powerful and even subvert the formal goals of the organization. Managers who fear such counterorganizational groups sometimes attempt to prevent informal group formation by designing the work or the physical setting within which it is carried out so as to eliminate meaningful interaction (such as in a noisy assembly line). Or leaders and key members may be systematically rotated out of the group to prevent any stable group structure from emerging. This technique was well illustrated by Chinese Communist procedures of managing military prisoners during the Korean war (Schein, 1956, 1961). Anytime a group of prisoners would form a coalition, the Chinese would move one or more key members to another part of the camp, thus gradually inducing a growing feeling of social isolation among the prisoners which made escapes or resistance much more difficult.

Types of Informal Groups

Informal groups in large organizations can be classified into several types, as observed by Dalton (1959) in his classic study of industry. The most prevalent have been labeled *horizontal cliques*, by which Dalton means an informal association of workers, managers, or organizational members who are more or less of the same rank, and work in more or less the same area. The bank-wiring room had two such cliques in it. Most organizations that have been studied, regardless of their basic function, have an extensive informal organization consisting of many such cliques.

A second type, which Dalton terms a *vertical clique*, is a group composed of members from different levels within a given department. For example, in several organizations that Dalton studied, he found groups that consisted of a number of workers, one or two foremen, and one or more higher level managers. Some of the members were actually in superior-subordinate relationships to one another. Vertical cliques apparently come into being because of earlier acquaintance of the members or because they need each other to accomplish their goals. For example, such groups often serve a key communication function both upward and downward.

A third type of informal group can be called a *mixed or random clique*, comprised of members of different ranks, from different departments, and from different physical locations. Such cliques may arise to serve common interests or to fulfill functional needs the formal organization does not meet. For example, the head of manufacturing may cultivate a relationship with the best worker in the maintenance department in order to be able to short-circuit formal communication channels when a machine breaks down and he or she needs immediate maintenance work. On the college campus we have seen the growth of informal groups which consist of students, faculty, and high-level administrators to work on problems that the formal committee structure cannot handle. Relationships outside the organizational context may be another important basis for the formation of cliques. For example, a number of members may live in the same part of town, or attend the same church, or belong to the same social club.

In summary, groups of all kinds will always be found in organizations, some formal ones created by deliberate design to do specific jobs, some informal ones created by the needs of people to interact, and some which form simply because of the probability of interaction created by physical proximity, similarity of interests, or other fortuitous factors.

FUNCTIONS FULFILLED BY GROUPS

One reason why groups are so common is that they fulfill such a wide range of functions both for their members and for the larger organization. It is useful to distinguish these kinds of functions and to remind ourselves that the basis of group formation is typically highly complex and "overdetermined" in that a given group can simultaneously fulfill a variety of formal organizational functions and meet a wide variety of members' personal needs.

Formal Organizational Functions of Groups

By *formal* organizational functions I mean those aspects of group activity that coincide with the organization's basic mission. Several such functions can be identified:

a. The group can be a means of *working on a complex, interdependent task* which is too difficult for any one individual to perform and which cannot be easily broken down into independent tasks. For example, to fly an airplane requires a crew composed of several members with specific but highly interdependent functions.

b. A group can be a means of *generating new ideas or creative solutions* when information is initially highly dispersed among several people and/or when some mutual stimulation is needed among members to be fully creative.

c. A group can serve critical *liaison or coordinating functions* among several departments whose work is to some degree interdependent. By bringing representatives of the department together into a committee, task force, or project team, it is possible to reduce communication breakdowns and maintain coordinated effort.

d. A group can be a *problem-solving mechanism* if the problem requires the processing of complex information, interaction among members with different information, and critical assessment of possible alternative solutions. Thus project teams, task forces, committees and ad hoc groups are used by organizations to tackle specific problems such as long-range planning, design and introduction of new products, development of product standards, or other criteria which have to be applied widely across the organization.

e. A group can be used to *facilitate the implementation of complex decisions*. For example, if a company has decided to move a factory from one site to another (typically a rather complex task), it has been found useful to create an implementation team comprised of representatives of all the major groups of workers in a factory to work out the logistics of the move. By involving these groups in the decision it was found that the move was made more efficiently with less time lost, less equipment broken, and fewer complaints from people who were displaced.

f. The group can be used as a *vehicle of socialization or training*. By bringing several people together into a training situation, a common message can be imparted and a common group perspective developed. As we will see later, there are risks in this strategy because the common group perspective eventually expresses itself in a counterorganizational form, but those risks have not been sufficient to keep organizations from using groups in their educational activities (Van Maanen & Schein, 1979).

The above list is not exhaustive. As a powerful tool in implementing a wide variety of task-related functions, the group is coming into its own in managerial circles. By bringing together the right people, at the right time, around the right set of questions, organizations have found it possible to greatly improve their overall effectiveness.

Psychological, Individual Functions of Groups

Organizational members bring with them a variety of needs, and groups can fulfill many of these needs. We can list the major functions fulfilled by groups in the following categories:

a. Groups are a primary means of fulfilling our *affiliation needs*, that is, our needs for friendship, support, and love. The original prototype of such a group, often called a "primary group" is, of course, the family. In adult life we continue to rely upon the family for the gratification of these needs, but we also find that we need friendship groups, work groups, and other relationships to fulfill our affiliation needs.

b. Groups are a primary means of developing, enhancing, and confirming our *sense of identity and maintaining our self-esteem*. Again, the family is the group in which these basic processes are begun, but various other kinds or formal and informal groups, many of them at our place of work, become an important source of determining or confirming our concept of who we are, what our status is, how valued we are, and, therefore, how high our self-esteem will be. Status symbols, uniforms, badges of office, and other similar external manifestations derive their importance from the fact that they help us to sustain our identity and our self-esteem.

c. Groups are a primary means of *establishing and testing social reality.* Through discussion with others and the development of shared perspectives and consensus, we can reduce uncertainty in our social environment. For example, when several workers share their insecurity about a hard-driving boss, develop a consensus that he or she is a slave driver, and develop strategies for dealing with him or her, this process *reduces* the uncertainty and the attendant anxiety of not understanding what is going on. Many group-held beliefs—for example, the belief among the Hawthorne plant's wiremen that if they produced more, management would lower the rate for each piece produced—may not have any actual foundation in past events, but nevertheless function as the current reality. As the famous sociological dictum put it, "If people define a situation as real, it will be real in its consequences."

d. Groups are a primary means of *reducing insecurity, anxiety, and sense of powerlessness.* The dictum that there is strength in numbers highlights the fact that not only do numbers provide actual strength in relation to an adversary, but there is ample evidence that just having others on our side makes us feel stronger, less anxious, and less insecure in the face of some kind of threat (Asch, 1951; Schachter, 1959). For example, it is clear that when workers feel insecure and exploited in a work situation they can band together into bargaining units or unions and thereby reduce their sense of powerlessness. Similarly, when workers informally agree to "restrict output" as they did in the bank-wiring room, they felt they were offsetting the power of management to control them through the incentive system.

e. Finally, groups can become for their members a *problem-solving, task-accomplishing mechanism* comparable to the formal functions identified earlier, but typically concerned with problems of self-interest, not those posed by management. Thus groups can serve as a means of gathering information, helping someone who is sick or tired, or avoiding boredom by inventing games or even participating in counterorganizational activities. Argyris (1964) cites a classic case of such worker "creativity." A group of workers in an electronics company resented the fact that their boss would visit various departments on a *random* basis to check on things. They used a large stock of the equipment they were manufacturing to set up a highly efficient early warning system to help them prepare for the boss's surprise "inspection." The boss never realized that many thousands of dollars worth of equipment were tied up in this internal group activity designed solely to accomplish a psychological task for the group members.

It is clear from reviewing the above functions why groups are so common and so important, even if they do not have formal, organizationally designed tasks to perform. Many of our most basic psychological needs are met in groups, and since so much of our daily adult life is spent in work settings of various kinds, it is not surprising that groups would become an integral part of such work settings.

Multiple or Mixed Functions

One of the most common findings from the research on groups in organizations is that most groups turn out to have both formal and informal functions; they serve the needs of both the organization and the individual members. Psychological groups, therefore, may well be the key unit for facilitating the integration of organizational goals and personal needs (Leavitt, 1975).

For example, a formal work crew such as is found in industry or in the Army (say, a platoon) often evolves into a psychological group that meets a variety of its members' psychological needs. If this process occurs, the group often becomes the source of much higher levels of loyalty, commitment, and energy in the service of organizational goals than would be possible if the members' psychological needs had to be met elsewhere. A key task for research and for management practice, then, is the determination of those conditions that will facilitate the fulfillment of psychological needs in *formal* work groups.

On the other hand, one of the most interesting and important organizational phenomena observed to date is the inverse of the development from formal to informal. In his research Dalton (1959) found many groups based on informal characteristics such as common background, religion, or membership in community organizations. Interestingly, managers used these informal networks as *formal communication channels* to obtain information quickly on conditions in various parts of the organization and to communicate to line operators what changes in production policy were in the offing. The actual mechanism might be the exchange of information at lunch, at the local meeting of the Rotary Club, over golf at the country club, or through an informal telephone conversation. According to Dalton, these contacts not only met many psychological needs but were clearly *necessary* for the maintenance of organizational effectiveness.

In summary, groups are important in organizations because of their potential for fulfilling both critical organizational and psychological functions. If organizations can be designed so that the psychological forces in groups work congruently with organizational objectives, there is greater potential of maximizing long-range organizational effectiveness and individual need fulfillment.

Let us next examine some of the factors that influence group formation, group effectiveness, and, most importantly, the degree to which integration of personal and organizational goals is possible.

FACTORS AFFECTING THE INTEGRATION OF ORGANIZATIONAL GOALS AND PERSONAL NEEDS IN GROUPS

A variety of factors will determine what kinds of groups will tend to exist in an organization and whether such groups will tend to fulfill both organizational and personal functions or only one or the other. These variables can be divided into three main categories: *environmental* factors—the cultural, social, physical, and technological climate in which the group exists; *membership* factors—the types of people in the group, categorized in terms of personal background, values, relative status, skills, and so on; and *dynamic* factors—how the group is organized, the leadership style(s), the amount of training members have received in leadership and membership skills, the kinds of tasks given to the group, its prior history of success or failure, its level of development, and so on.

Environmental Factors

Environmental factors such as the organization of the work, the physical location of workers, and the time schedule imposed will determine who will interact with whom and, therefore, which people are likely to form into groups in the first place. If groups are to be encouraged to fulfill organizational tasks, it follows that the work environment must permit and even encourage the emergence of "logical" groups. This end can be accomplished by actually designating certain groups as work teams, or by allowing groups to emerge through facilitating interaction and allowing enough free time for it to occur.

In many cases, the nature or location of a job itself requires effective group action, as in bomber, tank, or submarine crews, in groups who work in isolation for long periods of time—for example, a radar or weather station—or in medical teams in a hospital. In other cases, even though the technical requirements do not demand it, an organization often encourages group formation. For example, the Army, rather than replace soldiers one at a time, has begun to use four-man groups who go through basic training together as combat replacements. In the hotel industry, where it is crucial for the top management of a hotel to work well together, one company has begun a conscious program of training the top team together before they take charge of a hotel in order to ensure good working relations.

The degree to which such logically designed groups come to serve psychological needs will depend to a large extent on another environmental factor—the managerial climate. The managerial climate is determined primarily by the prevailing assumptions in the organization about employee motivation. If rational-economic assumptions are favored, it is unlikely that groups will be rationally utilized in the first place. According to those assumptions, groups should be undermined or destroyed in the interest of maximizing *individual* efficiency. If coordination is required, it is to be supplied by the assembly line or some other mechanical means. Consequently, a climate based on rational-economic assumptions is most likely to produce defensive, antimanagement groups. Such groups will arise to give their members the sense of self-esteem and security that the formal organization denies them.

An organization built on social assumptions will encourage and foster the growth of groups, but may err in creating groupings that are not logically related to task performance. This kind of organization often adheres to an underlying philosophy of job design and job allocation built on rational-economic assumptions, but then attempts to meet people's affiliative needs by creating various social groups that are extrinsic to the immediate work organization—company bowling leagues, baseball teams, picnics, and social activies. Such groups do not permit the integration of formal and informal group forces, however, because the groups have no intrinsic task function in the first place.

An organization built on self-actualizing assumptions is more likely to create a climate conducive to the emergence of psychologically meaningful groups because of the organization's stress on the intrinsic meaningfulness of work. However, such organizations—for example, research divisions of industrial concerns or university de-partments—often fail to carry these assumptions to their logical con-clusion. Typically, so much emphasis is given to providing challenge for each *individual* and so little emphasis is given to collective effort, that groups are not likely to be encouraged to develop.

The effective integration of organizational and personal needs undoubtedly requires a flexible climate that encourages the adoption of group strategies at some times but militates against them in other circumstances. Those organizations that have been able to use groups effectively tend to be very careful in deciding when to make use of a work team or a committee and when to set up conditions which promote or discourage group formation. There are no easy generalizations in this area, hence a diagnostic approach is the most likely to pay off. The type of task involved, the past success of the organization with group strategies, the people available, their ability to be effective group members, and the kind of group leadership available—all should be considered.

Membership Factors

Whether a group will work effectively on an organizational task and at the same time become psychologically satisfying to its mem-bers depends in part on the group's composition. For any effective work to occur, there must be a certain degree of consensus on goals, basic values, and on a medium of communication. If personal back-grounds, values, or status differentials prevent such consensus or communication, the group cannot perform well. It is particularly important that relative status be carefully assessed in order to avoid the fairly common pitfall of lower status members' withholding in-formation from higher status members because they do not wish to expose themselves or to be punished for saying possibly unpleasant things, or things they believe others do not wish to hear.

A typical example is the departmental staff meeting, in which the boss asks various subordinates how things are going in their units. Often subordinates will respond only with vague statements that "everything is all right," because they know that the boss wants and expects things that way and because they do not wish to be embarrassed in front of their peers by admitting problems. Conse-quently, for problem solving, such a group may not only be ineffec-tive but actually counterproductive.

Another typically difficult group is a committee composed of *representatives* of various other departments of the organization.

Each person is likely to be so concerned about his or her constituents, wishing to uphold their interests as its representative, that it becomes difficult for the members to become identified with the new committee.

A third kind of problem group, illustrating conflict of values, is the typical labor-management bargaining committee. Even though the group's mission may be to invent new solutions to chronic problems, the labor members typically cannot establish good communications with the management members because they feel management is condescending, devalues them as human beings, and basically does not respect them. These attitudes may be communicated in subtle ways, such as by asking that the meetings be held in management's meeting rooms rather than offering to meet on neutral territory or in a place suggested by the labor group.

For each of the above problems, the only remedy is to provide the members with enough common experiences to permit a communication system and a climate of trust to emerge. Such shared experience can be obtained by holding long meetings away from the place of work, thereby encouraging members to get to know each other in more informal settings, or by going through some common training experience. Experience-based training exercises or workshops serve not only to educate people about groups, but also to provide group members a common base of experience from which to build better working relationships (Dyer, 1977).

An inadequate distribution of relevant abilities and skills may be another important membership problem. For any work group to be effective, it must have within it the resources to fulfill its assigned task. If the group fails in accomplishing its task because of lack of resources and thereby develops a psychological sense of failure, it can hardly develop the strength and cohesiveness to serve other psychological needs for its members. All of these points indicate that just bringing a collection of people into interaction does not ensure a good working group. It is important to consider the characteristics of the members and to assess the likelihood of their being able to work with one another and serve one another's needs.[1]

Dynamic Factors

By dynamic factors, I mean those events and processes which occur during the life of the group itself or which lead up to the formation of the group, such as training people to become a group or

---

[1] I have not reviewed the literature on personality compatibility among group members because of lack of clear results from research in this area.

inducing certain group feelings. In this category would be variables such as group orientation and socialization procedures, the kind of group structure that emerges from the actual interactions of the members, and the success or failure the group experiences in attempting to fulfill its formal task (if it is a formal group) and to meet the psychological needs of its members.

Dynamic factors highlight the changing and changeable nature of groups. Groups are not static, rigid, or unchangeable. In fact, one of the major contributions of the field of group dynamics has been a body of knowledge and a related body of skills concerned with actually helping groups to change, grow, and become more effective. Instead of taking environmental and membership factors as fixed determinants of what a group can or cannot do, we have discovered that such factors can provide opportunities for group growth and can, if properly utilized, be turned into advantages rather than disadvantages. Entire texts have been written on the psychology of groups and how to work with them (Miles, 1959; Dyer, 1977; Schein & Bennis, 1965; Schein, 1969). We will not be able to review even a small portion of the large amount of information available, but perhaps the case illustrations cited will draw attention to some of the key variables and issues involved.

THE OIL REFINERY LABOR-MANAGEMENT CONFLICT. A large oil refinery was experiencing difficulty in its labor-management relations, and was threatened with the possibility that many of its employees would join a rather hostile and militant union. Several committees had been set up to find new solutions to the many problems brought up by the employees, but these committees invariably broke down in an antagonistic deadlock after a few meetings, with both labor and management members feeling that the other side was stubborn and recalcitrant.

Thus far, the story is fairly typical of many labor-management conflicts. However, this particular refinery had instituted a training program devoted specifically to helping trainees (1) become more familiar with the problems of being an effective group leader and/or member, and (2) obtain some insight into their own behavior in groups and their impact on other people. The program involved two weeks of full-time training in interpersonal relations and group dynamics, and resulted in considerable attitude change and personal insight for the trainees. The plan was eventually to have all members of management and the professional staff services attend the two-week program. But long before this goal had been accomplished, the labor crisis reached new proportions.

Senior management at this point decided to try still one more set of problem-solving committees, but this time, having gained some insight into group functioning, composed them and launched them in a very different manner. First of all, only management members who had been through the training program and who were therefore assumed to be more sensitive to group problems were put on the committees. Second, the groups were instructed not to arrive at decisions (in previous efforts the drive toward decisions had resulted in premature polarization of opinions), but merely to explore certain of the issues with the aim of *identifying alternatives*. Third, the management members were carefully instructed to allow the initiative for meeting times, locations, and agenda details to remain with the labor members.

From the outset, these committees had a very different kind of climate. They were oriented far more toward problem solving than toward worrying about which member had how much status. As a result, they generated proposals which met the desires of both workers and managers, and thus led to an overwhelming defeat of the militant union's effort to organize the refinery. Although it is difficult in such a case to identify the exact cause-and-effect relationships, there is little question that the training some members had received in how to be an effective group member and the greater insight management had as a result of the training in how to compose and launch groups helped substantially to resolve the conflict.

A similar example can be found in the area of higher education. As the result of severe riots on its campus in the late 1960s, one large university experienced a breakdown of communication between faculty, students, and administration. A planning team decided to hold a three-day conference away from the university for key representatives of the trustees, student body, faculty, and administration. The conference was designed by a group of invited consultants who were expert at group dynamics. Small problem-identification teams were constructed in such a way that each of the key groups would get to know members of the other groups in a more personal, informal setting. The output of the small groups was thus twofold: At the formal level they generated lists of priority problems which were then amalgamated into a master set of priorities in a plenary session; at the informal level, trust was reestablished among the various groups within the university, making possible further problem-solving activities back on the campus.

This case illustrates how a combination of dynamic factors such as leadership and group development, structural factors about when and where the meetings would be held and who would attend, and group process skills aided in the problem resolution. In the next several sections we will look at examples of each of these dynamic areas.

LEADERSHIP AND ORGANIZATIONAL FACTORS. Among the various dynamic factors that influence group behavior are those which derive from the leadership patterns or styles of group leaders and from how the group is organized and structured in the first place. These various factors are treated together because they are usually highly interrelated. There exists a vast research literature which has attempted to unravel these complex relationships, but we will identify only one or two of the major topic areas and some of the most interesting findings in each of them.[2]

Group Traditions versus Leader Style. One of the perennially fascinating problems in organizations concerns the question of whether group norms and traditions in an established group are stronger than the will of a new leader. A common situation in organizations involves the promotion or transfer of managers into new functions or geographical regions, which necessitates their taking over a group with its own history, traditions, and norms of how it likes to operate. Should the manager simply adapt to those norms, or impose his or her will on the group?

In a classic experiment reported by Merei (1949), the interplay between group traditions and leader strength was studied through an ingenious experimental design, using as subjects children 4 to 11 years old. Merei first observed the children to determine who were "natural" leaders and who were followers by observing the relative rate of giving versus following orders. "Follower" children were then put into groups and allowed to play together until they developed lasting habits and traditions (three to six meetings of 30 to 45 minutes each).

"Leader" children were selected by nursery school teachers on the criteria of being older, more domineering, more likely to be imitated by others, more aggressive, and higher in initiative. Twenty-six different leader children were then put into each of the twelve different groups at different times and under different conditions to observe the interplay between leader and group, with the following overall results:

1. In almost every case the group absorbed the leader, forcing its traditions upon him or her. Leader undertakings or desires either remained unfulfilled or gained acceptance only in a modified form suitable to the traditions of the group, in spite of the fact that the leader was older and more domineering.
2. Leaders accepted the traditions of the group but also found ways of influencing and changing them. At one extreme, a particularly strong

2 For examples of reviews the texts by Shaw (1971) and Cartwright and Zander (1968) are most useful.

group completely assimilated the leader child, who eventually gave up his leadership. At the other extreme, one girl leader completely dominated a group and immediately broke its traditions, but this group had been subjected on previous days to three other leader children and thus had already weakened traditions. Between these extremes were three types of leader behavior characteristic of most leadership styles:

a. *The order givers.* These types of leaders started out to give orders and boss everybody, were consistently ignored, and found themselves increasingly isolated. When they suddenly changed their behavior to adapt to the group traditions, they discovered they were able to give orders *within those traditions.* That is, they took over the group by ordering members to do what they would have done anyway, thus appropriating the leadership role without, however, changing the group traditions.

b. *The proprietors.* These types of leaders asserted themselves by taking possession of all the objects in the room or dominating individual children around ownership of these possessions but were completely unsuccessful in changing the games or the manner in which the objects were used. The group traditions remained the same and the leader children fitted into them, but the group placated the strong leaders by letting them possess the objects and deferring to them in a kind of ritual or ceremonial fashion. These leaders looked like they had really taken over, but in fact had unwittingly assimilated the group's traditions.

c. *The diplomats.* These types of leaders were, in a sense, the most interesting in that they showed evidence of accepting the group traditions on the surface *in order to change them.* Merei described the sequence as follows: the leader tries to do away with group traditions and lead it to new ones; the leader fails and is rejected; the leader then accepts the traditions and quickly learns them; within the frame of these traditions the leader soon assumes leadership, and, though reluctantly, the group follows him or her because he or she does a good job; the leader then introduces significant variations, loosening the tradition; finally, the leader introduces new elements into the group's rituals and thus changes the traditions.

Though Merei's work was done with children, it offers an excellent prototype of the kinds of forces one can observe at work in adult groups of all kinds. Neither the group nor the leader will always be dominant, but the interplay between a stable group with its own norms and traditions and a new leader will be very complex. Most managers have learned from their own experience that they have to deal with group norms in some fashion or other, but often the expectations managers bring back with them from leadership training programs about new leadership styles are ill-suited to the norms or past history of the groups to which they return. In such cases, the manager's new behaviorial role will quickly be unlearned, since neither the subordinates nor the boss is likely to reinforce the new behavior (Fleishman, 1953). In fact, it has been the frequency of this kind of phenomenon which has led most organizational consultants or managers who are concerned about *changing* an organization to think of changing group norms rather than individual leader behavior.

Group Structure. If the group cannot meet face-to-face at all times, it becomes important to consider the effect of structural factors such as the group's communication network on group functioning. For example, it has been shown that a person's feeling of participation is related to his or her position in a communications network; that group leadership may well emerge from the more central positions in such networks; that overcentralized communications are especially effective in implementing a given task but relatively inflexible in developing new solutions if the task changes; and that information is lost and distorted very rapidly as it travels through a number of separate communication links (Leavitt, 1951).

Other organizational structure issues which must be considered in group formation and performance are related to more general organizational phenomena which will be considered in Chapters 10 and 11. For example, members of an organization typically belong to several groups or units within that organization. The physical location of the different groups which stimulates or prevents interaction, the nature of the group task performed, the degree to which the group is temporary or permanent, the kinds of sanctions available to the group leader, the amount of time the group is together, and the degree to which roles are or are not formally structured—all will influence group formation and performance.

One example, drawn from a study of R&D groups, will help to clarify this complexity (Allen, 1977). R&D teams can be organized either (a) "functionally"—by putting people with a common technical background together geographically and under a common boss who controls important rewards such as career advancement, or (b) by "projects"—by putting diverse technical people together geographically and under a common project leader with a specific assigned task, for example, the design of a guidance system for a rocket. In the first case, both the project and the geographical location are seen as temporary, while in the second case the project takes on more permanence, geographical identity (thus favoring group formation), and potency because the project manager will be in more of a position of control.

Allen attempted to determine which form of organization would be more effective as measured by the group's technical output, and discovered that it depended upon the nature of the task and the nature of the technology (an external environmental factor). In a rapidly changing technology the functional form of organization was more effective, because it allowed the engineers to keep closer in touch with their own area of technology. On the other hand, on administrative tasks such as meeting cost and schedule targets, the project form was more effective, because the underlying technology of such administrative tasks does not change very rapidly and the project form permits much more immediate control of the relevant factors.

Putting the various findings together, Allen reached the conclusion that for long-term projects or in a rapidly changing technology, the functional form of organization will, on the whole, produce better results, while for short-term projects or in a slowly changing technology the project form will be more suitable. In both cases the individual engineers will belong simultaneously to a functional group and a project team (what has been called a "matrix" form of organization), but the relative effectiveness of each type of group will depend on geographical location, stimulation of interaction, and degree of power which is given to the functional or project manager, essentially structural characterisics of how the groups are organized.

GROUP DEVELOPMENT AND TRAINING. Probably the most important dynamic factor influencing the integration of individual and organizational needs is the degree to which leaders and members develop sensitivity and skill in managing group process. For example, leaders and members need to learn how difficult it is to really listen to another person and to empathize with him or her; how lack of respect and mistrust can arise from failure to listen; how in the early life of the group, members are likely to be preoccupied with individual needs for identity, security, attention, and status, and thus fail to be able to pay attention to the needs of others; how preoccupation with emotional needs early in the life of the group makes it very difficult to work constructively on a formal task; how premature structuring of the group or premature leader pressure for group output can lead to shallow solutions because the group is not psychologically prepared to work on a task; how group task and group maintenance factors have to be balanced in the life of a group for optimum task performance; and how different decision-making styles such as voting or seeking consensus create more or less effective task solutions. These and many other kinds of problems are chronic to any group, but members and leaders are often unaware both of the problem and of the fact that through training such problems can be overcome.

Though efforts to develop group sensitivies and skills can be traced back to the human relations movement of the 1920s and 1930s, it was not until Lewin and his followers developed what have come to be called "experiential" methods of training that this kind of skill development for leaders really took hold (Bradford et al., 1964; Schein & Bennis, 1965). The more traditional approaches to training had emphasized lectures, readings, demonstrations, and "practice" through role playing or similar devices. The experiential methods which developed around the workshops of the National Training Laboratories in Bethel, Maine, put more emphasis on learning from immediate, here-and-now kinds of experiences. Because these methods have been highly controversial and because they have played an important role in the development of group psychology, it is important to understand what assumptions and values lie behind them.

The experiential methods of training assume that:

1. People can learn best from an analysis of their own immediate, here-and-now psychological experiences.
2. The relevant facts from which such learning can best arise are the feelings, reactions, and observations of other people with whom one interacts, but which for a variety of reasons people tend systematically to withhold from each other.
3. A suitably designed training workshop can overcome the forces against sharing feelings, reactions, and observations and thus make available to participants learning at this more immediate and potent level.
4. The forces to be overcome are essentially culturally learned attitudes about the proper things people should say to one another and attitudes about how one learns (for instance, "one should not deliberately say something critical to another person," and "the way one learns is by listening to and reading the writings of an expert").

Experiential methods challenge and successfully change some of these attitudes, making it possible for participants to obtain personal insight into their own as well as others' reactions and feelings about commonly shared and observed group events.

Many kinds of concrete training devices are used to facilitate this kind of learning, ranging from role playing, followed by an analysis of each role player's performance, to unstructured sensitivity-training groups in which members experience the process of building a group literally from the beginning and analyze the process as they are going through it. In this process members learn how to observe and develop other group intervention skills.

Having obtained some insight and skills in the workshop, participants often discover that analogous events are occurring in their work groups and that they can constructively intervene to improve group functioning. Even such a simple thing as giving the group enough time to allow members to feel each other out and find a secure place for themselves in the group (which may take no more than an hour or two of low-pressure, informal talk) may make it possible thereafter for the group to work effectively on a high-pressure problem. It is this kind of personal insight which was generated by the refinery's training program and which made it possible for the management members to create a better climate for problem solving in their newly created labor-management committees.

One question which always arises in reference to experiential training concerns the *content* of what is learned. For example, does this form of training attempt to teach democratic leadership methods? Does it undermine the traditional prerogatives of authority positions, leading ultimately to greater "power equalization"? If so, is this not counterproductive in many organizational settings where authority must be upheld and must continue to be highly centralized?

The answers to these questions are complex. The ultimate values that are communicated through experiential training are (1) an increased commitment to a spirit of inquiry and a diagnostic approach to interpersonal and organizational situations, both of which are essentially the values of science; (2) a commitment to the value of open and honest communication wherever appropriate; and (3) a commitment to studying and influencing a group's *processes*—how it works—not only the *content* of what it is working on.

In terms of the spirit of inquiry, it may well be that the most important insight coming out of training is that a group should sometimes be run *autocratically* in order to achieve its goals. If this conclusion is based on a careful assessment of all factors, it is completely valid and *not inconsistent* with the philosophy of experiential training. But a commitment to open sharing of feelings and reactions does inevitably imply some democratization. The effective exercise of formal authority sometimes implies a limiting of communication to task-relevant information and a systematic exclusion of feelings in the interests of efficiency. To teach people the value of being more open and honest, then, may indeed undermine formal authority to some degree.

Whether or not such undermining of formal authority is desirable will in turn depend upon which kinds of information are withheld in the group process. One of the key things learned in studying group dynamics is that the process by which groups work—the communication patterns, decision-making methods, problem-solving techniques, norm-forming activities, interpersonal feelings and perceptions, the formation of likes and dislikes, and so on—are *not* all equally relevant to effective task performance. If one carefully distinguishes *task process* from *interpersonal process*, one often finds that the concealment of information about a problem the group is trying to solve (task process) is indeed very destructive, and members should be encouraged to be more open at this level. On the other hand, the concealment of who likes whom in the group (interpersonal process) may be quite irrelevant to task performance, and is probably best kept under wraps in an organizational context. The consultant, leader, or group member who is observing the various process events in the group must always make careful diagnostic judgments about which kinds of task or interpersonal processes are relevant to group goals and work on surfacing only the relevant data (Schein, 1969, 1978).

One of the reasons why many organizations have ceased to use sensitivity training extensively as a developmental tool is that consultants or trainers often failed to differentiate between task process—teaching members how to solve problems in groups more effectively—and interpersonal process—exploring how members really felt about each other and about themselves at a fairly deep level. The exploration of interpersonal processes has proved to be valuable for the *personal growth* of the participants, leading to a proliferation of various kinds of "encounter groups," but has proved to be of limited value in improving the ability of participants to lead or be members of *work groups*. The result has been that experiential methods as described above have come to be used in many more differentiated contexts from highly personally oriented "personal growth labs" to organizationally oriented team-building activities (Dyer, 1977). Although the underlying philosophy of sensitivity training is the same, its focus and the actual methods used vary dramatically according to whether one focuses on task process or interpersonal processes.

The general point is that one must be sufficiently aware of the important organizational factors and group goals to know when it is appropriate to be more open and honest *and* about what kinds of things. The paradox is that this kind of awareness and sensitivity, the skill of diagnosing what is going on in the group, can only develop from training programs which teach a spirit of inquiry, a sensitivity to group process, and the value of open exploration of perceptions and feelings *during the training period itself*.

In summary, as managers are learning more about groups and how they work, they are also learning more about how to provide training opportunities within the context of the work organization itself by having longer off-site meetings, process analysis periods at the end of group meetings, group-process–oriented consultants attending key meetings, and the like. What makes such activities successful is the focus on task process—the information gathering, problem-solving, and decision-making functions—and the avoidance of interpersonal issues except where there is clear evidence that such issues are hindering effective work performance.

WHEN NOT TO USE GROUPS

Though groups tend to be a universal human phenomenon, it is nevertheless very important to think clearly about when and how to use them, particularly in the formal sense of when to give a task or problem to a group and when not to. Three sets of phenomena have been studied which bear directly on this issue: (1) group versus individual problem-solving effectiveness; (2) groups versus individuals in the propensity to take risks; and (3) the problem of what has come to be called "group think"—or the tendency of the group to arrive at what may be a false consensus by overriding valid individual opinions.

Group versus Individual Problem Solving

A great deal of research has been devoted to the question of whether the group or isolated individuals whose work can be pooled is the more effective problem-solving instrument. No definitive answer has yet been reached, but some key variables have been identified. For example, it has been believed that a group can be more creative than individuals because of the mutual stimulation members provide each other, but this holds true only if there is a nonevaluative climate in the group, a decision-making structure appropriate to the task, enough time to explore the unusual idea, and the task is such as to require extensive data gathering or a complex evaluation of the consequences of various alternatives (Taylor, Berry, & Block, 1958).

Errors of judgment are more likely to be perceived before action is taken in a group setting than if it is left up to the individual to think through all alternative resolutions to a problem. In general, groups will be better than individuals when the problem has multiple parts and when the members have different and complementary skills or information which can be pooled in the problem-solving process. For example, many of the kinds of problems encountered by managers are effectively solved by groups because they require the input of financial, marketing, manufacturing, engineering, and human considerations. It is no accident that as business has become more complex, increasing use has been made of group problem-solving techniques, even though managers may dislike groups and be impatient with them.

One of the most important criteria for determining whether or not to use a group in making a decision involves an assessment of why and how the decision is to be *implemented*. People are more likely to carry out a decision that they have had a hand in making than one that has been imposed. Therefore, if effective implementation is critical, it is important to involve the implementers as much as possible, if only by asking them whether they see any problems with a proposed decision.

If it is decided to use a group to perform a task, the leader must recognize and understand some of the many dynamic, environmental, and membership factors operative within it. If the group is to perform effectively, it must be allowed to develop a climate in which members trust each other enough to be willing to share information and to honestly critique each other's ideas. The leader must ensure that the group's task or goals are clearly understood and that enough consensus has been obtained to make joint effort in a common direction possible. If the leader is not willing to invest the time and energy to help the group to develop, a group should not be used in the first place.

Group versus Individual Risk Taking

Folklore about groups has included two general propositions: (1) Important decisions should always be made by individuals rather than groups, because groups tend to be too conservative and incapable of acting "boldly"; (2) groups should never be allowed to make decisions because no one can then be held individually accountable. In a perceptive analysis, Reitz (1977) notes that these two propositions are in fact contradictory but that no one had really notices this or attempted to resolve the issue until the pioneering research of Stoner and Marquis at MIT in the 1960s. Their work led to a whole series of researches on what has since come to be called the "risky shift" phenomenon (Stoner, 1968; Marquis, 1962; Helmreich, Bakeman, & Scherwitz, 1973; Davis, Laughlin, & Komorita, 1976).

The essence of the risky shift phenomenon is the discovery that groups acting collectively will tend to take a *riskier* decision alternative across a wide range of problems than could be predicted by taking the average of all the individual responses. For example, if a football team had to decide whether to go for a risky touchdown play in order to win the game rather than settling for a safe tie, first the individual players and then the same individuals in a group *following discussion of the alternatives* would be asked how good the chances should be of making the touchdown before they would make that play. In experiments of this type it has consistently been shown that, on the average, individuals might go for the touchdown if the chances of success were 7 out of 10, while by contrast, following their discussion, the group might decide to go for the touchdown if the chances were only 4 out of 10, thus taking a more risky alternative. This experiment was repeated in different kinds of groups and on different kinds of decision tasks with essentially similar results, but a good theory of *why* the phenomenon occurs has not yet been well articulated.

One possibility is the diffusion of responsibility hypothesis that if no one individual is responsible, people are more willing to run risks. A second theory is that leaders are more likely to be risk takers and they will have greater influence in the group discussion than nonleaders. Neither of these theories has received consistent support. So far the closest to a satisfactory explanation is what might be called the "cultural amplifier" hypothesis. If taking a risk is a cultural value, then arguments in favor of that value are more likely to be upheld in group discussion than more conservative arguments. Since most of the decision problems first studied were of the type where taking a risk would, in our culture, be a positive value, the group tended to shift toward taking greater risk. However, it has been noticed that on some kinds of problems—for example, juries deliberating on the guilt or innocence of a defendant—the group will act more conservatively than the average individual. Marquis and Reitz (1969) experimented with a series of problems where cultural values would dictate more conservative decisions and found indeed that groups acted more conservatively on these issues than the individuals in the groups alone.

The important conclusion to be reached from all of this research is that the manager who brings a group together to reach consensus must be aware of group tendencies to be "cultural amplifiers" and must be careful not to bias the decision process by using a group only when he or she wants a certain kind of decision outcome in the first place. I have observed the "cultural amplifier" phenomenon in management groups particularly on decision tasks with unclear outcomes that require the use of partial information—for example, long-range planning, new product introductions, complex personnel policies, or diversification decisions. The more nebulous the criteria and the information needed to reach a clear-cut decision, the greater the risk that the group will act in the direction of the cultural values and override what may be a rational decision from the point of view of that particular organization.

Group Think

The tendency for groups to seek unanimity has been observed both in real-life groups such as political or religious movements (Schein, Schneier, & Barker, 1961) and in the laboratory experiments on group dynamics (Schachter, 1951). Members with deviant views are pressured in various ways to "conform" to the majority opinion, thus creating the possibility that the group decision will not reflect an accurate analysis but rather the dominant opinion, whatever that happens to be. Janis (1972) has conducted a series of historical researches on this phenomenon, termed "group think," and has shown that some major political decisions were reached on the basis of incomplete processing of relevant information and of *active suppression of minority views and dissent*, with disastrous consequences. Janis specifically identified the decision in 1950 to send General MacArthur to the Yalu river in Korea, ignoring the information that the Chinese would then enter the Korean conflict; the decision in 1941 not to prepare better for the Pearl Harbor attack in the face of information that such an attack might occur; and the 1962 decision to attempt the invasion of Cuba at the Bay of Pigs in the face of information that Castro was well prepared to handle such an invasion. In each case there was evidence that an inner group of advisers developed a unanimous opinion and that during various kinds of group meetings dissent was ignored, punished, or prevented, thus insulating the decision maker from a full review of the relevant information and options.

Janis identifies the symptoms of group think in the following way (Janis and Mann, 1977): (1) The group shares an illusion of invulnerability; (2) the group engages in collective rationalization to discount dissonant information; (3) the group comes to believe in the inherent morality of what it wants to do; (4) the group develops stereotypes of other groups and of dissenters which protects it from accurate analysis; (5) the group puts direct pressure on dissenters in order to silence them; (6) group members begin to censor their own thought, especially doubts they may have about the wisdom of proposed courses of action; (7) the group comes to believe in its unanimity because of lack of dissent and the belief that "silence means consent"; (8) some members of the group come to function in the role of "mindguards"—watchmen who "protect" the leaders from dissenting views by actively discouraging such dissenters from expressing their disagreement.

Conditions such as these are not universal in groups but can arise if certain antecedent conditions obtain. Specifically, a group is vulnerable to group think if it enjoys high cohesiveness, is insulated from other groups with different views, lacks methodical procedures for searching out relevant information and alternative solution, lacks systematic procedures for evaluating alternatives, has strong directive leaders who discourage dissent in the first place, and is under high stress but despairs of finding a solution better than the one being considered. The greatest danger inherent in this situation is that the group actually believes it is aware of the various alternatives, having no suspicions that dissent has been internally suppressed or prevented by "mindguards."

If a leader or manager is to prevent these circumstances from arising, it becomes crucial to set up conditions that encourage dissent, search, critical judgment, exploration of alternatives, and checking of assumptions. The checking of assumptions is one of the most critical functions to be performed in a group, especially when the group is silent and in apparent agreement. The leader or consultant must at those times directly ask the group whether the silence means that everyone agrees, and must actively explore alternatives and objections before assuming that consensus has been reached. This process is time-consuming but essential if the group is making an important policy decision.

If a leader is not prepared to hear group dissent, he or she probably should not use a group decision-making process in the first place. It is all too easy for a group to become an instrument of rubber stamping what the members think the leader wants, thus creating an illusion of a carefully thought-out decision which, in fact, has not been thought through at all. Here again training for managers in how to conduct meetings becomes essential, so that they can become aware of the symptoms of group think and learn how to counteract them if they occur.

SUMMARY

In this chapter we have reviewed what a psychological group is, described the types of formal and informal groups commonly found in organizations, analyzed both the formal organizational and individual psychological functions that groups perform, and discussed some of the factors that favor situations in which groups will perform both types of functions, thus acting as integrative forces in the organization.

Groups are not a universal solution for all types of problems. They should not be used if the problem does not specifically require a sharing of information and evaluation of alternatives, or if cultural amplification is to be avoided, or if the group climate runs the risk of creating group think by squashing dissent. Most importantly, groups should not be used if the leaders and members are unwilling to invest some time and energy in helping the group to develop into an effective working unit.

The effective use of groups requires group dynamics training for both leaders and group members. Such training is usually most effective if it uses experiential methods and if it helps to focus attention on group process, especially the problem-solving process.

Intergroup Problems in Organizations

10

The firs major problem of groups in organizations is how to make them effective in fulfilling both organizational goals and the needs of their members. The second major problem is how to establish conditions *between* groups which will enhance the productivity of each without destroying intergroup relations and coordination. This problem exists because as groups become more committed to their own goals and norms, they are likely to become competitive with one another and seek to undermine their rivals' activities, thereby becoming a liability to the organization as a whole. The overall problem, then, is how to establish collaborative intergroup relations *in those situations where task interdependence or the need for unity makes collaboration a necessary prerequisite for organizational effectiveness.*

SOME CONSEQUENCES OF INTERGROUP COMPETITION

The consequences of intergroup competition were first studied systematically by Sherif in an ingeniously designed setting (Sherif, Harvey, White, Hood, & Sherif, 1961). He organized a boys' camp in such a way that two groups would form and would gradually become competitive. Sherif then studied the effects of the competition and tried various devices for reestablishing collaborative relationships between the groups. Since his original experiments, there have been many replications with adult groups; the phenomena are so constant that it has been possible to make a demonstration exercise out of the experiment (Blake & Mouton, 1961). The effects can be described in terms of the following categories:

A. What happens *within* each competing group?

1. Each group becomes more closely knit and elicits greater loyalty from its members; members close ranks and bury some of their internal differences.
2. The group climate changes from informal, casual, playful to work and task oriented; concern for members' psychological needs declines while concern for task accomplishment increases.
3. Leadership patterns tend to change from more democratic toward more autocratic; the group becomes more willing to tolerate autocratic leadership.
4. Each group becomes more highly structured and organized.
5. Each group demands more loyalty and conformity from its members in order to be able to present a "solid front."

B. What happens *between* competing groups?

1. Each group begins to see the other group as the enemy, rather than merely a neutral object.
2. Each group begins to experience distortions of perception—it tends to perceive only the best parts of itself, denying its weaknesses, and tends to perceive only the worst parts of the other group, denying its strengths; each group is likely to develop a negative stereotype of the other ("they don't play fair like we do").
3. Hostility toward the other group increases while interaction and communication with the other group decreases; thus it becomes easier to maintain the negative stereotype and more difficult to correct perceptual distortions.
4. If the groups are forced into interaction—for example, if they are forced to listen to representatives plead their own and the others' cause in reference to some task—each group is likely to listen more closely to their own representative and not to listen to the representative of the other group, except to find fault with his or her presentation; in other words, group members tend to listen only for that which supports their own position and stereotype.

Thus far, we have listed some consequences of the competition itself, without reference to the consequences if one group actually wins out over the other. Before listing those effects, I would like to draw attention to the generality of the above reactions. Whether one is talking about sports teams, interfraternity competition, labor-management disputes, or interdepartmental competition as between sales and production in an industrial organization—or about international relations and the competition between the Soviet Union and the United States—the same phenomena tend to occur. These responses can be very useful to the group, by making it more highly motivated in task accomplishment, but they also open the door to group think. Furthermore, the same factors which improve intragroup effectiveness may have negative consequences for intergroup effectiveness. For example, as we have often seen in labor-management disputes or international conflicts, if the groups perceive themselves as competitors, they find it more difficult to resolve their differences, and eventually both become losers in a long-term strike or even a war.

Let us next look at the consequences of winning and losing, as in a situation where several groups are bidding to have their proposal accepted for a contract or as a solution to some problem. Many intraorganizational situations become win-or-lose affairs, hence it is of particular importance to examine their consequences.

C. What happens to the *winner*?

1. Winner retains its cohesion and may become even more cohesive.
2. Winner tends to release tension, lose its fighting spirit, become complacent, casual, and playful (the condition of being "fat and happy").
3. Winner tends toward high intragroup cooperation and concern for members' needs, and low concern for work and task accomplishment.
4. Winner tends to be complacent and to feel that the positive outcome has confirmed its favorable stereotype of itself and the negative stereotype of the "enemy" group; there is little motivation for reevaluating perceptions or reexamining group operations in order to learn how to improve them, hence the winner does not learn much about itself.

D. What happens to the *loser*?

1. If the outcome is not entirely clear-cut and permits a degree of interpretation (say, if judges have rendered it or if the game was close), there is a strong tendency for the loser to *deny or distort the reality of losing*; instead, the loser will find psychological escapes like "the judges were biased," "the judges didn't really understand our solution," "the rules of the game were not clearly explained to us," "if luck had not been against us at the one key point, we would have won," and so on. In effect, the loser's first response is to say "we didn't really lose!"
2. If the loss is psychologically accepted, the losing group tends to seek someone or something to blame; strong forces toward scape-goating are

set up; if no outsider can be blamed, the group turns on itself, splinters, surfaces previously unresolved conflicts, fights within itself, all in the effort to find a cause for the loss.

3. Loser is more tense, ready to work harder, and desperate (the condition of being "lean and hungry").

4. Loser tends toward low intragroup cooperation, low concern for members' needs, and high concern for recouping by working harder in order to win the next round of the competition.

5. Loser tends to learn a lot about itself as a group because its positive stereotype of itself and its negative stereotype of the other group are disconfirmed by the loss, forcing a reevaluation of perceptions; as a consequence, the loser is likely to reorganize and become more cohesive and effective once the loss has been accepted realistically.

The net effect of the win-lose situation is often that the losers refuse psychologically to accept their loss, and that intergroup tension is higher than before the competition began.

Intergroup problems of the sort we have just described arise not only out of direct competition between clearly defined groups, but are, to a degree, intrinsic in any complex society because of the many bases on which a society is stratified. Thus, we can have potential intergroup problems between men and women, between older and younger generations, between higher and lower ranking people, between blacks and whites, between people in power and people not in power, and so on (Alderfer, 1977). Any occupational or social group will develop "ingroup" feelings and define itself in terms of members of an "outgroup," toward whom intergroup feelings are likely to arise. Differences between nationalities or ethnic groups are especially strong, particularly if there has been any conflict between the groups in the past.

For intergroup feelings to arise we need not belong to a psychological group. It is enough to feel oneself a member of what has been called a "reference group," that is, a group with which one identifies and compares oneself or to which one aspires. Thus, aspirants to a higher socioeconomic level take that level as their reference group and attempt to behave according to the values they perceive in that group. Similarly, members of an occupational group upholds the values and standards they perceive that occupation to embody. It is only by positing the existence of reference groups that one can explain how some individuals can continue to behave in a deviant fashion in a group situation. If such individuals strongly identify with a group that has different norms they will behave in a way that attempts to uphold those norms. For example, in Communist prison camps some soldiers from elite military units resisted their captors much longer than draftees who had weak identification with their military units. In order for the Communists to elicit compliant behavior from these strongly identified prisoners, they had to first weaken the attachment to the elite unit—that is, destroy the reference group—by attacking the group's image or convincing the prisoner that it was not a group worth belonging to (Schein, 1961). Intergroup problems arise wherever there are any status differences and are, therefore, intrinsic to all organizations and to society itself.

REDUCING THE NEGATIVE CONSEQUENCES OF INTERGROUP COMPETITION

The gains of intergroup competition may, under some conditions, outweigh the negative consequences. It may be desirable to have work groups pitted against one another or to have departments become cohesive loyal units, even if interdepartmental coordination suffers. Often, however, the negative consequences outweigh the gains, and management seeks ways of reducing intergroup tension. Many of the techniques proposed to accomplish this come from the basic researches of Sherif, Blake, Alderfer, and others; they have been tested and found to be successful. The chief stumbling block remains not so much being unable to think of ways for reducing intergroup conflict as being *unable to implement some of the most effective ways.*

Destructive intergroup competition results basically from a conflict of goals and the breakdown of interaction and communication between the groups. This breakdown in turn permits and stimulates perceptual distortion and mutual negative stereotyping. The basic strategy of reducing conflict, therefore, is to locate goals which the competing groups can agree on and to reestablish valid communication between the groups. Each of the tactical devices that follows can be used singly or in combination.

Locating a Common Enemy

For example, the competing teams in a league can compose an all-star team to play another league, or conflicts between sales and production can be reduced if both can harness their efforts to helping their company successfully compete against another company. The conflict here is merely shifted to a higher level.

Bringing Leaders or Subgroups of the Competing Groups into Interaction

An isolated group representative cannot abandon his or her group position, but a powerful leader or a subgroup that has been delegated power not only can permit itself to be influenced by its counterpart negotiation team, but also will have the strength to influence the remainder of its home group if negotiation produces common agreements. This is the basis for "summit meetings" in international relations.

Locating a Superordinate Goal

Such a goal can be a brand-new task which requires the cooperative effort of the previously competing groups, or it can be a task like analyzing and reducing the intergroup conflict itself. For example, the previously competing sales and production departments can be given the task of developing a new product line that will be both cheap to produce and in great customer demand; or, with the help of an outside consultant, the competing groups can be invited to examine their own behavior and reevaluate the gains and losses from competition (Walton, 1969).

Experiential Intergroup Training

The procedure of having the conflicting parties examine their own behavior has been tried by a number of psychologists, notably Blake and Mouton (1962), with considerable success. Assuming the organization recognizes that it has a problem, and assuming it is ready to expose this problem to an outside consultant, the experiential workshop approach to reducing conflict might proceed with the following steps:

1. The competing groups are both brought into a training setting and the common goals are stated to be an exploration of mutual perceptions and mutual relations.
2. The two groups are then separated and each group is invited to discuss and make a list of its perceptions of itself and the other group.
3. In the presence of both groups, representatives publicly share the perceptions of self and other which the groups have generated, while the groups are obligated to remain silent (the objective is simply to report to the other group as accurately as possible the images that each group has developed in private).

177

4. Before any exchange has taken place, the groups return to private sessions to digest and analyze what they have heard; there is a great likelihood that the representatives' reports have revealed discrepancies to each group between its self-image and the image that the other group holds of it; the private session is partly devoted to an analysis of the reasons for these discrepancies, which forces each group to review its actual behavior toward the other group and the possible consequences of that behavior, regardless of its intentions.
5. In public session, again working through representatives, each group shares with the other what discrepancies it has uncovered and the possible reasons for them, focusing on actual, observable behavior.
6. Following this mutual exposure, a more open exploration is then permitted between the two groups on the *now-shared goal* of identifying further reasons for perceptual distortions.
7. A joint exploration is then conducted of how to manage future relations in such a way as to minimize a recurrence of the conflict.

Interspersed with these steps are short lectures and reading assignments on the psychology of intergroup conflict, the bases for perceptual distortion, psychological defense mechanisms, and so on. The goal is to bring the psychological dynamics of the solution into conscious awareness and to refocus the groups on the common goal of exploring jointly the problem they share. In order to do this, they must have valid data about each other, which is provided through the artifice of the representative reports.

Blake's model deals with the entire group. Various other approaches begin by breaking down group prejudices on an individual basis. For example, groups A and B, each proposing an alternative product (idea), can be divided into pairs composed of an A and a B member. Each pair can be given the assignment of developing a joint product that combines the best ideas from the A product and the B product. Or, in each pair, members may be asked to argue for the product of the opposing group. It has been shown in a number of experiments that one way of changing attitudes is to ask a person to play the role of an advocate of the new attitude to be learned (Janis & King, 1954). The very act of arguing for another product, even if it is purely an exercise, makes the person aware of some of its virtues which he or she can now no longer deny. A practical application of these points might be to have some members of the sales department spend time in the production department and be asked to represent the production point of view to some third party, or to have some production people join sales teams to learn the sales point of view.

Most of the approaches cited depend on a *recognition* of some problem by the organization and a *willingness* on the part of the competing groups to participate in some program to reduce negative consequences. The reality, however, is that most organizations neither recognize the problem nor are willing to invest time and energy in resolving it. Some of the unwillingness also arises from each competing group's recognition that in becoming more cooperative it may lose some of its own identity and integrity as a group. Rather than risk this loss, the group may prefer to continue the competition. This may well be the reason why, in international relations, nations refuse to engage in what may seem like perfectly simple ways of resolving their differences. They resist partly in order to protect their integrity—that is, save face. For all these reasons, the *implementation* of strategies and tactics for reducing the negative consequences of intergroup competition is often a greater problem than the initial development of such strategies and tactics.

PREVENTING INTERGROUP CONFLICT

Because of the great difficulties of reducing intergroup conflict once it has developed, it may be desirable to prevent its occurrence in the first place. How can this be done? Paradoxically, a strategy of prevention challenges the fundamental premise upon which organization through division of labor rests. Once it has been decided by a superordinate authority to divide up functions among different departments or groups, a bias has already been introduced toward intergroup competition; for in doing its own job well, each group must, to some degree, compete for scarce resources and rewards from the superordinate authority. The very concept of division of labor implies a reduction of communication and interaction between groups, thus making it possible for perceptual distortions to occur.

The organization planner who wishes to avoid intergroup competition need not abandon the concept of division of labor, but should follow some of the steps listed below in creating and handling the different functional groups.

1. Relatively greater *emphasis should be given to total organizational effectiveness* and the role of departments in contributing to it; departments should be measured and rewarded on the basis of their contribution to the total effort rather than their individual effectiveness.
2. *High interaction and frequent communication* should be stimulated between groups to work on problems of intergroup coordination and help; organizational rewards should be given partly on the basis of help rendered to other groups.
3. *Frequent rotation of members* among groups or departments should be encouraged to stimulate a high degree of mutual understanding and empathy for one another's problems.

4. *Win-lose situations should be avoided* and groups should never be put into the position of competing for some scarce organizational reward; emphasis should always be placed on pooling resources to maximize organizational effectiveness; rewards should be shared equally with all the groups or departments.

Most managers find the fourth point particularly difficult to accept because of the strong belief that performance can be improved by pitting people or groups against one another in a competitive situation. This may indeed be true in the short run, and may even on occasion work in the long run, but the negative consequences described above are undeniably the product of the win-lose situation. Thus, if managers wish to prevent such consequences, they must face the possibility that they may have to abandon competitive relationships altogether and seek to substitute intergroup collaboration toward organizational goals. The more *interdependent* the various units are, the more important it is to stimulate collaborative problem solving.

Implementing a preventive strategy is often more difficult, partly because most people are inexperienced in stimulating and managing collaborative relationships. Yet observations of organizations using the Scanlon Plan not only reveal that it is possible to establish collaborative relationships, even between labor and management, but also that when this has been done, organizational and group effectiveness have been as high as or higher than under competitive conditions. Training in how to set up collaborative relations may be a prerequisite for any such program to succeed, especially for those managers who have themselves grown up in a highly competitive environment.

THE PROBLEM OF INTEGRATION
IN PERSPECTIVE

I have discussed two basic issues in Part IV: (1) the development of groups within organizations which can fulfill both the needs of the organization and the psychological needs of its members; and (2) the problems of intergroup competition and conflict. To achieve maximum integration, the organization should be able to create conditions that will facilitate a balance between organizational goals and member needs and minimize disintegrative competition between the subunits of the total organization.

Groups are highly complex sets of relationships. There are no easy generalizations about the conditions under which they will be effective, but with suitable training, many kinds of groups can function at levels previously unimaginable. Consequently, training in group dynamics by experiential methods may be a more promising approach to effectiveness than attempting a priori to determine the right membership, type of leadership, and organization. Of course, all of the factors must be taken into account, and the training approach, although central, must be carefully chosen to preserve and enhance positive group qualities already present.

The creation of psychologically meaningful and effective groups does not solve all of the organization's problems, however, particularly if such groups compete and conflict with each other. We examined some of the consequences of competition under win-lose conditions and outlined two basic approaches of dealing with this problem: (1) reducing conflict by increasing communication and locating superordinate goals, and (2) preventing conflict by establishing from the outset organizational conditions to stimulate collaboration rather than competition.

The prevention of intergroup conflict is especially crucial if the groups involved are highly interdependent. The greater the interdependence, the greater the potential loss to the total organization of negative stereotyping, withholding of information, efforts to make the other group look bad in the eyes of the superior authority, and so on.

In concluding this section on groups, it should be emphasized that the preventive strategy does not imply absence of disagreement and artificial "sweetness and light" within or between groups. Conflict and disagreement at the level of the group or organizational *task* is not only desirable but essential for the achievement of optimal solutions to organizational problems. By contrast, when the task becomes less important than gaining advantage over the other person or group, interpersonal or intergroup relations suffer the most harmful effects. The negative consequences we described, most notably mutual negative stereotyping, fall into this latter category and undermine rather than aid overall task performance.

Interestingly enough, observations of actual conflictual situations suggest that task-relevant conflict which improves overall effectiveness is greater under collaborative conditions, because groups and members trust each other enough to be frank and open in sharing information and opinions. In the competitive situation, each group is committed to hiding its special resources from the other groups, thus preventing effective integration of all resources in the organization. Potentially constructive task conflict is suppressed under competitive conditions and the danger of group think is increased.

Organization
Structure
and
Dynamics

V

In these final chapters we will examine some of the more elusive aspects of organizational psychology, those having to do with the structure and design of organizations, with the relationships between organizations and their environments, with organizational effectiveness and health, and, finally, with the problem of organizational change, particularly as conceptualized by proactive programs that have come to be known collectively as Organizational Development. I will be adopting a very eclectic perspective here, drawing in material from sociology and administrative science as appropriate. If we are to get a grasp of these problems from a psychological vantage point, we must enlarge the scope of our analysis and examine our ideas about total systems interacting with complex environments.

Some readers will find these chapters more abstract and possibly less relevant because they deal with more far-reaching topics. But there is no more practical a set of problems facing the senior manager in most organizations than how to design and structure the organization. Managers need analytical insights into these matters to avoid a "seat of the pants," intuitive approach that results in piecemeal "decentralization"—for example, have "Pete report to Jane." Hopefully this analysis will both illustrate the kinds of criteria that need to be examined in thinking about organization design and simultaneously bring home to the reader the incredible difficulties involved in implementing organizational change once a decision to change has been reached.

184

We close with some general prescriptive statements about the conditions that must obtain for organizational "health," pointing out that the search for individual creativity and commitment cannot be ultimately successful if organizational health is lacking over the long run.

The Organization as a Complex, Open System

INTRODUCTION

In the early chapters of this book we presented a traditional definition of an organization as the "rational coordination of the activities of a number of people for the achievement of some common, explicit purpose, through division of labor and a hierarchy of authority." Most of what has been called "classical organization theory" or the theory of bureaucracy starts with some such definition. I then attempted to show why this definition does not do justice to the reality of what goes on in organizations. Pressures from the various environments within which organizations exist, the internal dynamics of organizations that result from human needs and desires and how these change over time, and the fact that people form into various kinds of formal and informal groups—all make the classical definition unrealistic and misleading. What is needed is a more dynamic definition of the organization, one that reflects the realities of human motivation, of group dynamics, and of intergroup phenomena.

Such a dynamic definition has been in the making since the early 1950s with George Homans's classic book *The Human Group* (Homans, 1950). Homans had been impressed by the degree to which systems-type thinking had influenced physiology, and applied these same ideas to an analysis of group and organizational phenomena. The most influential early statement of the systems position was probably Katz and Kahn's 1966 book, *The Social Psychology of*

Organizations, which explicitly defines organizations as open systems in constant interaction with their environments. These ideas drew heavily on other theorists, notably Trist and his co-workers (1963) and Rice (1963) of the Tavistock Institute in London, who had discovered in their coal mining studies and their redesign of Indian textile mills that one had to treat organizations as complex *sociotechnical* systems in which the environmental, technological, and social factors interacted in a complex way with interpersonal and task-related forces within the organization.

This chapter will review a number of these theories and argue explicitly for the importance of treating organizations as open systems, even though such a perspective makes it more difficult to analyze and change organizational phenomena. Because this field has expanded at a great rate during the last 20 years, I will not be able to review "organization theory" as a whole, but will attempt to present some of the more crucial theoretical interpretations that have emerged in recent years.

What makes theorizing and research so difficult in this area is that we do not yet have good taxonomies of all the factors that are operable in the organization and its environments. Different theorists have variously labeled such concepts as organization structure, organizational process, environment, technology, organizational goals, and so on. It should be recognized that we are in a very early stage of organizational science where careful observation and the building of appropriate taxonomies is just as important as testing hypotheses or attempting to develop precise theory. This chapter will review several such taxonomies and attempt thereby to show the inherent complexity of this area.

Sources of Complexity

One of the major difficulties is defining the appropriate boundaries of any given organization and determining its relevant environments. Where does a business concern—with its research departments, suppliers, transportation facilities, sales offices, and public relations offices—leave off and the community begin? Is the relevant environment society as a whole, the economic and political system, other companies in the same market, the immediate community, the union, or all of these? What is the relevant environment of a university? Is it the community in which the university is located, the families of its student body, the professional associations of its professors, or society in general as the consumer of its graduates and its research and scholarly output? If we are to understand the forces which act upon organizations as systems, we must be able to specify the environmental origin of such forces.

Second, organizations generally have several purposes or fulfill several functions. Some of these functions are primary while others are secondary; some are manifest and some are latent. The primary manifest function of a business concern is to make a product or service for profit. A secondary manifest function is to provide security and meaning for members of the community through the provision of jobs. The cultural and social norms which dictate this secondary function are just as much a part of the environment as are the economic forces which dictate a good product at a minimum cost. Yet these forces often impose conflicting demands on the organization.

If we attempt to analyze the functions of a university, we can identify several primary manifest functions, including transmission of knowledge, production of knowledge, and conservation of knowledge through libraries. In addition, the university, along with the rest of the educational system, has a primary *latent* function—the identification and labeling of talent for the various jobs that must be fulfilled within society. The education system acts as a kind of filter—it identifies and lets through only persons of certain qualifications. For society to maximize the talents of its members, some system must be used to identify talent. In our present society, the educational system seems to have acquired this function. The point of this example is to illustrate how the fulfillment of the manifest functions of teaching and research may at times actually conflict with the latent function of sorting and grading talent. Some of the difficulties experienced by organizations derive from the fact that they have multiple functions, some of which may conflict yet none of which they can abandon.

Third, the organization carries within itself representatives of the external environment. Employees are not only members of the organization which employs them, they are also members of society, other organizations, unions, consumer groups, and so on. From these various other roles they bring with them demands, expectations, and cultural norms which often conflict with the internal norms of the employing organization.

Fourth, the nature of the environment is itself changing very rapidly. We see this most clearly in the tremendous growth of *technology*, yet change is also proceeding rapidly in the *economic* sector because of the expansion of markets throughout the entire world; in the *sociopolitical* sector because of changing norms about the priorities which should guide technologically sophisticated countries like the United States; and in the *cultural values* sector because of changing norms about the role of work and career in people's total lives (Van Maanen, Schein, & Bailyn, 1977). From being relatively stable and predictable, portions of the environment have become what Emery and Trist (1965) call "turbulent." Turbulent environments require a different kind of capacity to respond on the part of organizations. In higher education, for example, professors typically respond to one set of norms deriving from cultural concepts of science and scholarship; meanwhile, students develop a different set of norms based on their frustration over unsolved problems within society and over a curriculum that often seems unrelated to the solution of those problems. To further complicate the situation, alumni in their role as financial donors to the university bring a third set of norms having to do with more traditional criteria concerning the prestige and quality of the organization.

For all of the above reasons, organization theorists have begun to build more complex models which attempt to take into account relationships between systems and their environments. These new systems models do not have the neatness or completeness of the classical concepts of organization, but they are a closer approximation of what researchers find when they actually study organizations.

SOME EARLY SYSTEM MODELS

The Homans Model

One especially useful model of social systems, whether at the level of the small group or the large organization, has been proposed by the sociologist George Homans (1950). According to Homans any social system exists within a three-part environment: a *physical* environment (the terrain, climate, layout, and so on), a *cultural* environment (the norms, values, and goals of society), and a *technological* environment (the state of knowledge and instrumentation available to the system for the performance of its task). The environment imposes or specifies certain *activities* and *interactions* for the people involved in the system. These activities and interactions in turn arouse certain feelings and *sentiments* among the people toward each other and the environment. The combination of activities, interactions, and sentiments that can be thought of as environmentally determined is termed the *external system.*

Homans postulated that activities, interactions, and sentiments are mutually dependent on one another. Thus, a change in any of the three variables will produce some change in the other two. Of particular interest here is the relationship postulated between interaction and sentiments, which is that the *higher the rate of interaction of two or more people, the more positive will be their sentiments toward each other*, or vice versa, the more positive the sentiment, the higher the rate of interaction. The seemingly obvious exception of two people who come to hate each other as a result of interacting is explained if we realize that over the long run these people will reduce their interaction as much as possible. If they are forced into continued interaction, they often find good sides to each other so that positive sentiment in the end grows with increased interaction.

Whether such hypotheses as the one cited are true or false is, for the moment, not as important as the dynamic conceptualization which Homans provides, because from it can be derived several other important concepts. Homans notes that with increasing interaction come not only new sentiments which were not necessarily specified by the external environment, but also new *norms* and shared frames of reference which generate new activities, also not specified by the external environment. In the Hawthorne studies, it was found that the workers developed games, interaction patterns, and sentiments which were not suggested and not even sanctioned by the formal work environment. Homans has called this new pattern which arises out of the external system, the *internal system*. The internal system corresponds to what most theorists have labeled the informal organization.

Homans further postulated that the internal and external systems are mutually dependent. This means that any change in either system will produce some change in the other. A change in work technology will produce a change in patterns of interaction, which in turn will change (or sometimes temporarily destroy) the internal system. For example, the longwall coal mining method destroyed some of the primary work groups. On the other hand, if the internal system develops certain norms about how life should be organized, it will often change the way the work is actually performed, how much of it will be done, and what quality will result. For example, the wiremen in one of the Hawthorne experiments developed patterns of job trading, a concept of a fair day's output, and their own leadership.

Finally, the two systems and the environment are mutually dependent. Just as changes in the environment will produce changes in the formal and informal work organization, so the norms and activities developed in the internal system *will eventually alter the physical, technical, and cultural environment*. For example, out of workers' informal problem solving may come ideas for technological innovations (change in technical environment), redesigned work layouts (change in physical environment), and new norms about what is a legitimate psychological contract between workers and management (change in cultural environment).

The most important aspect of this conceptual scheme is its explicit recognition of the various mutual dependencies. Empirical research studies have shown again and again how events in one part of the organization turn out to be linked to events in other parts or in the environment. Similarly, consultants have shown how changes initiated in one part of an organization produce unanticipated and often undesired changes in other parts. When Homans first proposed his theory, he showed how it could explain such diverse phenomena as workers' behavior in the bank-wiring room of the Hawthorne plant, the behavior of a street corner gang which had been studied and described in a classic study by William F. Whyte (1943), family patterns in preliterate tribes observed by anthropologists, and social change in a modern suburban community. The "elements" chosen— *activities, interactions, sentiments,* and *norms*—and their mutual dependencies in the *external* and *internal system* proved to have great taxonomic value because they could be used to describe such diverse organizational phenomena.

Many of the later "contingency theories" that we will examine are essentially extensions of Homans's proposition that different aspects of the environment create different patterns of activities, interaction, sentiments, and norms. However, Homans also recognized the very important fact that once norms and sentiments were formed, once the internal system was created, the organization in turn influenced its environment. In other words, open systems are not simply adaptive to whatever the environment provides, but are actively engaged in interaction with their environments. Unfortunately, not many organization theories have yet been able to conceptualize exactly *how* organizations influence their environments. Then, too, when organizations reach a certain size, such as General Motors or the Department of Defense, it is not entirely clear which way the predominant influence is flowing—is the environment influencing the organization or is the organization powerful enough to influence or even determine its own environment?

The Tavistock Sociotechnical Model

Some of the most vigorous proponents of the systems approach to organizational phenomena have been a group of social scientists associated with the Tavistock Institute in London.[1] Out of their

1 I will not review all of this work but the major contributions were made by Eric Trist, A.K. Rice, E. Jacques, Wilfred Brown, Fred Emery, P.G. Herbst, Gurth Higgin, and A.T.M. Wilson. For a review see Trist et al. (1963).

studies of changing technology they conceived the idea of a *so-ciotechnical system*, which in turn led to the development of more general "open systems" definitions of organizations.

The idea of a *sociotechnical* system implies that any productive organization or part thereof is a combination of *technology* (task requirements, physical layout, equipment available) and a *social sys-tem* (a system of relationships among those who must perform the job). The technology and the social system are in mutual interaction with each other and each determines the other. In keeping with this concept, it would make just as little sense to say that the nature of the work *determines* the type of organization that develops among workers, as it would be to say that the sociopsychological char-acteristics of the workers *determines* the manner in which a given job will be performed. As the Hawthorne studies and Trist's coal mining studies have shown, and as Homans has argued, each deter-mines the other to some degree.

The open systems model of organizations as discussed by Rice (1963) argues that any given organization "imports" various things from its environment, utilizes these imports in some kind of "con-version" process, and then "exports" products, services, and "waste materials" which result from the conversion process. One key import is the information obtained from the environment pertaining to the primary task—that is, what the organization must do in order to survive. Other imports are the raw materials, money, equipment, and people involved in the conversion to something that is exportable and meets some environmental demands.

If we now combine the two ideas of open systems and so-ciotechnical systems, we can see the importance of multiple chan-nels of interaction between the environment and the organization. Not only must the organization deal with the demands and con-straints imposed by the environment in terms of raw materials, money, and consumer preferences, it must also deal with the expec-tations, values, and norms of its members. Employees' capacities, preferences, and expectations of employees are, from this point of view, not merely "givens," but factors that are undoubtedly influ-enced by the nature of the job and the organizational structure they come up against. Consequently, one cannot solve work problems merely by better selection or training techniques. Rather, *the initial design of the organization must take into account both the nature of the job (the technical system) and the nature of the people (the social system).*

For example, in the coal mining studies previously cited, if it is true that mining induces anxiety and that anxiety can best be man-aged in small, cohesive work groups, then a technology which prevents such work group formation is likely to be ineffective. On the other hand, if one starts with the concept of open sociotechnical systems, one would ask, "What *combination* of technology, initial worker characteristics, and organizational structures would most likely result in an effective work organization?"

An answer to this question might require the reassessment of the relative importance of different environmental inputs with respect to the basic task. Economic demands and technological developments might both argue for a work method and structure that would undermine the social system. The organization planner might then have to reassess whether the costs of building an effective social organization to produce long-run economic gains outweigh the gains of short-run maximum efficiency. In order to make this reassessment, the planner would have to consider a variety of other environmental factors—for example, changing aspects of the labor force, particularly on such key variables as anxiety proneness; new technology in improving mine safety; trends in labor-management relations and union policies; and so on.

The sociotechnical systems approach has had a number of important effects on current organization theory and managerial practice. First, it spawned some very important experiments which were carried out in Europe on what has come to be called "industrial democracy." In the first phase of these experiments it was found that worker participation on boards of directors and in workers councils did not appreciably reduce feelings of alienation, probably because workers remained unable to contribute their input to the work technology itself (Emery and Thorsrud, 1969; Van Beinum and de Bel, 1968; Cummings & Srivastva, 1977).

When the researchers turned their attention to more direct involvement of the worker in the redesign of actual jobs—that is, toward participation in the day-to-day operations of the enterprise ("shop floor democracy")—it was found in experiments both here and abroad that such increased direct participation reduced alienation and increased productivity. In the United States, the work of Davis (1957, 1966) has led to a number of important experiments in the redesign of manufacturing plants, as well as to the concept of open systems planning as a tool for managers to rethink more broadly the strategy and operation of their work units (Hackman, 1977; Walton, 1972, 1974, 1975a; Beckhard & Harris, 1977; Clark & Krone, 1972; Krone, 1974).[2]

2 Open systems planning refers to a systematic analysis of environmental forces acting on a system, how the system responds, how it should ideally respond, and what must be done to improve the response systems to achieve the ideal state (Beckhard & Harris, 1977).

A second concept to develop from open sociotechnical systems design thinking was that of the autonomous work group. A whole work group is provided the opportunity to design and manage a total integrated task, thus permitting workers to meet their social and self-actualizing needs within the context of the work situation (Herbst, 1962). However, if an organization-wide system of autonomous work groups is to be implemented, a managerial climate must prevail in which self-regulating work structures are allowed to develop and evolve in response to further environmental changes (Cummings & Srivastva, 1977). So even though the focus of sociotechnical theory is the work itself, the implications for organizational functioning in terms of the continuing evolution of work designs are enormous.

> Since work systems relate to their environment through a boundary that both differentiates the system and mediates environmental exchanges, it is necessary to enact a boundary such that the system's primary task is separated or protected from external disruptions while the system regulates its exchanges with the environment. We refer to this process as "boundary management" and include it as an essential task of management. The second task involves the management of forces external to the system. Since work systems must relate to a succession of suitable environments if they are to survive and develop, it is necessary to plan for a desired environment and to initiate steps to bring it about. We refer to this second process as "open systems planning." When both tasks of management are performed effectively, sociotechnical systems are able to perform their primary tasks while managing their relationships with a succession of favorable environments. (Cummings & Srivastva, 1977) p. 107.

A third far-reaching implication of the sociotechnical systems way of thinking comes to light in Walton's (1975b) discussion of the innovative Kalmar plant of Sweden's Volvo Company. In order to improve working conditions and create autonomous work groups, Volvo's production technology had to be reexamined, and some of the product designs even had to be rethought. If a work group was to be able to assemble an entire electrical system of a car, the system had to be designed to make this more integrated task possible. The notion that one might start with work criteria to fit social and personal needs and then design products around such human need fulfillment is a far-reaching idea which comes out of systems thinking. Within the Kalmar plant the assembly line was replaced by a system of highly sophisticated, battery-driven car carriers called "assembly wagons." These served simultaneously as carrier and work table; they reduced the noise levels, tipped the cars when needed to make them more accessible to workers, increased safety, and increased worker autonomy because they could be "parked" or brought into the work area when workers were ready for them (Lindholm & Norstedt, 1975).

QUALITY OF WORK LIFE MOVEMENT. The experiments on work redesign and industrial democracy, combined with the growing body of work by psychologists, industrial engineers, and sociologists on the causes of and remedies for worker alienation in modern industrial society, have led to a major effort on the part of many consultants, researchers, and managers to improve the quality of life in the work place. An important statement of the philosophy of this movement and a series of cases illustrating work redesign was published by Davis and Cherns (1975). In a more recent analysis, Hackman (1977) notes that sociotechnical theory is one of the most general and elegant theories of job redesign, but its very generality creates some problems in that it becomes difficult to specify operationally just how a job is to be redesigned, how an autonomous work group is to be created, or how management structure and organization design are to be formulated to achieve the desired quality of work life. Though individual investigators—for example, Cummings and Srivastva (1977)—give specific operational criteria by which to analyze jobs and social systems, there is as yet no consensus of opinion.

Many important quality of work life experiments have been spawned by specific job redesign efforts such as those of Hackman (1977), Walton (1974, 1975), Ford (1973), Myers (1970), and others which are built on more direct specification of job characteristics such as those outlined in Chapters 4 and 5. Nevertheless, sociotechnical theory stands as one major seminal approach toward the redesign of work and ultimately the redesign of organizations themselves.

ORGANIZATIONS AS OVERLAPPING GROUPS, ROLE SETS, AND COALITIONS

A number of theorists and researchers have noted that to think of organizations in terms of individual decision makers arranged in various hierarchies or networks such as those depicted in the typical organization chart is out of line with the reality of organizational functioning. In other words, the organization chart represents only one of a number of communication channels between people in organizations; therefore, if we are to understand organizations as complex systems, we must start with more realistic building blocks. Three examples can be cited of this line of thinking.

Likert's Overlapping Group Model

The two key ideas Likert (1961, 1967) has contributed to organization theory are (1) that organizations can be conceptualized as systems of interlocking groups; and (2) that the interlocking groups are connected by individuals who occupy key positions of dual membership, serving as *linking pins* between groups.

This model draws our attention to two important points. First, the relevant environment for any given group or system is likely to be a set of other systems or groups, not something impersonal. This set is composed of three parts: (1) larger-scale systems, such as the whole complex of organizations performing a similar job, or even society as a whole; (2) systems on the same level, such as comparable organizations, consumer and supplier organizations, community groups, and so on; and (3) subsystems within the given system, including both formal and informal work groups.[3]

Second, Likert recognized that the organization is bound to its environment through key linking people who occupy positions in both the organization and some environmental system, and the parts of the environment may well be linked to each other through similar key people. To the extent that this model is correct, it suggests not only a relevant point of entry in analyzing system/environmental relations (the location of linking pins), but also implies an interdependent network among the parts of the environment. Consequently, if an organization is to understand and deal with its environment, it must seek out and understand these interdependencies.

Katz and Lazarsfeld's (1955) analysis of the "two-step" flow of communication provides a good example of this point. These investigators discovered that influence on consumer beliefs and preferences does not result from direct exposure of the individual to relevant information and advertising, but rather from exposure to "opinion leaders" in the community. Thus, if an opinion leader in the realm of fashions or political beliefs changes his or her outlook, a great many individual consumers will then follow suit. The effect of advertising on the opinion leader is, therefore, the critical variable.

If this phenomenon can be generalized, it argues that an organization must be responsive to the opinion leaders in its environment, not to its individual consumers, suppliers, or employees. These leaders then act as linking pins between the organization and various individuals. Similarly, if several groups are involved and their opinion leaders influence each other, it is important for the organization

---

3 It is beyond the scope of this book to analyze interorganizational relationships but some important work has been done in this field (Evan, 1978).

to know that the several groups are not independent portions of the environment. If it influences one, it may influence others as well.

The Kahn Overlapping Role-set Model

Kahn and his colleagues (Kahn, Wolfe, Quinn, Snoek, & Rosenthal, 1964) have pointed out that while the overlapping group model is closer to organizational reality, it still misses the important point that psychological groups and formal groups may be different. In Likert's model, no clear provision is made for distinguishing between types of groups, making it difficult to accurately identify the key linking pins. Kahn has proposed that instead of groups, one should consider what sociologists have termed *role sets*. If one considers the formal positions in an organization as "offices," and the behavior expected of any person occupying an office as his or her "role," one can then ask, What other offices are linked to the particular one under consideration in the operating organization? Or, to put it in terms of the role concept, one can ask, Given a focal person fulfilling an organizational role, with whom else is that person connected or associated in performing the role? The set of people—superiors, subordinates, peers, and outsiders—with whom role-related relationships exist then constitutes the role set. The organization as a whole can then be thought of as a set of overlapping and interlocking role sets, some of which transcend the boundaries of the organization.

The behavior of members of an organization can then be studied in terms of (1) *role overload*—where the sum total of what role senders expect of the focal person far exceeds what he or she is able to do; (2) *role conflict*—where different members of the role set expect different things of the focal person; or (3) *role ambiguity*—where members of the role set fail to communicate to the focal person expectations they have or information needed to perform the role, either because they do not have the information or because they deliberately withhold it.

The kinds of expectations members of a role set hold, the manner in which they attempt to influence focal persons, the focal persons' perceptions of sender expectations and influence attempts, their reactions to these, and their attempts to cope with the feelings and tensions that may be generated can then be related to organizational factors (rank, type of job, reward system, and so on), to personality factors in either focal persons or role senders, and to interpersonal factors that characterize the nature of the relationship between the role senders and the focal persons (degree of trust, relative power, dependence, and so forth).

For example, in their study, Kahn and his colleagues show that role conflict will be greater if the role set includes some members who are inside and some who are outside the organizational boundaries. Role conflict and ambiguity also tend to be greater the higher the rank of the focal person in the organization structure. On the other hand, the coping responses of the focal person subject to role overload, conflict, or ambiguity often reduce tension but at the expense of organizational effectiveness. For example, the person who perceives conflict may deal with it by ignoring or denying some of the legitimate expectations that some members of his role set have communicated, resulting in a portion of the job remaining undone. In general, people do not attempt to resolve conflict by bringing together the various role senders whose demands are conflicting, thus making it impossible to achieve an integrative solution.

Kahn's study underlines the great degree of interdependence among organizational variables like rank, location of position in the structure, role expectations, coping patterns in response to perceived conflict, and effectiveness of role performance. Kahn's focus on the concept of role also highlights the possibility that more abstract concepts of organization (for instance, overlapping role sets) are amenable to empirical research.

Cyert, March, and Simon's Theory of the Firm

Cyert and March (1963) and March and Simon (1958) in their highly influential studies of how organizations set goals and make decisions, reached the conclusion that an organization is, in reality, a complex coalition of individuals and groups with diverse goals, needs, desires, talents, and orientations. In order to understand goal setting and decision making, one must recognize from the outset that there exists within organizations a process of continuous bargaining for power, and that coalition members use various forms of *side payments* to induce others to join with them in the pursuit of their particular goals. For example, side payments can take the form of offers of money, status, position, or authority, so that in essence one can think of a "managerial coalition" bargaining with an "employee coalition" to induce the latter to join and work for the organization through the offer of wages and benefits of various sorts. Similarly, in bargaining with stockholders, management attempts to induce investment in the firm by offering as side payments good dividends on shares of stock. Obviously the ability to make side payments, the possession of money or other scarce resources which are desired by another group, gives a coalition more power in the total organization.

Commitments of resources as side payments to various coalitions (for example, high wages to employees or high dividends to stockholders) become a constraint on the possible future actions of the organization; they reduce the organization's flexibility by limiting its resources. Of course, as organizations interact with their various environments and as coalitions relate to each other and to the organization, they learn to revise their goals. Thus the total goal-setting process of the organization can be seen to be a process of bargaining, limited by prior commitments and influenced by organizational learning. For the organization to survive and adapt, it needs "organizational slack"—that is, resources *not* committed by prior decisions. If there is no surplus production capacity, no extra talent or uncommitted money to invest in new programs, the coalitions within the organization will basically be stymied in any attempt to change the course of the organization.

One of the great advantages of the organizational models that evolved from this line of thinking is that they mesh more readily with the organizational and decision-making models that predominate in political science and public administration. In studying public organizations such as government bureaus, foundations, hospitals, and community organizations, it has always been clearer that organizations are composed of complex coalitions that bargain for power with each other and, therefore, that the process of setting organizational goals and policies has to be conceptualized in terms of bargaining compromises rather than the rational pursuit of primary goals (Janis & Mann, 1977; Allison, 1971; Lindblom, 1959, 1965; Hickson, Butler, Axelson, & Wilson, 1978). One of the real weaknesses of organization theories built on an analysis of business organizations is that they overemphasized the pure "rationality" of the organization and underemphasized the degree to which organizational decisions result from complex negotiations between various individuals, groups, and role sets, many of which have membership both inside and outside the organization. Simon's concept of the manager as one who *satisfices* (reaches a workable decision) rather than maximizes—because rationality is always limited or bounded— is one of the most important insights which has come out of this line of thinking (Simon, 1960).

THE NEOSTRUCTURALISTS—NEW EFFORTS
TO BUILD FORMAL ORGANIZATION
THEORY

The classical structuralist approach to organization theory derived from an analysis of "bureaucracy" and led to a whole host of principles of organization based on a static system in a static environment. Some of these principles included "unity of command" (every person must have only one boss); "span of control" (no supervisor should have more than a certain number of subordinates reporting to him or her—usually 10 to 15); "authority should equal responsibility" (a boss should have control over those things for which he or she is responsible), and so on.

A number of sociologists, organization theorists, and management analysts saw merit in these principles and began to combine them with ideas from the more dynamic open systems theory. There is as yet no one approach that can claim to be a total theory of organization, but the various pieces are important enough to be reviewed separately.

As has been pointed out, the difficulty in building theory is to identify the key elements or variables that are operative and then to develop good taxonomies for such variables—taxonomies that help us sort out *observable organizational realities*. Probably the most powerful of such taxonomies is Etzioni's classification of types of organizational authority and member involvement (see pp. 45–46). The work we will discuss now is consistent with and builds on the Etzioni typology.

Focus on Organization/Environment
Interaction—Thompson and Duncan

Systems theory has focused organization analysis on the interaction of the organization with its environment, but a comprehensive listing of relevant variables is not yet available. Thompson and McEwen (1958), building on the bargaining models of March, Simon, and Cyert, asserted that how an organization will set its goals will ultimately be a function of the degree to which it can control its environment versus being controlled by it. Figure 11.1 shows their basic environmental control dimension, examples of the types of organizations typical of different positions along the continuum, and the basic kind of goal-setting process that is appropriate at each segment along the dimension.

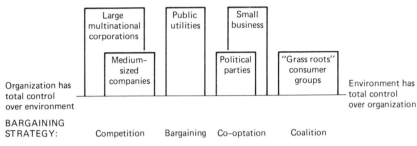

Fig. 11.1 Power continuum in organizational-environmental relations (based on Thompson and McEwen, 1958).

Thus, for example, a large multinational company which, by virtue of its size, is relatively high in the degree to which it controls its environment can afford to engage in pure competitive behavior motivated primarily by rational self-interest. Medium-size organizations that must coexist with a number of others in their environment are forced into more of a bargaining stance. Public utilities or political parties, which have still less control of their environment, often attempt to deal with that environment by "coopting" certain troublesome portions of the environment. For example, a political party may merge with a competing faction in order to gain strength, or a company may promote a dissident union leader into management ranks. Finally, loosely organized groups such as consumer cooperatives, which have relatively little control over their environment, can only cope by forming coalitions with other such groups in an attempt to increase their power relative to other environmental groups.

This kind of analysis helps one to understand, for example, the response of business firms to government regulation, consumer movements, and advocacy groups such as Ralph Nader's. If the firm feels it can control the environment, it will fail to respond to initial regulatory attempts. Weak consumer groups may then lobby certain congressional committees in an attempt to coopt a more powerful environmental element. Should its lobbying tactics work, the firm will have less power and be forced to adopt more of a bargaining-type response.

A somewhat more general model of the impact of the environment on the organization was provided by Duncan (1972, 1973). His analysis attempted to specify which characteristics of the environment would create problems for an organization because they would increase "environmental uncertainty."

1. Lack of information on which factors in the environment will be most relevant to the organization's functioning; for example, lack of knowl-

202

edge of consumer attitudes in regard to a new product; inability to determine whether political instability in some part of the world will affect certain market areas; inability to determine which sociopolitical factors might affect the price of oil; inability to forecast future technology in key areas.

2. Inability to assign probabilities to given known environmental factors; for example, inability to determine how likely it is that OPEC nations will raise the price of oil; inability to determine the likelihood that the government will strictly enforce its equal employment opportunity regulations.

3. Lack of information on the costs of an incorrect decision; for example, lack of information on the costs of building new factories overseas if the local governments decide to nationalize all of their local industry and expropriate foreign companies; lack of information on the costs of lawsuits against the company if employees decide they have been discriminated against on the basis of age, sex, or minority status.

These factors are then combined into a fourfold classification of types of environmental uncertainty (Figure 11.2) based on two further dimensions for analyzing the environment: *simplicity to complexity* and *stability to instability*. Thus, Duncan hypothesized that the lowest perceived uncertainty of the environment occurs in simple, static environments where there are only a few relevant factors

	Simple	Complex
Static	CELL 1: Low Perceived Uncertainty 1. Small number of factors and components in the environment 2. Factors and components are somewhat similar to one another 3. Factors and components remain basically the same and are not changing	CELL 2: Moderately Low Perceived Uncertainty 1. Large number of factors and components in the environment 2. Factors and components are not similar to one another 3. Factors and components remain basically the same
Dynamic	CELL 3: Moderately High Perceived Uncertainty 1. Small number of factors and components in the environment 2. Factors and components are somewhat similar to one another 3. Factors and components of the environment are in continual process of change	CELL 4: High Perceived Uncertainty 1. Large number of factors and components in the environment 2. Factors and components are not similar to one another 3. Factors and components of environment are in a continual process of change

Fig. 11.2 A model of degree of environmental uncertainty based on degree of complexity and stability of the environment. *Source: R. B. Duncan, "The characteristics of organizational environments and perceived environmental uncertainty,"* Administrative Science Quarterly, *1972, 17, 320.*

which are relatively predictable and stable (cell 1). The highest perceived uncertainty is experienced by organizations operating in a complex environment—that is, one characterized by a large number of dissimilar factors that are continuously changing (cell 4). Duncan also found that stability is more important than complexity in determining uncertainty; in other words, environments with a few unstable factors were seen as more uncertain and threatening (cell 3) than environments with many, dissimilar but relatively more stable factors operating (cell 2).

For example, it would be easier for a company simultaneously to deal with political, social, and economic factors if they changed relatively slowly than to deal with only a single economic factor such as the price of energy if it was changing very rapidly and unpredictably. Thus, Duncan's table can be used as a first step in deciding what kind of organizational strategy to adopt under specific circumstances, from pure competitive behavior to coalition formation. To follow the previous example, the more the price of energy continues to fluctuate unpredictably, the more one would expect large organizations to attempt to form coalitions with energy producers, a strategy aptly coined in the phrase, "If you can't beat 'em, join 'em."

A further analytical insight is offered in Thompson's (1967) analysis of decision-making strategy as a function of (1) *goal consensus* among the dominant coalitions in an organization, and (2) the degree to which there is certainty about how to accomplish a given goal. The first of these variables resembles Cyert's and March's theory of the firm, but by combining it with the dimension of certainty—and Duncan's analysis of how certainty can begin to be measured—one can derive a more powerful taxonomy of *managerial decision types*. Figure 11.3 shows the basic typology and identifies four kinds of managerial decisions or leadership styles:

PREFERENCES REGARDING
POSSIBLE OUTCOMES

		Certainty	Uncertainty
BELIEFS ABOUT CAUSE-EFFECT RELATIONS	Certain	Computational strategy	Compromise strategy
	Uncertain	Judgmental strategy	Inspirational strategy

Fig. 11.3 Types of managerial decisions needed under different conditions of uncertainty. *Source: J. D. Thompson,* Organizations in Action *(New York: McGraw-Hill, 1967), p. 134. Used by permission.*

1. *Computational:* If there is high goal consensus and high certainty about how to achieve goals, one can routinize decision making much as one routinizes mathematical problem solving once the rules are known. Thus a shared decision can be reached to develop a new product for which the technology is known and for which a clear market exists.
2. *Compromise:* If there is high certainty about how to achieve various different kinds of goals but low consensus on which goals should be sought, management finds itself having to make compromises and engage in various kinds of bargaining behavior of the kind that Cyert and March identified. One such situation might be compromise on which of several products to develop where the technology for each is well-known but where lack of consensus exists on the size of the profit margins each will yield in the short and long run.
3. *Judgmental:* If there is high goal consensus but the environmental/organizational interaction is such that there is low certainty about how to achieve a given goal, what is needed is good judgment on how to maximize the probabilities of desired outcomes and minimize the probabilities of undesired outcomes. Thus, judgment is needed where the market for a given product is clear and where profit goals are clearly agreed upon but the costs of developing the product are highly uncertain because of changing technology.
4. *Inspirational:* If there is neither consensus on goals, nor any degree of certainty on how to achieve a given goal, what is needed is an inspirational leader who combines the ability to pull diverse coalitions together and the judgment to make the decisions with the highest probabilities of desired outcomes. The decisions which entrepreneurs make in the face of high environmental uncertainty to go ahead with certain products and market strategies are of this type.

What this kind of analysis makes clear is that the various normative theories which attempt to specify "correct" leadership or managerial behavior, or "correct" ways to organize, often make inadequate assumptions about the state of the organization/environment interaction. If one sees the full range of possibilities in that interaction, one can also see why there are so many organizational structures and decision-making styles observable in organizations. This point will become even clearer when we examine organizational tasks and their related technologies.

Focus on Organizational Goals—
March and Simon, Perrow

A number of theorists have focused on and refined the concept of organizational goals. Early in the chapter we saw that one way of looking at goals is to use the sociological concept of *manifest* and *latent* functions—the functions organizations or institutions fulfill for society, some of which are made explicit and public, while others remain implicit and private.

March and Simon (1958) make a similar distinction when they attempt to differentiate the following types of goals:

1. *Official goals:* Those goals which are publicly stated by the organization's founders or leaders and often find expression in its official charter.
2. *Operative goals:* Those goals which reflect the real intentions of the leaders or dominant coalitions of the organization, but which are often concealed from the public. For example, a business may state as its official goal to maximize profits in order to give maximum returns on investments to stockholders. But its real intentions may be to survive and grow by capturing a larger share of the market, goals which entail heavy reinvestments and lower dividends, or an organization may state that it is an equal opportunity employer but its real intentions may be minimal compliance with the law.
3. *Operational goals:* Those goals which can actually be measured concretely and thus permit some assessment of how well the organization is performing against agreed-upon criteria. Thus, the goal of "growth" may be an operative goal, but it does not become operational until it is stated as an increase of 5 percent in sales over the next 12 months, or the addition of three new factories in five years in order to increase production capacity by 20 percent, and the like.

Distinctions such as these have been found necessary by students of organizations because of the difficulty of describing an organization by just one set of goals. One clearly finds managers behaving in ways that are inconsistent with official goals, and one often finds in organizations behavior which seems self-defeating from the point of view of official or even operative goals. Unless one can specify what the organization is concretely measuring itself on, one cannot really understand what actual goals are being pursued.

A further set of goal distinctions has been proposed by Perrow (1970) in an effort to clarify the multiple levels of analysis at which goals have to be studied if one is fully to understand organizational decisions:

1. *Societal goals:* The point of reference here is society in general and these goals are therefore like the manifest or latent functions of an organization previously referred to. Examples would be to produce goods and services, to maintain order, to generate and maintain cultural values.
2. *Output goals:* The point of reference here is that segment of the public

in direct contact with the organization—the clientele for whom the products or services are created. Examples would be the creation of consumer products, business services, health care, educational programs, and so on, what sociotechnical systems theorists tend to call the "primary task" or "core mission" of the organization.

3. *System goals:* The point of reference here is the organization itself and the concern is with the *manner in which it functions,* independent of the particular outputs it creates. Examples would be the goals of growth, efficiency, obtaining market share, certain profit levels, being a certain kind of organization in terms of style or climate, being a leader in the industry, and so on. It is these kinds of goals which often given the organization its particular "personality" and which, if they are confused with output goals, can cause a great deal of difficulty. If, in attempting to maintain a certain style, the organization loses sight of its important output goals, it may unwittingly threaten its own survival.

4. *Product characteristic goals:* The point of reference here is the actual product or service, whether the emphasis is on quality or quantity, variety, styling, availability, uniqueness, innovativeness, or whatever. In one sense these goals are more specific derivatives of the output and system goals in that certain combinations of what the organization is basically creating and its style will dictate product characteristics.

5. *Derived goals:* The point of reference here is the organizational leadership itself and what it chooses to do with the power and resources it accumulates while pursuing the other goals. For example, an organization may use its power and wealth for certain political goals, or to build up the community in which it operates, or to support the arts or local educational institutions, or to provide maximum personal development for its own employees. Organizations generate power and resources which they can choose to use in consistent ways to influence the external or internal environment, and these goals are independent of the goals that generated the power or resources in the first place.

Perrow concedes that these categories are not always clearly distinguishable in a particular case, but it is very important to make the analytical distinctions in order to understand what actually happens to organizations as they evolve and develop. It is particularly important when organizations engage in strategic planning activities that they learn to distinguish their societal and output goals—those things which ultimately justify the survival of the organization in the total society—from the secondarily generated system, product, and derived goals. Many of the essential components of planning exercises should be especially geared to helping top managements first to identify clearly what their output goals are and what justifies their continued existence as an organization before they discuss system, product, or derived goals.

Focus on Technology and Organizational Tasks

One of the most persistent questions in organization theory has been, What is the best way to organize something? or, alternatively stated, By what criteria should one determine organizational structure? Early classical theories attempted to derive general principles about such things as optimal number of subordinates, but observations of organizations had shown that effectiveness did not necessarily correlate with the degree of adherence to these principles, forcing students of organizations to look for other kinds of variables to explain the relationship between organizational form and effectiveness.

An obvious candidate for such an explanatory variable was the nature of the *task* the organization was supposed to perform, that is, *the goals the organization set for itself and the technology involved in the accomplishment of those goals.* A number of researchers in England began to study large numbers of organizations in different industries in order to determine how organizational form related to effectiveness. Thus, for example, Burns and Stalker (1961) distinguished between those firms with fairly stable production technologies and those with rapidly moving, dynamic technology (for example, electronics products). In the more stable technological environment a more "mechanistic" managerial style worked well, characterized by rigidly prescribed structure, well-defined duties, clear power and lines of authority for each organizational role, a strong hierarchy of command, and primarily vertical hierarchical communications. By contrast, in the more dynamic technological environment, they found that a more "organic" style was better suited, characterized by a relatively flexible structure, continual adjustment and redefinition of individual tasks through interaction with others, more lateral than hierarchical communications and control, and a wide dispersion of power based on technical expertise rather than organizational rank.

Woodward (1965) studied approximately 100 British firms to determine whether their organizational structures were related to three major types of technology which she distinguished:

1. *Unit and small batch* technology, in which customized products are made for individual customers
2. *Large batch and mass production* technology such as that found on the assembly line
3. *Process* technology, which involves the transformation of raw materials through a series of continuous (chemical) processes

Woodward found that the companies with different technologies demonstrated characteristic patterns and that the most effective companies within each group were the ones closest to the median for that category, suggesting that there *were* optimal organizational forms. For example, with increasing technological complexity, as one moves from unit to mass to continuous-process technology, the number of subordinates under a given executive increased, the number of levels in the organizational hierarchy increased, the ratio of administrators, supporting staff and specialists increased, relative labor costs decreased, and so on. A more formal, structured approach seemed best suited to mass production technology, while a more flexible organization seemed better suited to both unit and process technologies.

Subsequent studies by Pugh (1973), Hickson and his colleagues (1969), and others called the Aston Group showed that the effects of technology tended to apply only to those parts of the organization intimately involved with that technology—typically the production departments—and that one could not infer organizational structures in other functional departments such as accounting and marketing, or in the firm as a whole unless it was very small. They argued for a more contingent set of relationships, namely, that technology will influence organization only if organizational size and type of department are controlled for.

In a more recent study, Mahoney and Frost (1974) focused on specific departments rather than total organizations and used the three-part typology of technologies proposed by Thompson (1967):

1. *Long-linked technologies,* in which there is a series of interdependent steps such as in the assembly line or in continuous process work
2. *Mediating technologies,* in which the work unit links otherwise independent units into a system through the creation of standard operating procedures (for example, a bank which brings depositors and borrowers together into a system through mediating the transactions between them)
3. *Intensive technologies,* in which each task sequence is uniquely applied to the particular needs of a given client based on feedback from earlier steps (for example, the professional service organization such as a hospital which provides many specialized services in particular combinations on behalf of an individual patient).

Using managerial judgments as to which factors contributed most to effectiveness, Mahoney and Frost found that in *long-linked technologies* such as in data processing, the important factors were planning, efficient utilization of employee skills for task performance, and tight supervisory controls (resembling Burns and Stalker's "mechanistic system"). In *mediating* technologies such as clerical departments in an insurance company, effectiveness was related more to the ability to remain flexible and adaptive to the needs of the moment. In *intensive* technologies such as research laboratories, managers related overall effectiveness more to effective utilization of employees, the building of cooperation and team spirit, the personal development of employees, and careful staffing of projects (more similar to Burns and Stalker's "organic" system).

In summarizing these and many other research studies on the relationship of technology to organization structure, Steers (1977) concludes that there is no simple, consistent relationship between technology and structure, though there is some evidence that more complex, unstable technologies are less likely to be associated with more formal hierarchical structures.

Perrow's Integrative Framework

Though the research evidence is not yet conclusive, enough trends have been identified to enable some theorists to construct a generalized framework for analyzing the relationship between technology, environmental uncertainty, and organizational form. For example, Perrow (1970) starts with two characterisics of organizational tasks (basic underlying dimensions of technology):

1. The degree to which the task is *routinized* and has *few exceptions*
2. The degree to whch the task to be performed is based on *analyzable principles* and *known ways of solving problems* (versus having constantly to invent new solutions because of variations in the problems posed)

These two dimensions enable Perrow to sort various kinds of technologies into a fourfold table as shown in Figure 11.4. In cell 1 we have what might best be characterized as the "craftsmanship" approach. The raw material and the basic product remain essentially the same, but individual customers may want some special feature. Examples might include a factory producing fine glassware, a musical instruments factory, or other industries which Woodward would classify as "unit or small batch" production. For such organizations a decentralized production organization in which the lowest technical levels have relatively low job discretion while supervisors have high power and high discretion appears to be most typical.

TASK VARIABILITY

		Uniform and Stable: Few exceptions	Non-Uniform and Unstable: Many exceptions
METHODS FOR RESOLVING UNCERTAINTY	Unanalyzable Search: Cause and effect not well understood	1 Craft (decentralized)	2 R&D Non-Routine Manufacturing (flexible, polycentralized)
	Analyzable Search: Cause and effect well understood	4 Routine Continuous process (formal, centralized)	3 Engineering (flexible, centralized)

Fig. 11.4 Types of production technologies (Perrow, 1970).

Cell 2 is what Perrow calls "nonroutine manufacturing" or, at the extreme, R&D types of work which require a much more flexible organization, the kind that Burns and Stalker would have called "organic structures." Organizations in these industries ideally display high discretion at both the technical and the managerial level, high interaction, decentralization of decision making according to expertise, a high degree of interdependence and, therefore, a high need for effective coordinating structures.

Cell 3 involves custom-made products, but in areas well known for their amenability to technical and analytical solution. Hence we are here dealing with engineering firms that design customized equipment for manufacturing firms and production organizations that apply such designs to making drill presses, electric motors, and so on. In this model the technical level has relatively more discretion because it possesses the problem-solving techniques needed to design and manufacture the process. Coordination is achieved through high interaction with and feedback from the consumer. The organization is flexible but also centralized because of the known problem-solving routines.

Cell 4 is the traditional routine manufacturing operation involving mass production or continuous process operation where the technology is well understood. Thus, both of Woodward's other types, the "large batch assembly" and the "continuous process" fall into this cell, since both share what Thompson has termed *long-linked* technologies and a high degree of sequential interdependence. Firms in this cell display the greatest tendency toward the formal, centralized, bureaucratic form of organization where coordination is achieved primarily through rules and plans; however, it should be noted that, at the extremes, in continuous process technologies such as automated oil refineries, this does not hold true. At the extremes the relationships are instead adaptive to the particular characteristics of the task being performed, so that in the oil refinery there is a high formalization but also high decentralization down to skilled operators who have high levels of responsibility and high discretion within a well-defined set of rules (Blauner, 1964).

The real contribution of Perrow's model is that it integrates much of the work on task, environmental, and technological characteristics into a single framework which makes it possible to sort out the characteristics of organizational tasks in a more systematic fashion. However, the data to support this more complex taxonomy remain to be gathered, and some dynamic theories as to *why* organizations need to structure themselves in the way they do are not fully developed in Perrow's model.

SUMMARY

In this chapter we have reviewed early open systems models of organizations and some of the many efforts to produce taxonomies that illustrate the complex relationships between the organization's environments, its mission, goals, and tasks, and its internal structure. What a review of these taxonomies shows is once again the complexity of the phenomena we are dealing with. If it is hard to get a simple, clear view of human nature, and if it is hard to get a simple clear view of the process of leadership and influence, and if it is hard to understand the dynamics of groups, it is even harder to get a simple, clear view of something as complicated as the overlapping, diffuse set of coalitions, role sets, and formal and informal groups, all of which are trying to achieve multiple goals in a turbulent, complex environment—the thing we call organizations.

Nevertheless, we live in an organizational society and if we do not make at least an effort to understand organizational phenomena we run the danger of becoming victimized by them. It is small comfort to complain about bureaucracy, to laugh at organizational inefficiency, or to fear organizational power to control our lives. What we must seek is sufficient understanding to be able to influence organizations. In the taxonomies and concepts presented above we have laid a foundation for such understanding. But the concepts are rather static and global. In the next chapters we turn to more dynamic concepts of organization change and development, and to models of organizations which are less global.

The Organization as a Dynamic, Developing System

12

INTRODUCTION AND PURPOSE

In this chapter I will present several developmental models of organizations which lead to a redefinition of what we mean by *organization*. These models make it possible to think about organizations as dynamic systems because they emphasize some of the *processes* that occur in organizations *over time* as they face different kinds of external and internal events. Lawrence and Lorsch provide one key set of concepts in elucidating the effects of "differentiation" and "integration"; Galbraith shows how different kinds of organizational design decisions can be related to information-processing requirements as an organization grows and becomes more complex; Kotter develops a dynamic diagnostic model which ties together many of the structural elements identified in the last chapter and lays a foundation for how to intervene constructively if one wishes to influence organizations.

Following these models I will review a concept of organizational health and propose an organizational coping model which leads to an analysis of "organization development" and the concept of action research.

DYNAMIC MODELS OF ORGANIZATIONS

Focus on the Effects of Differentiation and Integration: Lawrence and Lorsch

Lawrence and Lorsch (1967) developed a way of thinking about organizations which made it possible to explain *why* different kinds of organizations are more or less effective in different kinds of environments or technologies. Their key premise is that each functional part of an organization, be it production, research, or sales, deals with a *different* part of the total environment and the people in that area develop a cognitive point of view which reflects their particular adaptation to that specific part of the environment. This process is called *differentiation* and is exemplified by the contrast between research and sales. A research person, for example, usually has a long time horizon, is often in a technological environment where a breakthrough is difficult, will make many false starts and will take months or years to get results even in a dynamic technology, and is oriented toward recognition from professional colleagues; the sales manager in that same company has a very short time horizon, is oriented toward a variety of customers, gets knowledge of results very quickly, and is concerned about issues which are of little interest to the research person and which change daily or weekly even in fairly stable sales environments (for example, pricing policy).

The other key process which every organization must deal with is *integration*, the bringing together of these widely differing cognitive styles and problem-solving approaches into a coherent, goal-oriented set of activities. In studying a wide range of organizations, Lawrence and Lorsch found that effective organizations dealt with such differences by developing integrative structures which served to *mediate and coordinate* rather than to compel each of the functions to adopt a common point of view. Thus, within any given organization there are usually several different kinds of tasks to be performed, which reflect different environmental and technological characteristics. A key to effective total performance is the manner in which one integrates the different tasks into a coherent organizational strategy.

Every organization must determine its optimum degree of differentiation in terms of the particular characteristics of its different environments, and must choose an appropriate means of integration based on an analysis of which functions give the organization its particular competitive advantage in the marketplace. Some businesses, for example, may conclude that the key to their future success lies in new product development, which means that those functions in need of special integrative strategy would be R&D, engineering, and production. Other businesses might conclude that the key to their future is the development of new markets for old products, which would require integration among sales, marketing, and production. Still other businesses might decide that their success will depend upon increasing their ability to produce for existing markets, a strategy that might require high integration among finance (to raise the money to build new plants), production, and personnel (to ensure that an effective labor force will be available).

Integrative mechanisms can be individual managers, committees, or entire departments, depending upon the size of the task. When individual managers had to fulfill integrative roles at the "interface" between departments, it was found that the successful integrator had empathy for both points of view, derived his or her influence from being closely related to the departments rather than being a high-ranking officer of the company, tended to be open and confrontive rather than suppressing or avoiding potential areas of conflict, and tended to push decisions down to the lowest level where relevant information was available.

In summary, whereas Woodward, Thompson, Duncan, and Perrow (see Chapter 11) were concerned with basic models of the technological environment that related departmental structure to a specific aspect of the environment, Lawrence and Lorsch have shown that total organizations, particularly large ones, usually do *not* reflect the organizational arrangements which may be appropriate to the production function. The manner in which the *total* organization is structured will reflect the resolution of the multiple problems of (1) how best to differentiate (geographically, by technology, by product or service groupings, or on some other basis); (2) how to locate the critical interfaces between differentiated units (those which are most necessary to ensure the organization its competitive advantage); and (3) what mechanisms to use to integrate or coordinate across the critical interfaces or boundaries that have been identified.

Focus on Information Processing— Galbraith's Theory of Design

Galbraith's (1973, 1977) model begins with the assumption that the organization is a complex system whose primary problem of relating to its environment is the acquiring and utilization of *information*. In effect, the various models of technology and the environment reviewed in the last chapter can all be seen as information-processing models, and the problem of organization design can be viewed as a matter of information utilization in the service of organizational goals.

The design of organization structure is a process that occurs over time. It is a process of deciding how to maintain a coherence between strategy choices, choices about division of labor (differentiation), about the processes of coordinating the different units (integration), about how to integrate individuals into the organization, and, finally, about how to change any and all of the above in order to adapt to changes in the environment.

Starting with the basic propositions of contingency theory that (1) there is no one best way to organize, and (2) not all the ways to organize are equally effective, Galbraith notes that the key problem facing the organization is "task uncertainty" defined as the "difference between the amount of information required to perform the task and the amount of information already possessed by the organization" (1977, pp. 36–37). This definition is entirely consistent with the taxonomies proposed by Duncan and Perrow but puts the problem squarely into a dynamic context by focusing on a diagnosis of how much information is needed and how much information is already available. Thus, the degree of product or technological diversity determines the number of different variables about which the organization must collect information. Internal factors deriving from the number of different specialities involved in task accomplishment are also related to product diversity and technological complexity. The other major factor which Galbraith considers is more closely related to March, Simon, and Cyert's model of decision making—the degree to which product quality, quantity, and the meeting of schedules interact with other organizational goals and are constrained by prior commitments (money or resources tied up in other products) or by bargaining outcomes (getting the cooperation of a powerful coalition where little initial goal consensus exists).

> The greater the uncertainty, the greater the amount of decision making and information processing. It is hypothesized that organizations have limited capacities to process information and adopt different organizing modes to deal with task uncertainty. Therefore, variations in organizing modes are actually variations in the capacity of organizations to process information and make decisions about events which cannot be anticipated in advance. (Galbraith, 1977, p. 39)

Figure 12.1 shows nine alternative ways for dealing with increasing amounts of uncertainty. These mechanisms can be seen as developmental and evolutionary as an organization moves from being simple and small to being complex and large.

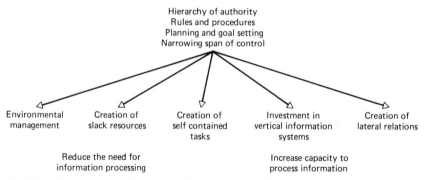

Fig. 12.1 Organizational design strategies for dealing with increasing amounts of uncertainty (Galbraith, 1977).

1. *Hierarchy of authority.* If two or more people need to coordinate their efforts, the simplest and most efficient mode of processing the information between them is direct communication. However, if they are geographically dispersed, or there are too many people for direct communication, or the people do not have goal consensus (the essence of the organizing activity), the next simplest processing mechanism is to build a hierarchy and to have all information flow downward through a single superior. This mechanism can be reproduced by building a multilayered system such as the typical multilevel formal organization. However, each communication channel can carry only a certain amount of information, and unkown amounts of distortion will occur in the transmission of information unless the information is relatively simple and distortion-free. If task uncertainty requires the communication of more complex information, the organization must use a more complex information-processing system.

2. *Rules, programs, and procedures.* The basic purpose of rules, programs, and procedures is to keep the information channels free from irrelevant information in order to permit the upward transmission of data relating to exceptional circumstances. Thus, in a fairly predictable, simple task environment all contingencies can be identified ahead of time and manuals written which tell employees what to do in the case of each contingency. Only if something comes up not covered in the manual should the employee communicate upward for resolution of the issue by management. Thus with rules, programs, and procedures one also finds training programs and systems designed to ensure standardized behavior by employees, for example, guidelines developed by industrial engineers for assembly-line workers or by airplane designers for pilots. Such a system, of course, reduces the discretion of lower levels of the organization and

217

can often lead to problems of low morale and alienation from work—unless employees *want* to be only minimally involved in their work.

Galbraith notes the important point that each mechanism identified is *added* to the previous ones, not put in place of it; thus rules, programs, and procedures exist and function *in addition* to the hierarchy, not in place of it. But they minimize the amount of information the hierarchy must deal with. As task uncertainty increases, the hierarchy becomes overloaded with exceptions not covered by the rules and time delays occur in providing solutions, thus again requiring the addition of new information-processing mechanisms.

3. *Planning and goal setting.* As information-processing needs increase, one response is to delegate more discretion to lower levels where the information exists, but this will only work if the organization has a way of ensuring that the employee with more discretion will make the correct response from the point of view of the *overall goals of the organization*. Two mechanisms for ensuring such responses are (1) to increase the amount of craft and professional training of employees so that they will internalize the appropriate goals; and (2) to increase the amount of planning to ensure that employees will understand ahead of time where the organization is trying to go.

Thus in the automated oil refinery as contrasted with the automobile assembly plant, employees are much more professionalized and highly trained, enjoy much more discretion in dealing with unanticipated events, and are involved much more in the planning process. Planning serves to set targets and goals for the lower level unit, which then allow individuals or autonomous work groups to decide appropriate courses of action to achieve those goals. This approach is, in a sense, the essence of "management by objectives," where it is the goal of every management level to involve the subordinate sufficiently in the target-setting process to ensure that the subordinates will know the targets, will have accepted them, and will therefore work to achieve them when unanticipated situations arise, making it possible to give each subordinate more discretion (increase the amount of "delegation").

Once again it is important to note that those things which can be covered by rules and standardized procedures continue to be covered, and the hierarchy still exists to handle exceptions and to adjust plans if unanticipated events arise. It is also likely that as the organization grows and handles more of its decisions through plans and procedures, it will (1) generate the need for some staff specialists to handle the administration of those plans and procedures, which means (2) that the number of administrative and staff people will increase with task uncertainty and organizational size, (3) that fewer line managers will be needed, but (4) that because those line managers are freed of some administrative responsibilities, they may each be able to handle more subordinates, thus making the overall organization more efficient.

4. *Changing the hierarchy by reducing span of control.* If the organization still continues to be overloaded, it can cope by reducing the span of control, that is, by giving each manager fewer people to supervise. However, this increases the total number of managers (a possible explanation for the observed phenomenon that as organizational size and complexity increases the ratio of managers to direct employees tends to increase). This mechanism is thus expensive and not very efficient, since the total number of organizational links across which information must now be passed *increases*. Organizations that find themselves in this situation soon begin to search for a better alternative. Basically there are two possibilities: mechanisms that reduce the need for information processing and mechanisms that increase the capacity to process more information (refer again to Figure 12.1).

5. *Environmental management.* Organizations can adjust their basic strategy to deal with the information overload by trying to control portions of their environment. For example, if the production process is constantly disrupted by unpredictable deliveries of raw materials or if sales are unpredictable because of unreliable distribution channels, the organization can "integrate vertically," by which is meant that it can bring into itself more parts of the environment to gain control over those unpredictable elements. A wire manufacturing company can acquire a copper mine to ensure a constant supply of raw materials, or a food manufacturing company can acquire a trucking company to ensure reliable distribution of its products. Instead of relying on the production of new technology in the universities, companies can develop their own research and development laboratories. If the problem is high labor costs due to unpredictable strikes and turnover caused by political unrest, companies begin to become politically active to influence government or union policies. If the problem is fluctuating raw materials costs such as the recent problems with the price of oil, companies begin to become politically active to influence foreign policy toward greater price stabilization. All of these devices can be seen as efforts to reduce the environmental uncertainty and thus the information-processing overload within the organization. However, all of these devices may be too costly, forcing still other responses.

6. *Creation of slack resources.* One way of reducing the stress of information overload is to reduce performance standards, either by

letting schedules slip or by hiring (buying) additional resouces specifically to deal with these peak periods. Thus a machine shop that
is dealing with fluctuating orders or a design group that is dealing
with constantly changing design requirements can add extra machines or extra engineers to handle periods of overload or it can
slow down whenever a change occurs (thus letting the schedule slip)
in order to solve the change problem. It has been empirically observed that most organizations maintain some slack resources to deal
with task uncertainty. Whether or not this mechanism will solve the
information-processing problem will, of course, depend upon its cost
relative to the other mechanisms identified.

  7. *Creation of self-contained tasks.* As organizations grow, acquire more tasks and product lines, deal with more complex technologies, and thus have more information to process, they are
typically observed at a certain stage in their evolution to make a
major design change from a "functional" to a "product" (or market)
form of organization. The essence of this organizational change is to
reduce the overload on the various functions (for example, engineering, manufacturing, marketing, and sales) that results from too great
a span of products or geographical territories. By setting up smaller,
self-contained units, the necessary tasks are accomplished on a product or geographical basis that allows each new unit to be relatively
autonomous.

  Consequently, each unit has only to process the information
relevant to its product, market, or region, and the total amount of
information processing once again becomes manageable. This organizational step has also been termed "decentralization" or "divisional-
ization," because the organization typically subdivides into relatively
more self-contained units and manages each of the units in terms of
total unit performance. The parent organization is then enabled to
deal with a wider range of tasks and geographic regions, but may
generate new problems because of the potential duplication of resources within each unit. The timing of such a reorganization decision is, therefore, strategically very complicated, and one sees many
large organizations creating hybrid forms in which sales or manufacturing may be decentralized by product or territory but marketing or
finance may continue to be centralized to take advantage of coordinated effort across units and to minimize cost.

  Within organizational units the same process can be observed
with the creation of project teams with a variety of resources at their
disposal, or with autonomous work groups given responsibility for
managing their own operations, including quality control, pricing,
acquisition of raw materials, and distribution of finished products to
other parts of the organization.

Each of the above organizational design decisions represents an effort to reduce the amount of information that must be processed by each unit, but since the costs of such decisions may be prohibitive, two further mechanisms are considered to increase the capacity of the organization to process information.

8. *Investment in better vertical information systems.* Since the hierarchical form of organization *can* if utilized properly disseminate information fairly reliably and rapidly, one solution is to revamp information systems to provide higher capacity for rapid, accurate information transmission. Thus, if exceptions based on environmental variability force constant revision of rules and plans, it becomes necessary to get quick, reliable information to the top of the organization where plans can be readjusted and rules and procedures changed. To accomplish this the organization must add people, computers, information systems, and analytical procedures whose primary functions are to (1) gather information on new events, variances from expected events, and information relevant to present plans and procedures, (2) digest this information, (3) get it to the upper levels of the hierarchy efficiently, and to (4) disseminate new plans and procedures efficiently and reliably back to the lower levels. The rapid growth of information, control, and decision support systems, often based on complex, computerized data-processing systems, can thus be viewed as a response to the problem of adjusting plans rapidly and effectively in the face of growing task uncertainty and potential information overload (Keen & Scott-Morton, 1978).

9. *Creation of lateral relations, integrating roles, and matrix organizations.* The final, most interesting, and most complex organizational design decision involves a partial abandonment of the hallowed principle that organizational authority must be hierarchically arranged. If task uncertainty and information overload dictate that managers or workers talk to each other on the basis of *who has relevant information* rather than who reports to whom, it becomes possible for the organization to legitimize such communication by encouraging various forms of lateral communication, by creating linking or liaison roles between groups at the same level, by conducting meetings, or by creating task forces for the purpose of information exchange.

If such linking or integrating roles become crucial in the processing of information and decision making, the organization may have difficulty deciding where the integrator fits into the hierarchy. For example, in a geographically decentralized manufacturing organization which makes multiple products in each of its locations, it may be necessary for coordination purposes to have an "integrative" production manager whose job is to ensure that certain policies which are geographically determined (for example, raw materials procurement) are consistent with other policies determined by individual product line managers in the home office—such as production quotas, schedules, and quality standards. The question arises, should the production manager report to the geographically based "site manager," who is responsible for everything at that particular plant, or to the product line manager at headquarters, who is responsible for making maximum profits on the product line. Depending upon local circumstances either solution may be used. However, "matrix" organizations have also sprung up, in which persons occupying integrative roles are officially told that they have *two* bosses and are genuinely accountable to both of them. In a true matrix all decisions are negotiated with both bosses, and both bosses are involved in the performance review of employees who have such dual reporting relationships.

In a recent study, Davis and Lawrence (1977) have depicted such organizational structures as diamond-shaped (see Figure 12.2), highlighting the fact that a true matrix is a genuine departure from traditional hierarchical organizational forms. The essence of the difference and what defines a matrix organization is a "multiple com-

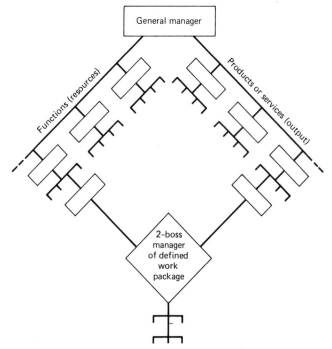

Fig. 12.2 Example of matrix design (Davis and Lawrence, 1977).

mand system" in which people have two or even more bosses to whom they are equally accountable. Such an organizational form permits higher information-processing capacity without duplication of people, but, on the other hand, forces people into new behavior patterns. A matrix organization can only function if both bosses and subordinates learn how to manage in a multiple command structure.

SUMMARY. Galbraith has presented the design options available to an organization in a sequential and developmental fashion, starting with the notion of simple hierarchy, the introduction of rules and plans, increase of discretion by professionalization of employees, reduction of span of control in the hierarchy, managing the environment, the creation of slack resources, decentralization into units which can manage self-contained tasks, investment in improved vertical information systems, and, finally, the creation of various lateral relations such as groups, linking roles, integrators, and the matrix form of organization. He reminds us of two important points: (1) introducing a new form of information processing in no way eliminates the previous form but merely adds to it, and (2) every organization must cope with uncertainty and information-processing requirements by some means. If the process is not explicitly managed, if the organization does not choose one of the methods as most appropriate, it will automatically fall back on the use of slack resources because inability to keep abreast of information-processing needs will simply slow the organization down, increase budget overruns, and reduce performance levels until the information is processed. "Not to decide is to decide, and it is to decide on slack resources as the strategy to remove hierarchical overload" (Galbraith, 1973, p. 55).

All of these considerations are particularly important when organizations embark upon new strategies such as broadening their product lines, entering new geographical areas, deciding to acquire other organizations as part of a financial expansion, and otherwise increasing their total task complexity. The resulting increase in information that will have to be processed should be explicitly planned for as part of the overall strategy.

Focus on Organizational Diagnosis— Kotter's Organizational Dynamics

One of the major problems facing both students of organizations and managers trying to improve their functioning is the lack of overview models and diagnostic categories in terms of which to analyze what is going on. Kotter (1978) has pulled together many of the major variables of organization theory into the diagnostic model shown in Figure 12.3, which can be used to analyze short-run, moderate-range, and long-term organizational dynamics. The basic conceptual elements used in the model are:

1. *Key organizational processes*: "... the major information-gathering, communication, decision-making, matter/energy-transport, and matter/ energy-converting actions of the organization's employees and machines" (p.10)
2. *The external environment*: "An organization's task environment can be defined as all possible suppliers (of labor, information, money, and materials, and so on), markets, competitors, regulators, and associations that are relevant in light of the organization's current products and services.... The wider environment ... can be defined by such indicators as public attitudes, the state of technological development, the economy, the occupational system, the political system, the demo-

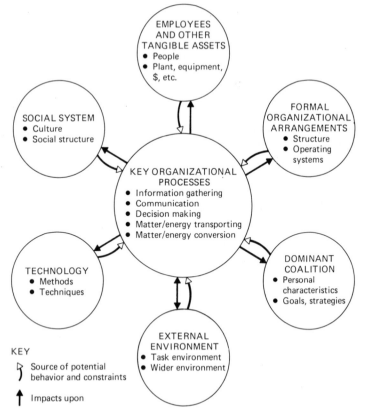

Fig. 12.3 Basic conceptual elements for analyzing short-run dynamics. (Kotter, 1978.)

graphic characteristics of people and organizations, the society's social structure, current price levels, laws, and so on" (p. 12)

3. *Employees and other tangible assets*: ". . . the size (or number) and internal characteristics of an organization's employees, plant and offices, equipment and tools, land, inventories, and money" (p. 14)

4. *Formal organizational arrangements*: ". . . all formal systems that have been explicitly designed to regulate the actions of an organization's employees (and machines)" (p. 15)

5. *The social system*: ". . . culture and social structure. Culture can be defined as those organizationally relevant norms and values shared by most employees (or subgroups of employees). Social structure is defined as the relationship that exists among emplyees in terms of such variables as power, affiliation, and trust" (p. 17)

6. *Technology*: ". . . the major techniques (and their underlying assumptions about cause and effect) that are used by an organization's employees while engaging in organizational processes, and that are programmed into its machines" (p. 18)

7. *The dominant coalition*: ". . . the objectives and strategies (for the organization), the personal characteristics, and the internal relationships of that minimum group of cooperating employees who oversee the organization as a whole and control its basic policy making" (p. 20)

Short-run organizational dynamics (up to a few months) are created by specific cause-and-effect relationships between the key organizational processes and each of the six other elements. In other words, if there is a change in any of these elements such as a drop in demand for the product (environment), or a change in employee skill levels, or the introduction of a new incentive system (formal arrangements), or a change in employee morale (the social system), or the introduction of new product technology, or a key managerial change, there will be an immediate impact on the way in which the organization makes decisions and processes information (see Figure 12.4 for an example). In turn, any change in organizational processes will cause changes in the six other elements. One can thus track the effects of a triggering event such as a drop in the demand for a product through several successive effects on internal processes to more far-reaching effects on other such elements as the state of morale or the internal social system—much as Homans postulated an interaction between internal and external systems. What Kotter has added, however, is a more refined set of categories and a further theory about how to think about longer range dynamics.

Moderate-range dynamics (up to several years) result from lack of congruence among the six structural elements which surround the organizational processes. For example, if the basic strategy of the

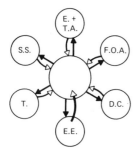

1. Demand from the external environment drops, causing incoming orders to go down.

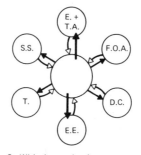

2. With the production process continuing at the same rate, the drop in orders causes deliveries to go down and shipments to inventory to go up.

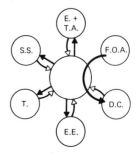

3. A formal control system maintains a process that causes top management to be alerted to these changes.

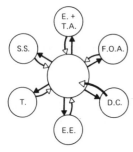

4. After watching the situation for a few weeks, top management intervenes in the process to slow production and reduce the work force.

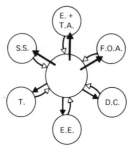

5. Their decisions are implemented—the production plan is changed, people are laid off, and the "no large layoff" belief is shattered.

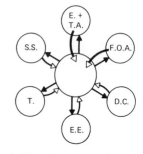

6. These changes cause the production process to slow.

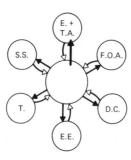

7. Shipments exceed production, causing inventories to go down.

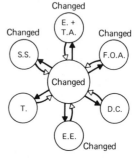

8. The system restabilizes with the states of five of the elements changed.

Fig. 12.4 Examples of short-run cause and effect sequences. (Kotter, 1978.)

226

dominant coalition is based on incorrect assumptions about the external environment, or if the formal reward or control system is inconsistent with employee educational levels or cultural attitudes, or if the tangible assets available to the organization are not sufficient to make a complex product (technology), and so on, the organization will gradually begin to experience disequilibrium and will have to seek ways to "co-align" its basic structural elements. Such a process will take time and will involve more complex organizational change processes than the reactive changes characteristic of short-term dynamics.

Long-term dynamics (decades) result from the fact that each of the structural elements becomes more differentiated and complex as the organization evolves, and this evolution for each element can be toward a more or less adaptive state. Given that some of the elements will inevitably exert more of a dynamic or driving force on the total organization than others, it is likely that over time the elements will become less congruent or coaligned, and a need will arise for some of the elements to adapt to changes necessitated by the driving effects of other elements. The ability of those elements to make the adaptation will then determine the long-range ability of the organization as a whole to remain viable in a changing environment.

The driving element(s) can be any one of the seven factors or a combination thereof. Perhaps it is the dominant coalition (an aggressive entrepreneur) or a rapidly changing technology. Or perhaps the social system has been modified by legislation to alter the kinds of work employees find acceptable; or, again, perhaps the organization's formal arrangements are too tradition oriented, and rules and regulations about work procedures need to be reviewed. Wherever the driving force is coming from, it will take considerable time to determine whether the other elements will be able to adapt. And, since the source of the driving force is not always known and may change, it may be crucial to consider how each of the basic elements can remain adaptable; for example, by maintaining a product mix that utilizes several technologies, by keeping multiple channels open to all segments of the environment, by keeping assets in good shape and well maintained, by ensuring that formal arrangements are flexible and differentiated according to the different tasks faced by the organization, by developing the social system toward norms of high trust, adaptability, and flexibility, and by developing within the dominant coalition a learning attitude and a variety of skills.

In summary, Kotter's model provides a systematic check list of elements to analyze, types of interactions among elements to consider in terms of a time horizon, and developmental goals to seek if long-run adaptation is to be maximized. This type of model takes the open systems point of view to its logical conclusion in identifying the wide variety of interactions that must be analyzed if adaptability is to maximized.

TOWARD A REDEFINITION OF "ORGANIZATION"

This chapter has tried to show how research and theorizing about organizations in the last several decades has progressively tended toward a view of the organization as an open, complex system in dynamic interaction with multiple environments, attempting to fulfill goals and perform tasks at many levels and in varying degrees of complexity, evolving and developing as the interaction with a changing environment forces new internal adaptations. This line of thinking can best be summarized by stating a series of general propositions rather than attempting a single all-encompassing definition of what is an organization.

1. The organization must be conceived of as an open system, which means that it is in constant interaction with all its environments, taking in raw materials, people, energy, and information, and transforming or converting them into products and services that are then exported to these various environments.

2. The organization must be conceived of as a system with multiple purposes or functions that involve multiple interactions between the organization and its various environments. Many of the activities of subsystems within the organization cannot be understood without considering these multiple interactions and functions.

3. The organization consists of many subsystems that are in dynamic interaction with one another. Instead of analyzing organizational phenomena in terms of individual behavior, it is becoming increasingly important to analyze the behavior of such subsystems, whether they be conceived in terms of coalitions, groups, roles, or some other conceptual elements.

4. Because the subsystems are to varying degrees interdependent, changes in one subsystem are likely to affect the behavior of other subsystems.

5. The organization exists in a set of *dynamic* environments comprised of a number of other systems, some larger, some smaller than the organization. The environments place demands upon and constrain the organization and its subsystems in various ways. The total functioning of the organization cannot be understood, therefore,

without explicit consideration of these environmental demands and constraints, and the manner in which the organization copes with them in the short run, moderate-range, and long term.

6. The multiple links between the organization and its environments make it difficult to specify clearly the boundaries of any given organization. Ultimately, the concept of organization is perhaps better conceived in terms of the stable *processes* of import, conversion, and export rather than in terms of such *structural* characteristics as size, shape, function, or design.

Increasing Organizational Effectiveness

WHAT IS ORGANIZATIONAL EFFECTIVENESS?

Throughout this book we have used the term *organizational effectiveness* but have avoided defining it because of its inherent ambiguity and complexity. If a person, group, or some larger system such as an organization has a single clear-cut goal, one can measure progress toward that goal. Effectiveness could then be defined in terms of how quickly or cheaply or efficiently goal progress was occurring. But two problems immediately surface when one attempts such a definition: First, what if the person, group, or organization has chosen the wrong goal by some broader criterion—for example, trying to be the world's fastest runner without any basic talent in running, or trying to sell a product to a consumer group that does not want that product? Second, one rarely, if ever, finds a real-life situation in which there is only *one* goal operating. It is a characteristic of all human systems to have multiple goals, all of which are generally operating simultaneously, and among which the priorities are shifting constantly. Progress toward any goal can be measured, and that measure has usually been defined as the *efficiency* of an organization. But choosing the right priorities among goals, ensuring that the ultimate *functions* of the organization are met, is a more complex process, one that approximates the concept of effectiveness.

230

Early theories of organization were content to specify single goals or functions for organizations, such as maximizing profits, providing useful products for society, increasing productivity, or achieving high employee morale. What has undermined these types of criteria as viable measures of effectiveness is (1) the discovery that seemingly rational organizations behave in ways that appear to be highly inefficient if the sole criterion is profit maximization or productivity, and (2) that real organizations do have multiple functions and multiple goals, that some of these are actually in conflict with each other, and that the organization tolerates and "works through" the conflicts. Thus, maximizing profit may rationally entail cutting labor costs, but this action may have the side effect of undermining morale. Lowered morale may mean worker alienation and eventually increased threat of sabotage or strikes, which in turn lowers productivity and eventually reduces profit. The dilemma of effectiveness, then, is clear. Is effectiveness the ability to maximize profit in the short run (which would require a definition of "short run"), or does effectiveness have something to do with the ability to *maintain* profits over some longer period of time to which the concepts of survival and growth are more applicable?

Or, to take another kind of example, if we think of organizations like universities, teaching hospitals, or prisons, we can immediately name several functions or goals, *all of which are primary and essential*. The university must simultaneously teach and create valid knowledge through research; the teaching hospital must take care of and cure patients, and must, at the same time, provide learning opportunities for interns and residents; the prison must keep criminals out of circulation but also provide opportunities for rehabilitation. Is the effectiveness of the organization to be judged by its performance on one function, on both separately, or on some complex integration of the several functions?

One attempted resolution to these dilemmas has been to define effectiveness in terms of systems-level criteria. Acknowledging that every system has multiple functions and also exists within an environment that provides unpredictable inputs, a system's effectiveness can be defined as its *capacity to survive, adapt, maintain itself, and grow*, regardless of the particular functions it fulfills. A number of students of organizations such as Argyris, Trist, Rice, Kahn, and Bennis have argued explicitly for this type of conception. Perhaps the clearest statement of effectiveness criteria in these terms has been given by Bennis (1962). He introduces these ideas in relation to the traditional approaches of measuring output and satisfaction at a given point in time and introduces the more general concept of "health":

If we view organizations as adaptive, problem-solving, organic structures, then inferences about effectiveness have to be made, not from static measures of output, though these may be helpful, but on the basis of the processes through which the organization approaches problems. In other words, no single measurement of organizational efficiency or satisfaction—no single time slice of organizational performance—can provide valid indicators of organizational health. (Bennis, 1962, p. 273)

Instead, Bennis proposes the following three criteria of health, criteria which, interestingly, closely mirror formulations about individual mental health proposed by Jahoda (1958):

1. *Adaptability:* The ability to solve problems and to react with flexibility to changing environmental demands.
2. *A sense of identity:* Knowledge and insight on the part of the organization of what it is, what its goals are, and what it is to do. Pertinent questions include, To what extent are goals understood and shared widely by members of the organization? To what extent is self-perception on the part of the organization's membership in line with perceptions of the organization by others?
3. *Capacity to test reality:* The ability to search out, accurately perceive, and correctly interpret the real properties of the environment, particularly those which have relevance for the functioning of the organization.
4. *Integration:* A fourth, often-cited criterion that in effect underlies the others is a state of "integration" among the subparts of the total organization, such that the parts are not working at cross-purposes.

For Argyris (1964) this last criterion is central, and he devotes most of his research and theorizing to finding those conditions which will permit an integration of individual needs and organizational goals. What he regards as unhealthy or ineffective are restrictions on output, destructive competition, and apathy that results in employees' fulfilling personal needs at the expense of organizational goals. McGregor (1960) has argued in a similar vein for the integration of personal and organizational goals. According to his theory, if management develops practices built on a more valid set of assumptions about human motivation, it will facilitate the integration of concern for production with concern for people. Organizational effectiveness, according to Blake and Mouton (1964), is achieved when management succeeds in being both production and people centered. To support this theory, they have developed training programs explicitly to develop this managerial style. Finally, Lawrence and Lorsch (1967) point to an optimal degree of differentiation and integration among the critical subdivisions of an organization as the best criterion of organizational effectiveness.

In summary, a systems-level criterion of organizational effectiveness must be a *multiple criterion* involving *adaptability, sense of identity, capacity to test reality*, and *internal integration.*

To the extent that effectiveness is a multiple criterion, it would be a mistake to assume that if one just selected the right people and trained them to do the job, effectiveness would be ensured. It would be equally erroneous to assume that just the establishment of a mutually satisfactory psychological contract with employees, or just the reduction of intergroup competition, or just leadership training, or just the right organization structure, any of these alone, would guarantee effectiveness. Rather, the systems conception leads us to a different way of thinking about the problem: Viewed as a total system, *how does an organization cope with its environment?* How does it obtain information and process it validly? What mechanisms exist for translating information, particularly about alterations in the environment, into changed operations? Are the internal operations flexible enough to cope with changes? How can the organization's capacity to cope be improved?

ORGANIZATIONAL COPING

An Adaptive Coping Cycle

That sequence of activities or processes which begins with a change in some aspect of the organization's internal or external environment and ends with a more adaptive, dynamic equilibrium for dealing with the change can be thought of as the organization's *adaptive coping cycle.* By identifying the various stages or processes of this cycle, we should be able to pinpoint those areas in which an organization may typically fail to cope adequately. Consultants and researchers may then be able to help in a variety of ways to increase organizational effectiveness.

For purposes of analyzing the cycle, one can think of five conceptually separable stages, but in reality all of them go on more or less simultaneously, since the organization is in a constant dynamic interaction with its multiple environments.

1. *Sensing* a change in some part of the internal or external environment.
2. *Importing* the relevant information about the change into those parts of the organization that can act upon it, and *digesting* the implications of that information.

3. *Changing* production or conversion processes inside the organization according to the information obtained while *reducing or managing* undesired side effects in related systems, and *stabilizing* the change.
4. *Exporting* new products, services, and so on, which are more in line with the originally perceived changes in the environment.
5. *Obtaining feedback* on the success of the change through *further sensing* of the state of the external environment and the degree of integration of the internal environment.

Let us illustrate this process by means of brief examples. Suppose a manufacturing concern producing electronic equipment learns that its products will be in much greater demand because the space program is stepping up (stage 1). This information must now be reviewed seriously by those members of the organization who are in a position to do something about it. In other words, it is not sufficient for market research to have the information if it cannot convince general management of the significance for the firm of this development (stage 2). If management becomes convinced, it must change its production processes to enable the company to produce more of the equipment (stage 3), but these changes must be accomplished without producing other undesirable internal changes (for example, a strike in response to unreasonable demands for increased production), and they must be stabilized. In other words, the organization must be able to change without destroying itself. The increased production must then be marketed and sold (stage 4). Finally, sales figures and future-demand figures must then be analyzed to determine whether the organizational change has been "successful" in terms of increased sales, and the internal environment must be assessed to determine whether unanticipated costs in the form of lowered morale or intergroup competition have been minimized (stage 5). The adaptive coping cycle as described is thus a more general example of systems coping, as compared with Kotter's organizational dynamic model, but the two are entirely consistent conceptions.

For another and different type of example, let us take a college fraternity as the organization. The fraternity leadership might sense in the college administration a shift in policy toward shutting down fraternities unless scholastic standards are raised (stage 1). Stage 2 would then be to get the membership to recognize the real danger to the survival of the fraternity. Stage 3 might be a program of changing norms by reducing emphasis on social activities and increasing emphasis on scholastic activities, without producing undesired changes such as total loss of prestige among other fraternities. In connection with these stages, the fraternity leaders might also recognize the necessity of convincing other fraternities on the campus to develop similar programs in their own houses, because of the likelihood that university policy would respond only to changes in the whole fraternity system. Stage 4 would be the actual improvement in grades, test performance, and classroom behavior, while stage 5 would be a matter of checking with the administration about whether the fraternity's standing was improving, whether policy would again change, and what fraternity member attitudes now were.

Both examples cited start with some changes in the external environment. The coping cycle is no different, however, if the first step is the recognition that something is not right in the *internal* environment. Thus, an organization may sense that employee morale is too low, or that several departments are destructively competing with another, or that a technologically sound process is not being correctly applied, or that management attitudes and practices are failing to elicit adequate motivation and loyalty among employees. Once the organization perceives some change or problem within itself, it must then digest this information and follow a logical course of change as outlined in the five stages. The diagnostic models we reviewed in Chapter 12 are very useful in pinpointing where to look for potential sources of change pressure.

Problems and Pitfalls in the Adaptive Coping Cycle

By considering the adaptive coping cycle as a series of stages, one can identify several points at which difficulties may arise in maintaining and improving effectiveness. Certain problems and pitfalls are characteristically associated with each stage.

1. Failure to sense changes in the environment or actually misperceiving what is happening is one of the most common causes of organizational failure. Many businesses can adjust to new conditions provided the organization can sense when the time is ripe to develop new products, services, or procedures. If the organization has multiple primary functions, as does a university, it becomes especially important to accurately sense changing attitudes about education, the feelings of alumni about contributions, the role of the university in the community, its reputation within the academic community, the morale of its faculty, and so on. Consulting and applied research specialities like market research, consumer psychology, and public opinion polling have developed partly in response to organizational needs for more accurate sensing of internal and external environmental changes.

2. Failure to transmit the relevant information to those parts of the organization which can act upon it is a frequent occurence in large-scale organizations where staff units may be unable to impart certain information to line management. For example, many personnel departments have become convinced that the management process would be more effective if line management would adopt complex assumptions about the nature of employee motivation. But unless this knowledge can be imparted in a meaningful way to line managers, one cannot say that the information has really been imported into the system or properly digested. This example illustrates another difficulty. To change one's assumptions about human nature involves changing a long held set of attitudes, self-images, and working procedures. Such a change will typically be strongly resisted because of its threatening nature—that is, the implication that the former way of functioning has been erroneous. To get the information imported and digested, therefore, might involve a major and lengthy program of influencing attitudes, self-images, and working procedures and must be based on a realistic change model such as will be described later in this chapter.

The difficulties of importing information into the relevant system have led to the use of external consultants or researchers as information transmitters and "change agents." A staff group that strongly senses the existence of a problem may find itself hiring a consultant to reidentify the problem and import it to other parts of the system. The consultant uses his or her prestige to help import the information into those parts of the system that have the power to do something about it, and to help those involved digest the implications of the information.

3. Failure to influence the conversion or production system to make the necessary changes often results from lack of recognition that such changes are necessary and from deeply rooted sources of resistance to change. Organization planners or top managers often naively assume that simply announcing the need for a change and giving orders for the change to be made will produce the desired outcome. In practice, however, resistance to change is a ubiquitous organizational phenomenon. Whether it be an increase in production that is desired, an adaptation to some new technology, or a new work methodology, it is generally found that those workers and managers who are directly affected will resist the change or sabotage it if it is forced upon them.

The major reason for resistance to change is that the conversion or production parts of any organization are themselves systems—they generate ways of working, stable interpersonal relationships, and common norms, values, and techniques of coping and surviving in their own environment. In other words, the subsystems of an organization operate according to the same coping principles as does the whole organization. If the *subsystem* is to change, it must *sense* a change in management policy, be able to *import* this information into itself, *manage* its own change, *stabilize* it, *export* better results in terms of the desires of management, and *obtain feedback* on how it is doing. The line manager desiring the change can, from this point of view, accomplish more by viewing his or her role as that of helping the system to cope rather than giving orders or issuing directives. There is some evidence that one of the best ways to help implement a change is to involve the affected system directly in the decision-making process. The more such a system participates in decisions about how to manage the change, the less likely it is to resist the change and the more stable the change is likely to be (Lewin, 1952; Coch & French, 1948; Bennis, Benne, & Chin, 1969).

The failure to achieve a stable change occurs most frequently when innovations are made in one subgroup without working through the consequences for other subgroups in the organization. Cases can be cited of changes in administrative procedure in one department which were so threatening to another department that they had to be abandoned to preserve the overall morale of the organization (Bavelas & Strauss, 1962). Because the various parts of an organization tend to be linked, a proposed change in one part must be carefully assessed in terms of its likely impact on other parts. Wherever possible, the linkage between systems should be used to positive advantage; that is, if a desired change is successfully implemented in one of the systems, it will tend to spread by itself to other parts of the systems.

A good example of this process would be in changing managers' assumptions about workers' attitudes. If top management can be helped to alter their attitudes, then, because of their strategic linkage to all parts of the organization, their resultant behavior change would *automatically* act as a force on all of their subordinates toward similar changes. The same change in attitudes in the middle or near the bottom of the hierarchy may fail to spread or even to maintain itself because of inadequate upward and lateral linkage to other systems.

4. Once changes have been made within the organization, there remains the problem of exporting the new results. In the case of business concerns, this is a problem of sales and marketing. In the case of other organizations, it may be a problem of communicating as rapidly as possible to the relevant environmental systems the changes which have occurred. It does little good for the fraternity to change its norms of scholastic achievement if it takes so long before

grades improve that the administration has already decided to close the fraternities.

If the organization wants to export information, the problem is one of "advertising." But because advertising typically involves gaining a competitive advantage over another organization, forces toward distorting information are generated, thus reducing the credibility of what is communicated. One role that "third parties" or consultants have played here has been to export *reliable* information about changes in the system. Thus, a neutral faculty member may be appointed jointly by the administration and the fraternity to evaluate changes in members' attitudes. Similarly, we send "political observers" to countries requesting foreign aid to evaluate the validity of their claims that they are changing toward democratic forms of government; government agencies send representatives to industrial firms that claim to have developed the capacity to provide a weapons system or some other product efficiently and cheaply. In all these cases, what is involved is accurate export of information about changes in the system which may not be immediately visible in such indexes as higher production rates or new products and services.

5. Failure to obtain feedback on the success of the change is a common pitfall. The problems here are essentially the same as the problems of sensing changes in the environment in the first place. We need only add that many organizations have explicitly created systems to assess the impact of changes and thus to provide to themselves the necessary feedback information. In the case of internal changes, there may be a research group in the employee relations department whose prime job is to survey employees periodically to determine how they are reacting to changes in management policy; political organizations will run polls immediately after a change in political platform to determine the public's reaction; production control units will assess whether a new process is producing the desired increase in efficiency; and so on. The danger is to assume that because one has decided to do something different that it will work out and not to check on actual results.

In summary, for each stage in the adaptive coping cycle, one can identify characteristic pitfalls and problems. The important point is that the maintenance and increase of organizational effectiveness depends on successful coping, which means that all of the stages must be successfully negotiated somehow. It does little good to have the best market research department in the world if the organization is unable to influence its own production system; nor does it help to have a highly flexible production or conversion operation which cannot sense or digest information about environmental changes.

ORGANIZATIONAL CHANGE
AND DEVELOPMENT

As organizations came to be perceived as dynamic, coping systems, the concepts of how they change and how such change can be influenced and managed began to be refined. In fact, one of the most rapidly expanding areas of organizational psychology during the last several decades has been what has come to be called variously "organization development," "action research," or "applied behavioral science." This section will briefly review the development of this area, examine the assumptions and change theories upon which it rests, and show how the concepts discussed in the previous sections of the book relate to it.

There is little question that the intellectual father of contemporary theories of applied behavioral science, action research, and planned change is Kurt Lewin. His seminal work on leadership style and the experiments on planned change which took place in World War II in an effort to change consumer behavior launched a whole generation of research in group dynamics and the implementation of change programs (Marrow, 1969). Of particular relevance to organizational psychology were the classical change studies done at the Harwood Manufacturing Company, which demonstrated the importance of the involvement in the *planning* of change of those workers who would ultimately be most influenced by the change (Coch & French, 1948; Marrow, Bowers, & Seashore, 1967). The roots of this field are clearly in the systems models that have been advocated throughout this book, but it also represents the coming together of a number of historical strands each of which has influenced in important ways what practitioners of "planned change and organization development" do today:

1. The field of *group dynamics*, especially as developed by Lewin and his followers (Cartwright & Zander, 1968).
2. The field of *sociometry*, out of which developed the concept of role playing and other kinds of social interventions (Moreno, 1934; Jennings, 1950).
3. The field of *applied anthropology*, from which came a strong tradition of careful observation of social systems and an understanding of the subtle internal dynamics of such systems (Whyte, 1943; Horsfall & Arensberg, 1949).
4. *Leadership training and sensitivity training* as developed by the National Training Laboratory in the 1950s and 1960s (Bradford, 1974; Schein & Bennis, 1965).
5. *Clinical and counseling psychology* as developed by Rogers (1961),

Perls and his co-workers (1965), Berne (1964) and others who strongly influenced the consulting and training models used by organizational consultants.

6. *Organizational self-studies* such as those initiated in the 1930s through the 1950s by companies such as Western Electric, American Telephone and Telegraph, Exxon, Union Carbide, General Electric, and Proctor & Gamble. This research brought together organizational psychologists such as Roethlisberger, McGregor, Likert, Blake, Shepard, and Beckhard with far-seeing managers who were willing to explore new approaches to the management of change within their organizations. Out of these contacts came some major action research experiments which helped to refine change theory and intervention skills.

7. *Organization structure and design theories* such as those reviewed which helped to provide theoretical underpinnings for much of the work on organizational processes and linked some of the more classical sociological and anthropological theories to the more applied concepts which were evolving (Simon, 1960; Perrow, 1970; Thompson & McEwen, 1958).

8. *Intergroup and interorganizational theories* which have derived both from the seminal studies of Sherif and his colleagues (1961, 1969) on intergroup conflict and competition, and from the tradition within political science of examining intergroup bargaining and power relationships (Allison, 1971; Lindblom, 1959; Dahl, 1957).

When the field of organization development (OD) became popular with organizations in the 1960s it was dominated by a number of "fads" such as sensitivity training, team building, survey-feedback, transactional analysis, management by objectives, and so on. The faddish use of these techniques has declined somewhat, but the perspective OD gives to managing the process of change has become part of the thinking of most senior managers whether or not they use any of the specialized devices. It is important to recognize the distinction between OD as a philosophy and way of approaching problems versus OD as a set of techniques, because it is the philosophy and the underlying set of assumptions on which it is built that has its roots in research and organization theory. Any given technique such as survey-feedback or sensitivity training can exemplify some of these assumptions but is not automatically consistent with them. Two sets of such assumptions need to be examined, those dealing with action research and those dealing with resistance to change.

Action Research

The essence of the idea of action research goes back to two assumptions which were first espoused by Kurt Lewin:

1. There is nothing so practical as a good theory.
2. If you want to study an organization (system, group) try to change it.

In effect, Lewin was saying that organizations are dynamic systems that we cannot really understand unless we intervene somehow in those dynamics. But intervention cannot and should not be a random process because that would be neither efficient nor ethical. Instead, intervention should be based on a theoretical model of how the system works, and the model should, in ideal circumstances, predict the consequences of the intervention. Whether or not those consequences materialize as predicted then becomes a check on the initial theory. The model of theorizing, intervening, gathering data on the effects of the intervention, and then checking the theory prior to developing the next intervention is the sequence of activities which describes the *action research model*.

Several further assumptions are implicit in this model.

3. Pure research models involving control groups and controlled experimental manipulation are neither feasible nor desirable when dealing with human systems.

They are not feasible because (1) we do not have precise enough measurement to determine what would constitute a "control group" for something as complex as an organization; (2) we cannot support ethically the position that an intervention which is deemed to be of some benefit to organization A can validly be withheld for control purposes from organization B; (3) even if we could measure and justify the control conditions, it is unlikely that we could control the environment to isolate the true causes of variation in the independent and dependent variables; and (4) *any* intervention is likely to affect how an organization functions in multiple ways, so that it becomes difficult to isolate the specific effects of specific interventions (recall the problems of the "Hawthorne effect").

4. A science of groups and organizations can be built on "quasi-experimental" models and an action research philosophy by carefully designing organizational interventions (not experimental treatments) and studying their effects.

Careful design of the interventions implies well-thought-out theory, and studying the effects of the intervention implies the use of objective observation, interviews, measurements, and whatever other techniques are *appropriate* to the evaluation of the intervention to make it as nearly bias-free as possible. However, the true dilemma of the action research model is revealed in the next assumption.

5. Any measurement (unless it is completely unobtrusive) made to evaluate the effects of a prior intervention itself becomes automatically the next intervention.

In human systems the act of being surveyed, interviewed, or observed influences the system. Therefore, whatever measurement or observation system is used should itself be congruent with one's basic intervention theory or one is unwittingly making an undesirable intervention in the process of evaluating a prior intervention. For example, if management decides to evaluate a new supervisory program by means of a survey of employees, it is quite possible that the survey itself will not only measure attitudes toward the new program but actually form those attitudes—the type of question asked, the encouragement to think about the program, the degree of anonymity of the questionnaire, the possibility of sharing data across groups of employees, all will potentially and in unknown ways influence the group surveyed. Not only is it potentially impossible to determine whether a given effect is due to the supervisory program or the survey itself, but after the survey the human system is a different system anyway with new attitudes which now must be taken into account. This phenomenon leads to a sixth critical assumption.

6. The ethics of research interventions cannot be separated from the ethics of consultant/therapist interventions.

This assumption is one of the most important to understand because it is most often ignored in organizational research programs. If any measurement of a human system is to some degree an intervention into that system, then we can only justify a given measurement on the grounds that the measurement itself is a desirable intervention. And what is desirable must be judged on clinical criteria not research criteria. In other words, before a researcher can justify any particular research intervention in an organization, that researcher should be able to justify that particular intervention from a consultant or therapist perspective. If the intervention *could* be harmful from this point of view, then the research itself should be questioned and perhaps abandoned.

For example, an organization-wide program of interviews or survey questionnaires designed to "measure" company morale should not, by this logic, be conducted unless the organization and the researcher jointly decide that *the intervention of measuring everybody is itself a desirable intervention* into the system. The consequences of measuring everyone should be explored independently of the desirability of gathering the basic information, and the researcher should take the role of consultant in this discussion in order to help the organization make a sensible decision.

The logic that pertains here applies not only to groups and organizations but also to individuals. The clinician who uses a variety of techniques to treat a patient learns a great deal about the individual from observing the disparate effects of treatment. But at the same time the clinician must not experiment indiscriminately; he or she must be guided by what is considered ultimately beneficial to the individual. In the same way, the organizational researcher must adopt the role of clinician and be guided by the ethics of clinical practice. Since *any* interaction with the system becomes an intervention, we should be alert to the fact that even *diagnostic* interventions can become potent *action* interventions.

Planned Change Theory

In order to plan effective interventions one needs some kind of comprehensive change theory which explains how to initiate change, how to manage the total change process, and how to stabilize desired change outcomes. The problem of initiating change is especially salient because of the common observation that people resist change, even when the goals are apparently highly desirable. There are many theories of change reflecting a spectrum from revolution to evolution (Hornstein, Bunker, Burke, Gindes, & Lewicki, 1971; Bennis et al., 1969). For purposes of understanding how planned change occurs in groups and organizations of the kind we have discussed here, it is most useful to start with the model first proposed by Lewin (1952) and Lippitt and his collaborators (1958) in their analysis of planned change. Schein subsequently elaborated this model and used it to try to understand various phenomena, ranging from the coercive persuasion of prisoners of war to the kinds of change that occur in educational or developmental settings (Schein, Schneier, & Barker, 1961; Schein, 1961; Schein & Bennis, 1965; Schein, 1972). Several assumptions underlie this model:

1. Any change process involves not only learning something new, but *unlearning* something that is already present and possibly well integrated into the personality and social relationships of the individual.

2. No change will occur unless there is motivation to change, and if such motivation to change is not already present, the induction of that motivation is often the most difficult part of the change process.

3. Organizational changes such as new structures, processes, reward systems, and so on occur only through individual changes in key members of the organization; hence organizational change is always mediated through individual changes.

4. Most adult change involves attitudes, values, and self-images, and the unlearning of present responses in these areas is initially *inherently* painful and threatening.

5. Change is a multistage cycle similar to the adaptive coping cycle previously reviewed, and all stages must be negotiated somehow or other before a stable change can be said to have taken place.

Stage 1: Unfreezing—the Creation of Motivation to Change

The creation of motivation to change is a complex process that involves three specific mechanisms, all of which must be operating in order for the individual to feel "motivated" to unlearn present behavior or attitudes:

Mechanism 1: Present behavior or attitudes must actually be *disconfirmed*, or must fail to be confirmed over a period of time. In other words, the individual discovers that his or her assumptions about the world are not validated or that some behavior does not lead to expected outcomes and may even lead to undesirable outcomes. Such disconfirmation can arise from any of a wide variety of sources and is the primary source of pain or discomfort that initiates a change process. If everything is working fine there is no discomfort and hence no motivation to change. The most serious ethical questions surrounding the intervention process have to do with the question of when it is legitimate to *induce* discomfort by providing the person with information that will be discomforting. If others have done the disconfirming and the person then comes to the consultant for help, there is obviously less of an ethical issue.

Mechanism 2: The disconfirmation must set up sufficient guilt or *anxiety* to motivate a change. If the discomfort is at a low level, it is easily dealt with by denial or by avoidance of the disconfirming source. However, if the person realizes that he or she has really failed to live up to some important value or ideal (guilt) or is in danger of being overwhelmed by inner feelings or may miss some important rewards he or she is seeking (anxiety), then the discomfort becomes a real motivator. However, the person may still seek to use defenses to avoid the pain of change.

Mechanism 3: The creation of *psychological safety*, either by reducing barriers to change or by reducing the threat inherent in the recognition of past failures, is the critical third ingredient. The role of change agent here is to make the person feel secure and capable of changing without reducing the power or validity of the disconfirming information. No matter how much pressure is brought to bear on a person to change, no change will occur until that person feels it is safe to give up the old responses and to enter the uncertainty of learning something new. Probably the single most difficult aspect of initiating change is the balancing of painful disconfirming messages with reassurance that change is possible and can be embarked upon with some sense of personal safety. Once the person has accepted the disconfirming message and has become motivated to change because he or she feels it is safe to change, some new learning can take place.

Stage 2: Changing—Developing New Attitudes and Behaviors on the Basis of New Information and Cognitive Redefinition

The effect of creating a motivation to change is to open the person up to new sources of information and new concepts or new ways of looking at old information (cognitive redefinition). This process occurs through one of two mechanisms:

Mechanism 1: Identification with a role model, mentor, friend, or some other person and learning to see things from that other person's point of view. One of the most powerful ways of learning a new point of view or concept or attitude is to see it in operation in another person and to use that person as a role model for one's own new attitudes or behavior. Change agents sometimes become the target of identification which is why it is so important that the consultant's behavior be totally congruent with the new attitudes or behaviors to be learned. However, identification can also be a very limiting way of learning in that it focuses the person too much on a single source of information.

Mechanism 2: Scanning the environment for information specifically relevant to one's particular problem and the selection of information from multiple sources is more difficult but often produces more valid change. What we learn from a role model may not fit our particular personality. What we learn by scanning fits by definition, since we only use relevant information and remain in control of what we use.

It should be noted that change is a cognitive process which is facilitated by the obtaining of new information and concepts. But the person will not pay attention to that information or try to learn new concepts unless there is real motivation to change. Thus, many change programs err in moving directly to stage 2 without first testing whether they can in fact tap any motivation to change. If motivation is not there, the change program must move to the more difficult emotional level of attempting to create circumstances which will induce motivation.

Stage 3: Re-Freezing—Stabilizing the Changes

It is often found that programs designed to induce attitudinal changes do have observable effects during the training period but do not last once the person is back in a normal routine. The problem usually is that the new things learned either did not fit into the person's total personality or are in varying degrees out of line with what his or her significant relationships will tolerate. The manager learns a new attitude toward subordinates but the manager's own boss and subordinates are really more comfortable with the old attitudes, so they immediately begin to disconfirm the new attitudes and thus initiate a new cycle of change back toward the original state. Thus, to ensure the stability of any change requires specific attention to the integration of the new responses.

Mechanism 1: The person should have an opportunity of testing whether the new attitudes or behaviors really *fit his or her self-concept*, are congruent with other parts of the personality, and can be integrated comfortably. It should be noted that one advantage of scanning over identification as a change mechanism is that from the start the person is more likely to select only those responses which fit him or her. The consultant or change agent should be cautious about pronouncing initial change as stable, especially if it is based on identification or imitation.

Mechanism 2: The person should have an opportunity to test whether *significant others will accept and confirm* the new attitudes and behavior patterns; alternatively, the change program should be targeted at sets of people or groups who will be able to reinforce the new behaviors in each other. The second approach is one of the reasons why team training in organizations may be more powerful than individual training: It ensures that behavior patterns learned and reinforced in concert will become part of each member's behavioral repertoire. This kind of change may require a good deal more give-and-take and thus may be initially slower but it will last longer.

Within this framework, the consultant or change agent has to employ various tactics to ensure that each stage and/or mechanism will be properly negotiated. If the target is organizational change, not merely individual change, further models are needed to determine with whom to begin a change process—how powerful is a certain individual, how well linked to others in the organization, how ready to change? The complexity of organizational change derives not only from the difficulty of estimating the probability of a specific change in *individual* attitudes but from the complexity of *orchestrating change in various individuals* to produce an organizational outcome.

The Role of the Consultant in Organization Development—Process Consultation

Having examined the assumptions which underlie the two concepts of action research and planned change, we can now conclude our discussion of organization development by examining further the role of change agent or consultant in the total process of organization change. If we accept the assumption that individuals, groups, and organizations as a whole are best thought of as complex dynamic systems, and if we accept the second assumption that "health" or effectiveness must ultimately be defined by some kind of ability to cope effectively, it follows that *the role of the change agent or consultant is to help the system improve in its inherent capacity to cope.* This logic leads to the concept of *process consultation,* in which the role of the consultant is to help the organization diagnose itself, to select its own coping responses, and to determine its own progress (Schein, 1969, 1978). The consultant must be an expert at helping the organization to help itself, which means awareness of systems dynamics and processes, and real expertness in the skills of helping.

It is much less clear whether the consultant should ever assume the role of expert or "doctor," which would imply that the change agent knows what is best for the organization. The organization development philosophy would argue that it is more valid for the consultant to be worried about the *internal integration* of the organization. The process consultant should *surface* inconsistent strategies which may, for example, maximize profit in the short run at the expense of morale in the long run. But by this same logic the consultant should also point out strategies that may be maximizing short-run morale at the expense of long-run profit. It should *not* be the role of the consultant to influence the organization toward one or the other of those goals per se.

To summarize so far, I do *not* believe it should be the role of the OD consultant to humanize the organization or to argue for participative management or Theory Y or any other specific theory. I *do* believe it is the role of the OD consultant to surface whatever problems the individual manager or the organization as a whole may be experiencing around efforts to obtain self-insight, to cope effectively, to test reality, and to integrate its efforts toward long-range effectiveness. The theoretical basis for this argument is that (1) clients want basically to promote a self-image of being able to help themselves; (2) only the client knows what kind of remedial action will ultimately work; and (3) the skills of self-diagnosis and coping are the most important things to learn. On a practical level one could also point out that the state of knowledge of how organizations work is, at the present time, not sufficient for consultants to make expert recommendations even if they thought that was their role.

Research on the effects of OD interventions has been sparse and inconclusive, partly because of the technical difficulties presented by the action research format. The problems in evaluating the effects of different kinds of organizational interventions are akin to those of evaluating teaching strategies or methods of psychotherapy. Organization development is a "clinical area" in which the accumulation of carefully documented cases will eventually provide insight into what works. While such clinical data are being accumulated, change agents must carefully assess their own assumptions and, if they work from assumptions other than those mentioned in connection with action research and planned change, should have a well-thought-out model of their own to justify whatever interventions they make.

CONCLUSION: ORGANIZATIONAL CONDITIONS FOR EFFECTIVE COPING

This chapter began with some general criteria of organizational effectiveness or health. We then specified the coping processes that appear necessary in a rapidly changing environment in order to maintain or increase effectiveness, and went on to describe organization development as one major method of improving the coping process. In this concluding section, I would like to outline what *internal organizational conditions* appear to be necessary for effective coping to occur. To some extent the argument becomes circular, because some degree of health must be present for health to maintain itself or increase. The organizational conditions we identify will, therefore, resemble somewhat the ultimate criteria of health cited earlier:

1. Successful coping requires the ability to take in and communicate information reliably and validly.
2. Successful coping requires internal flexibility and creativity to make the changes which are demanded by the information obtained.
3. Successful coping requires integration of and commitment to the multiple goals of the organization, from which comes the willingness to change when necessary.
4. Successful coping requires an internal climate of support and freedom from threat, since being threatened undermines good communications, reduces flexibility, and stimulates self-protection rather than concern for the total system.
5. Successful coping requires the ability to continuously redesign the organization's structure to be congruent with its goal and tasks.

These five conditions are not easy to achieve in a complex system such as a large organization, but some guidelines for their achievement can be outlined. I would like to present these guidelines in terms of the basic variables provided in the previous chapters of this book.[1]

1. If we look first at the *recruitment and socialization* of human resources, we can ask whether the methods currently being used for the selection, testing, and training of employees are likely to produce the kind of image in the minds of employees that the organization wants? If these methods communicate indifference to personal needs and capacities, it is possible that employees will learn early in their career to withhold involvment, to make their performance routine, and to respond to demands for changes by feeling threatened and anxious rather than helpful and committed. If the organization is genuinely concerned about building long-range effectiveness, must it not develop a system for hiring and socializing employees which makes them feel wanted, secure, meaningfully engaged in their jobs, and positively committed to organizational goals? Furthermore, must it not also build into its career development system a concern for genuine psychological growth in order to ensure the flexibility and creativity that may be required at some future time? It would appear that one of the best ways to guarantee an ability to cope with an unpredictable environment would be to encourage all members of the organization to be open to change (that is, to develop), even at the expense of some short-run efficiency.

2. Turning next to the *utilization of employees and the psychological contract*, it would appear evident that if the organization

---

[1] In the next several pages I will talk of "the organization" as if it were an entity to highlight the fact that the collective decisions of key managers eventually come to be perceived as what "the organization" is doing.

expects its members to be committed and flexible and to work toward optimal interpersonal relationships for the sake of overall organizational effectiveness, it is in effect asking them to be morally involved in the enterprise, to be committed to organizational goals and to put intrinsic value on them. Clearly, if the organization expects this kind of commitment, it must for its part provide rewards and conditions consistent with such involvement. It cannot obtain commitment, creativity, and flexibility simply by handing out a larger paycheck; there must be the possibility of obtaining non-economic rewards such as autonomy, genuine responsibility, and opportunities for challenge and psychological growth.

Probably the most important thing the organization can do in this regard is to develop assumptions about people which fit reality. This, in turn, implies some willingness to find out what each person is like and what he or she truly wants at different career and life stages. By making broad generalizations about people, managers not only run the risk of being wrong about the empirical realities, but, perhaps worse, such generalizations insult employees by assuming that they are all basically alike. If managers begin to expose and test their assumptions, they will not only begin to develop a method for learning what the facts are, but will also communicate a degree of concern for workers that will reduce their feelings of being threatened or demeaned. As assumptions become increasingly realistic, management and leadership practices will begin to build the kind of climate that is needed for reliable and valid communication, creative effort, flexibility, and commitment over the long run.

3. Next, let us look at the problem of *groups and intergroup relations*. There is little question that groups are an integral part of any organization and that the basic choice is not whether to have them but, rather, how to create conditions under which group forces work toward organizational goals rather than counter to them. One aspect of the solution is alluded to in the first two guidelines, for the evidence seems quite clear that if employees feel threatened, demeaned, and unappreciated they will form together into *anti*management groups. To prevent such groups from forming, therefore, requires management practices that are less threatening toward employees and more likely to enable them to integrate personal needs and organizational goals.

A second part of the answer lies in training for effective group membership and leadership. Though most of us have had much experience in groups, it is unlikely that we have had the opportunity to focus clearly on those factors that make groups more or less effective. If members of the organization develop a better understanding of how groups work, they are less likely to form groups that are bound to fail. If groups are formed that can achieve some degree of psychological success, and if this success is perceived to be in part the result of good management, then group forces are more likely to coalesce with organizational goals. It takes more than good intentions to make an effective group. It requires knowledge of how groups work and skill in managing group processes.

When we turn to problems of intergroup competition, it seems clear that competition between the units or groups *of a single organization or system* must in the long run reduce effectiveness, because competition leads to faulty communication, to greater pressures for conformity and hence less flexibility, and to commitment to subgroup rather than total organizational goals. The dilemma is that competition also produces very high levels of motivation and productivity. As many case examples have shown, however, when organizational units are stimulated into competition, the short-run gains of increased production are greatly outweighed by the long-run losses of reduced intergroup communication and internal flexibility. What organizations must develop are programs that obtain motivation and commitment in an integrative manner, that keep communication channels between subparts open, that maintain the focus on total organizational performance rather than individual or subgroup performance, and that permit conflict to be confronted and worked through. Because it is very difficult to undo intergroup conflict, it is better to avoid it in the first place.

4. One of the most difficult aspects of the *design of organizations* is how to keep the right people communicating about the right tasks at the right time and with the right problem-solving and collaborative attitudes. The problem of organization design and structure is thus completely intertwined with the processes used to manage the people in whatever structure is chosen. To remain healthy an organization must see the problem of perpetual *redesign* of its structure as an essential coping mechanism, yet one of the most difficult and frustrating because restructuring is both time- and energy-consuming.

5. Finally, let us look once again at *leadership*. First, leadership is best thought of as a function within the organization rather than the trait of an individual. It can be distributed among the members of a group or organization, and is not automatically vested in the chairperson or whoever has formal authority. Good leadership and good membership, therefore, blend into each other in an effective organization. It is just as much the task of a member to help the group reach its goals as it is the task of the formal leader.

Second, organizational leadership has a unique obligation to manage the relationships between a system and its environment, particularly in reference to the key functions of setting goals for the organization and defining the values or norms in terms of which the organization must basically develop its sense of identity. This function must be fulfilled by those members who are in contact with the organization-environment boundary and who have the power to set policy for the organization. As such, it is a critical responsibility that usually falls to the organization's top executives. If the organization does not have clear goals and cannot develop a sense of identity, there is nothing to be committed to and nothing to communicate about. At the same time, top executives do not have to *impose* goals and identity unilaterally. There is no reason why the organization cannot develop its goals and identity collaboratively and participatively, engaging every member down to the lowest echelons in the process if it chooses to do so. What the top executives must do is to ensure that goals are set somehow, but they may choose a variety of ways of allowing this to occur.

I have tried to argue for an approach to organizational effectiveness which hinges upon good communication, flexibility, creativity, and genuine psychological commitment. These conditions are to be obtained by (1) recruitment, selection, and socialization practices that stimulate rather than demean people; (2) more realistic psychological relationships based on a more realistic psychological contract and the recognition of developmental changes in people; (3) more effective group action; (4) perpetual redesign of organization structures; and (5) better leadership in terms of the activities of goal setting and value definition. The argument is not based on the assumption that this would be nice for people or would make them feel better. Rather, the argument is that open systems work better if their members are in good communication with each other, are committed, and are creative and flexible.

Bibliography

Alderfer, C. P. *Existence, relatedness, and growth: Human needs in organizational settings.* New York: Free Press, 1972.

Alderfer, C. P. Group and intergroup relations. In J. R. Hackman, & J. L. Suttle (Eds.), *Improving life at work.* Santa Monica, Calif.: Goodyear, 1977.

Allen, T. J. *Managing the flow of technology.* Cambridge, Mass.: MIT Press, 1977.

Allison, G. T. *Essence of decision.* Boston: Little-Brown, 1971.

Argyris, C. *Personality and organization.* New York: Harper & Row, 1957.

Argyris, C. *Understanding organizational behavior.* Homewood, Ill.: Dorsey, 1960.

Argyris, C. *Integrating the individual and the organization.* New York: Wiley, 1964.

Argyris, C. Leadership, learning, and changing the status quo. *Organizational Dynamics*, Winter 1976, pp. 29–43.

Argyris, C., & Schon, D. *Theory in practice: Increasing professional effectiveness.* San Francisco: Jossey-Bass, 1974.

Argyris, C., & Schon, D. A. *Organizational learning: A theory of action perspective.* Reading, Mass.: Addison-Wesley, 1978.

Asch, S. E. Effects of group pressure upon the modification and distortion of judgments. In H. Guetzkow (Ed.), *Groups, leadership, and men.* Pittsburgh: Carnegie Press, 1951.

Bailyn, L., & Schein, E. H. Where are they now and how are they doing? *Technology Review*, 1972, 74, 3–11.

Bailyn, L., & Schein, E. H. Life/career considerations as indicators of quality of employment. In A. D. Biderman & T. F. Drury, *Measuring work quality for social reporting.* New York: Wiley (Sage Publications), 1976.

Bailyn, L. & Schein, E. H. *Living with technology: Issues at mid-careers.* Cambridge, Mass.: MIT Press, 1980.

Baldridge, J. V. *Power and conflict in the university.* New York: Wiley, 1971.

Bales, R. F. Task roles and social roles in problem solving groups. In N. Maccoby et al. (Eds.), *Readings in social psychology, 3d ed.* New York: Holt, Rinehart, & Winston, 1958.

Balzer, R. *Clockwork.* Garden City, New York: Doubleday, 1976.

Barash, D. P. *Sociobiology and behavior.* New York: Elsevier, 1977.

Barnard, C. I. *The functions of the executive.* Cambridge, Mass.: Harvard University Press, 1938.

Bass, B. M. *Organizational psychology.* Boston: Allyn & Bacon, 1965.

Bateson, G. *Steps to an ecology of mind.* New York: Ballantine, 1972.

Bavelas, A., & Strauss, G. Group dynamics and intergroup relations. In K. Benne, & R. Chin, (Eds.), *The Planning of Change.* New York: Holt, Rinehart, and Winston, 1962.

Beckhard, R. *Organization development: Strategies and models.* Reading, Mass.: Addison-Wesley, 1969.

Beckhard, R., & Harris, R. T. *Organizational transitions: Managing complex change.* Reading, Mass.: Addison-Wesley, 1977.

Benne, K. D., & Sheats, P. Functional roles of group members. *Journal of Social Issues,* 1948, *4,* 41–49.

Bennis, W. G. Revisionist theory of leadership. *Harvard Business Review,* 1961, *39,* 26ff.

Bennis, W. G. Toward a truly scientific management: The concept of organizational health. *General Systems Yearbook,* 1962, *7,* 269–282.

Bennis, W. G. *Changing organizations.* New York: McGraw-Hill, 1966.

Bennis, W. G. *The unconscious conspiracy: Why leaders can't lead.* New York: AMACON, 1976.

Bennis, W. G., Benne, K. D., & Chin, R. *The planning of change,* 2nd ed., New York: Holt, Rinehart, and Winston, 1969.

Berne, E. *Games people play.* New York: Grove Press, 1964.

Blake, R. R., & Mouton, J. S. Reactions to intergroup competition under win-lose conditions. *Management Science,* 1961, *7,* 420–435.

Blake, R. R., & Mouton, J. S. Headquarters-field team training for organizational improvements. *Journal of the American Society of Training Directors,* 1962, *16.*

Blake, R. R., & Mouton, J. S. *The managerial grid.* Houston, Tex.: Gulf Publishing, 1964.

Blake, R. R., & Mouton, J. S. *Consultation.* Reading, Mass.: Addison-Wesley, 1976.

Blau, P. M., & Scott, W. R. *Formal organizations.* San Francisco: Chandler, 1962.

Blauner, R. *Alienation and freedom.* Chicago: University of Chicago Press, 1964.

Bradford, L. P. *National training laboratories: Its history 1947–1970.* Bethel, Maine: National Training Laboratories, 1974.

Bradford, L. P., Gibb, J. R., & Benne, K. D. (Eds.) *T-Group theory and laboratory method.* New York: Wiley, 1964.

Burns, T., & Stalker, G. M. *The managment of innovation.* London: Tavistock Publications., 1961.

Cartwright, D. (Ed.) *Studies in social power.* Ann Arbor, Mich.: University of Michigan Press, 1959.

Cartwright, D., & Zander, A. *Group dynamics: Research and theory.* New York: Harper & Row, 1968.

Chander, A. D., Jr. *Strategy and structure.* Cambridge, Mass.: MIT Press, 1962.

Clark, J. V., & Krone, C. G. Towards an overall view of organization development in the early seventies. In J. Thomas & W. G. Bennis, (Eds.), *Management of change and conflict.* Baltimore: Penguin Books, 1972.

Coch, L., & French, J. R. P. Overcoming resistance to change. *Human Relations,* 1948, *1,* 512–532.

Cooley, C. H. *Human nature and the social order.* New York: Scribners, 1922.

Cummings, T. G., & Srivastva, S. *Management of work: A socio-technical systems approach.* Kent, Ohio: Kent State University Press, 1977.

Cyert, R. M., & March, J. G. *A behavioral theory of the firm.* Englewood Cliffs, N.J.: Prentice-Hall, 1963.

Dahl, R. A. The concept of power. *Behavioral Science,* 1957, *2,* 201–218.

Dalton, G. W., Thompson, P. H., & Price, R. Career Stages: A model of professional careers in organizations. *Organizational Dynamics,* 1977, *6,* 19–42.

Dalton, M. *Men who manage.* New York: Wiley, 1959.

Davis, J. H., Laughlin, P. R., & Komorita, S. S. The social psychology of small groups: Cooperative and mixed motive interaction. *Annual Review of Psychology,* 1976, *27,* 501–541.

Davis, L. E. Toward a theory of job design. *Journal of Industrial Engineering,* 1957, *8,* 305–309.

Davis, L. E. The design of jobs. *Industrial Relations*, 1966, *6*, 21–45.

Davis, S. M. *Comparative management*. Englewood Cliffs, N.J.: Prentice-Hall, 1971.

Davis, L. E., & Cherns, A. B. *The quality of working life, 2 vols.* New York: Free Press, 1975.

Davis, S. M., & Lawrence, P. R. *Matrix.* Reading, Mass.: Addison-Wesley, 1977.

Drucker, P. F. *The practice of management.* New York: Harper & Row, 1954.

Dubin, R. Industrial workers' worlds. *Social Problems*, 1956, *3*, 131–142.

Dubin, R. Work in modern society. In R. Dubin, (Ed.), *Handbook of work, organization, and society.* Chicago, Ill.: Rand-McNally, 1976.

Duncan, R. B. The characteristics of organizational environments and perceived environmental uncertainty. *Administrative Science Quarterly*, 1972, *17*, 313–327.

Duncan, R. B. Multiple decision-making structures in adapting to environmental uncertainty: The impact on organizational effectiveness. *Human Relations*, 1973, *26*, 273–291.

Dyer, W. G. *The sensitive manipulator.* Provo, Utah: Brigham Young University Press, 1972.

Dyer, W. G. *Team building.* Reading Mass.: Addison-Wesley, 1977.

Emery, F. E., & Thorsrud, E. *Form and content in industrial democracy.* London: Tavistock Publications, 1969.

Emery, F. E., & Trist, E. L. The causal texture of organizational environments. *Human Relations*, 1965, *18*, 21–32.

Etzioni, A. *Complex organizations.* New York: Holt, Rinehart and Winston, 1961.

Evan, W. M. (Ed.). *Inter-organizational relations.* Philadelphia: University of Pennsylvania Press, 1978.

Farris, G. Organizational factors and individual performance: A longitudinal study. *Journal of Applied Psychology*, 1969, *53*, 87–92.

Festinger, L., Schachter, S., & Back, K. *Social pressures in informal groups: A study of a housing project.* New York: Harper & Row, 1950.

Fiedler, F. E. *A theory of leadership effectiveness.* New York: McGraw-Hill, 1967.

Fiedler, F. E. Validation and extension of the contingency model of leadership effectiveness: A review of empirical findings. *Psychological Bulletin*, 1971, *76*, 128–148.

Fiedler, F. E., Chemers, M. M., & Mahar, L. *Improving leadership effectiveness: The leader match concept.* New York: Wiley, 1976.

Fleishman, E. A. Leadership climate, human relations training, and supervisory behavior. *Personnel Psychology*, 1953, *6*, 205–222.

Fleishman, E. A. Twenty years of consideration and structure. In E. A. Fleishman & J. G. Hunt (Eds.), *Current developments in the study of leadership*. Carbondale, Ill. Southern Illinois University Press, 1973.

Ford, R. N. Job enrichment lessons from AT & T. *Harvard Business Review*, January–February, 1973, pp. 96–106.

Frost, C., Wakeley, J. H., & Ruh, R. A. *The Scanlon plan for organization development*. East Lansing, Mich.: Michigan State University Press, 1974.

Galbraith, J. *Designing complex organizations*. Reading, Mass.: Addison-Wesley, 1973.

Galbraith, J. *Organization design*. Reading, Mass.: Addison-Wesley, 1977.

Gellerman, S. W. *Motivation and productivity*. New York: American Management Association, 1963.

Ghiselli, E. E. *Explorations in managerial talent*. Pacific Palisades, Calif.: Goodyear, 1971.

Gibb, C. A. Leadership. In G. Lindzey & E. Arenson, (Eds.), *Handbook of social psychology*, 2nd ed. Reading, Mass.: Addison-Wesley, 1969.

Goffman, E. *The presentation of self in everyday life*. New York: Doubleday, 1959.

Goffman, E. *Behavior in public places*. New York: Free Press, 1963.

Goffman, E. *Interaction ritual*. Chicago: Aldine, 1967.

Grusky, O. Authoritarianism and effective indoctrination: A case study. *Administrative Science Quarterly*, 1962, *7*, 79–95.

Hackman, J. R. Work design, In J. R. Hackman & J. L. Suttle (Eds.), *Improving life at work*. Santa Monica, Calif.: Goodyear, 1977.

Hackman, J. R., & Lawler, E. E. Employee reactions to job characteristics. *Journal of Applied Psychology Monograph*, 1971, pp. 259–286.

Hackman, J. R., & Oldham, G. R. Development of the job diagnostic survey. *Journal of Applied Psychology*, 1975, *60*, 159–170.

Hackman, J. R., & Oldham, G. R. *Work redesign*. Reading, Mass.: Addison-Wesley, 1979.

Haire, M. Psychological problems relevant to business and industry. *Psychological Bulletin*, 1959, *56*, 169–194.

Hall, D. T. *Careers in organizations*. Pacific Palisades, Calif.: Goodyear, 1976.

Hall, E. *The silent language*. New York: Doubleday, 1959.

Hall, E. *The hidden dimension*. New York: Doubleday, 1966.

Hall, E. *Beyond culture*. New York: Anchor, 1977.

Harbison, F., & Myers, C. A. *Management in the industrial world*. New York: McGraw-Hill, 1959.

Harrell, T. W., & Harrell, M. S. The personality of MBA's who reach general management early. *Personnel Psychology*, 1973, *26*, 127–134.

Harris, F. G., & Little, R. W. Military organization and social psychiatry. *Symposium on Preventive and Social Psychiatry.* Washington, D.C.: Walter Reed Army Institute of Research, 1957.

Harris, T. A. *I'm ok: you're ok.* New York: Avon, 1967.

Helmreich, R., Bakeman, R., & Scherwitz, L. The study of small groups. *Annual Review of Psychology,* 1973, *24,* 337–354.

Hemphill, J. K. *Leader behavior description.* Columbus, Ohio: Ohio State University, 1950.

Herbst, P. G. *Autonomous group functioning.* London: Tavistock Publications, 1962.

Hersey, P., & Blanchard, K. H. *Management of organizational behavior,* 3rd ed. Englewood Cliffs, N.J.: Prentice-Hall, 1977.

Herzberg, F. *Work and the nature of man.* Cleveland: World Publishing Co., 1966.

Herzberg, F. One more time: How do you motivate employees? *Harvard Business Review,* January–February 1968, pp. 53–62.

Herzberg, F., Mausner, B., & Snyderman, B. *The motivation to work.* New York: Wiley, 1959.

Hickson, D. J., Butler, R. J., Axelson, R., & Wilson, D. Decision coalitions. In B. King, S. Streufert & F. E. Fiedler (Eds.), *Managerial control and organizational democracy.* New York: Wiley, 1978.

Hickson, D. J., Pugh, D. S., & Pheysey, D. C. Operations technology and organizational structure: An empirical re-appraisal. *Administrative Science Quarterly,* 1969, *14,* 378–397.

Holland, J. L. *The psychology of vocational choice.* Waltham, Mass.: Blaisdell, 1966.

Holland, J. L. *Making vocational choices: A theory of careers.* Englewood Cliffs, N.J.: Prentice-Hall, 1973.

Homans, G. *The human group.* New York: Harcourt, Brace, 1950.

Homans, G. *Social behavior: Its elementary forms.* New York: Harcourt, Brace, 1961.

Hornstein, H. A., Bunker, B. B., Burke, W. W., Gindes, M., & Lewicki, R. J. *Social intervention.* New York: Free Press, 1971.

Horsfall, A., & Arensberg, C. Teamwork and productivity in a shoe factory. *Human Organization.* 1949, *8,* 13–25.

Hosking, D., & Schriesheim, C. Review of Fiedler et al., *Improving leadership effectiveness: The leader match concept* (New York: Wiley, 1976). *Administrative Science Quarterly,* 1978, *23,* 496–504.

House, R. A. A path-goal theory of leader effectiveness. *Adminstrative Science Quarterly,* 1971, *16,* 321–338.

Hughes, E. C. *Men and their work.* Glencoe, Ill.: Free Press, 1958.

Jahoda, M. *Current concepts of positive mental health.* New York: Basic Books, 1958.

Janis, I. L. *Victims of group think.* Boston: Houghton-Mifflin, 1972.

Janis, I. L., & King, B. T. The influence of role playing on opinion change. *Journal of Abnormal and Social Psychology,* 1954, *69,* 211–218.

Janis, I. L., & Mann, L. *Decision making.* New York: Free Press, 1977.

Jasinski, F. J. Technological delimitations of reciprocal relationships: A study of interaction patterns in industry. *Human Organization,* 1956, *15,* No. 2.

Jennings, H. H. *Leadership and isolation,* 2nd ed. New York: Longmans Green, 1950.

Kahn, R. L., Wolfe, D. M., Quinn, R. P., Snoek, J. D., & Rosenthal, R. A. *Organizational stress: Studies in role conflict and ambiguity.* New York: Wiley, 1964.

Katz, D., & Kahn, R. L. *The social psychology of organizations.* New York: Wiley, 1966.

Katz, D., Maccoby, N., & Morse, N. C. *Productivity, supervision, and morale in an office situation.* Ann Arbor, Mich.: Institute for Social Research, 1950.

Katz, E., & Lazarsfeld, P. F. *Personal influence.* Glencoe, Ill.: Free Press, 1955.

Katz, R. The influence of group conflict on leadership effectiveness. *Organizational behavior and human performance,* 1977, *20,* 265–286.

Katz, R. Job longevity as a situational factor in job satisfaction. *Administrative Science Quarterly,* 1978, *23,* 204–223.

Katz, R., & Van Maanen, J. The loci of work satisfaction. *Human Relations,* 1977, *30,* 469–486.

Keen, P. G. W., & Scott-Morton, M. S. *Decision support systems: An organizational perspective.* Reading, Mass.: Addison-Wesley, 1978.

Koontz, H., & O'Donnell, C. *Principles of management,* 5th ed. New York: McGraw-Hill, 1972.

Kotter, J. P. The psychological contract. *California Management Review,* 1973, *15,* 91–99.

Kotter, J. P. *Organizational dynamics: Diagnosis and intervention.* Reading, Mass.: Addison-Wesley, 1978.

Krone, C. G. Open systems redesign. In J. D. Adams, (Ed.), *Theory and method in organization development: An evolutionary process.* Arlington, Va.: NTL Institute for Applied Behavioral Science, 1974.

Ladd, E. C., & Lipsett, S. M. *The divided academy.* New York: McGraw-Hill, 1975.

Larson, L. L., Hunt, J. G., & Osborn, R. N. The great leader behavior myth.

Proceedings of the Academy of Management, 1975, pp. 170–172.

Lawler, E. E., III. *Pay and organizational effectiveness*. New York: McGraw-Hill, 1971.

Lawler, E. E., III. Pay, participation, and organizational change. In E. L. Cass & F. G. Zimmer (Eds.), *Man and work in society*. New York: Van Nostrand Reinhold, 1975.

Lawrence, P. R., & Lorsch, J. W. *Organization and environment: Managing differentiation and integration*. Boston: Harvard Graduate School of Business Administration, 1967.

Lawrence, P. R., & Lorsch, J. W. *Developing organizations: Diagnosis and action*. Reading, Mass.: Addison-Wesley, 1969.

Leavitt, H. J. Some effects of certain communication patterns on group performance. *Journal of Abnormal and Social Psychology*, 1951, 46, 38–50.

Leavitt, H. J. *The social science of organizations: Four perspectives*. Englewood Cliffs, N.J.: Prentice-Hall, 1963.

Leavitt, H. J. Suppose we took groups seriously? In E. L. Cass & F. G. Zimmer, (Eds.), *Man and work in society*. New York: Van Nostrand Reinhold, 1975.

Lesieur, F. *The Scanlon plan*. New York: Wiley, 1958.

Levinson, H. *Men, management, and mental health*. Cambridge, Mass.: Harvard University Press, 1962.

Levinson, H. *The exceptional executive: A psychological conception*. Cambridge, Mass.: Harvard University Press, 1968.

Lewin, K. Group decision and social change. In G. E. Swanson, T. N. Newcomb, & E. L. Hartley (Eds.), *Reading in social psychology*, rev. ed. New York: Holt, 1952.

Lieberman, S. The effects of changes in roles on the attitudes of role occupants. *Human Relations*, 1956, 9, 385–402.

Likert, R. *New patterns of management*. New York: McGraw-Hill, 1961.

Likert, R. *The human organization*. New York: McGraw-Hill, 1967.

Lindblom, C. E. The science of muddling through. *Public Administration Review*, 1959, 19, 79–99.

Lindblom, C. E. *The intelligence of democracy*. New York: Free Press, 1965.

Lindholm, R., & Norstedt, J. *The Volvo report*. Stockholm: Swedish Employers' Confederation, 1975.

Lippitt, R., Watson, J., & Westley, B. *The dynamics of planned change*. New York: Harcourt, Brace, 1958.

Lorenz, K., & Leyhausen, P. *Motivation of human and animal behavior*. New York: Van Nostrand Reinhold, 1973.

Lowin, A., & Craig, J. R. The influence of level of performance on managerial style. *Organizational Behavior and Human Performance*, 1968, *3*, 440–458.

Luthans, F. *Introduction to management: A contingency approach.* New York: McGraw-Hill, 1976.

Mahoney, T., & Frost, P. The role of technology in models of organizational effectiveness. *Organizational Behavior and Human Performance*, 1974, *11*, 122–138.

Maier, N. R. F. *Psychology in industrial organizations.* Boston: Houghton-Mifflin, 1973.

March, J. G., & Simon, H. A. *Organizations.* New York: Wiley, 1958.

Marquis, D. G. Individual responsibility and group decisions involving risk. *Industrial Management Review*, 1962, *3*, 8–23.

Marquis, D. G., & Reitz, H. J. Effects of uncertainty on risk taking in individual and group decisions. *Behavioral Science*, 1969, *4*, 181–188.

Marrow, A. J. *The practical theorist: The life and work of Kurt Lewin.* New York: Basic Books, 1969.

Marrow, A. J., Bowers, D. G., & Seashore, S. E. *Management by participation.* New York: Harper & Row, 1967.

Maslow, A. *Motivation and personality.* New York: Harper, 1954.

Mayo, E. *The social problems of industrial civilization.* Boston: Harvard University Graduate School of Business, 1945.

McClelland, D. *The achieving society.* Princeton, N.J.: Van Nostrand, 1961.

McClelland, D., & Burnham, D. H. Power is the great motivator. *Harvard Business Review*, March–April 1976, pp. 100–110.

McGregor, D. M. *The human side of enterprise.* New York: McGraw-Hill, 1960.

McGregor, D. M. *The professional manager.* New York: McGraw-Hill, 1967.

McKelvey, B., & Kilmann, R. H. Organization design: A participative multivariate approach. *Administrative Science Quarterly*, 1975, *20*, 24–36.

Mead, G. H. *Mind, self, and society,* edited by C. W. Morris. Chicago: University of Chicago Press, 1930.

Merei, F. Group leadership and institutionalization. *Human Relations*, 1949, *2*, 23–39.

Miles, M. *Learning to work in groups.* New York: Teachers College, Columbia University, 1959.

Mintzberg, H. *The nature of managerial work.* New York: Harper & Row, 1973.

Moreno, J. L. *Who shall survive?* Washington, D. C.: Nervous and Mental Diseases Publishing Co., 1934.

Myers, M. S. *Every employee a manager.* New York: McGraw-Hill, 1970.

National Commission on Productivity and Work Quality. *A plant-wide productivity plan in action: Three years of experience with the Scanlon plan.* Washington, D.C., 1975.

Osipow, S. H. *Theories of career development,* 2nd ed. New York: Appleton-Century-Crofts, 1973.

Ouchi, W. G., & Jaeger, A. M. Social structure and organizational type. In M. W. Meyer & Associates (Eds.), *Environments and organizations.* San Francisco: Jossey-Bass, 1978.

Pearlin, L. I. Alienation from work. *American Sociological Review,* 1962, *27,* 314–326.

Pelz, D., & Andrews, F. M. Organizational atmosphere, motivation, and research contribution. *American Behavioral Scientist,* 1962, *6,* 43–47.

Perls, F., Hefferline, R., & Goodman, P. *Gestalt therapy.* New York: Delta, 1965.

Perrow, C. B. *Organizational analysis: A sociological view.* Belmont, Calif.: Brooks-Cole, 1970.

Pigors, P., & Myers, C. A. *Personnel administration,* 8th ed. New York: McGraw-Hill, 1977.

Pugh, D. S. The measurement of organization structure. *Organizational Dynamics,* 1973, *1,* 19–34.

Reitz, H. J. *Behavior in organizations.* Homewood, Ill.: Irwin, 1977.

Rice, A. K. *Productivity and social organization: The Ahmedabad experiment.* London: Tavistock Publications, 1958.

Rice, A. K. *The enterprise and its environment.* London: Tavistock Publications, 1963.

Roe, A. *The psychology of occupations.* New York: Wiley, 1956.

Roethlisberger, F. J., & Dickson, W. J. *Management and the worker.* Cambridge, Mass.: Harvard University Press, 1939.

Rogers, C. *On becoming a person.* Boston: Houghton-Mifflin, 1961.

Schachter, S. Deviation, rejection, and communication. *Journal of Abnormal and Social Psychology,* 1951, *46,* 190–207.

Schachter, S. *The psychology of affiliation.* Stanford, Calif.: Stanford University Press, 1959.

Schein, E. H. The Chinese indoctrination program for prisoners of war. *Psychiatry,* 1956, *19,* 149–172.

Schein, E. H. Management development as a process of influence. *Industrial Management Review,* 1961, *2,* 59–77.

Schein, E. H. How to break in the college graduate. *Harvard Business Review,* November–December 1964, pp. 68–76.

Schein, E. H. Organizational socialization and the profession of management. *Industrial Management Review,* 1968, *9,* 1–15.

Schein, E. H. *Process consultation: Its role in organization development.* Reading, Mass.: Addison-Wesley, 1969.

Schein, E. H. The reluctant professor: Implications for university management. *Sloan Management Review*, 1970, *12* (1), 35–49.

Schein, E. H. The role innovator and his education. *Technology Review*, 1970, *72*, 33–37.

Schein, E. H. The individual, the organization, and the career: A conceptual scheme. *Journal of Applied Behavioral Science*, 1971, *7*, 401–426.

Schein, E. H. *Professional education: Some new directions.* New York: McGraw-Hill, 1972.

Schein, E. H. How "career anchors" hold executives to their career paths. *Personnel*, 1975, *52* (No. 3), 11–24.

Schein, E. H. *Career dynamics.* Reading, Mass.: Addison-Wesley, 1978. (a)

Schein, E. H. The role of the consultant: Content expert or process facilitator? *Personnel and Guidance Journal*, February 1978, pp. 339–343. (b)

Schein, E. H., & Bennis, W. G. *Personal and organizational change through group methods.* New York: Wiley, 1965.

Schein, E. H., & Ott, J. S. The legitimacy of organizational influence. *American Journal of Sociology*, 1962, *67*, 682–689.

Schein, E. H., Schneier, I., & Barker, C. H. *Coercive persuasion.* New York: Norton, 1961.

Schrank, R. *Ten thousand working days.* Cambridge, Mass.: MIT Press, 1978.

Seashore, S. F. *Group cohesiveness in the industrial work group.* Ann Arbor, Mich.: Survey Research Center, University of Michigan, 1954.

Shaw, M. E. *Group dynamics: The psychology of small groups.* New York: McGraw-Hill, 1971.

Sherif, M., Harvey, O. J., White, B. J., Hood, W. R., & Sherif, C. *Intergroup conflict and cooperation: The robbers' cave experiment.* Norman, Okla.: University Book Exchange, 1961.

Sherif, M., & Sherif, C. *Social psychology.* New York: Harper & Row, 1969.

Silberbauer, E. R. *Understanding and motivating the Bantu worker.* Johannesburg, South Africa: Personnel Management Advisory Service, 1968.

Simon, H. A. *The new science of management decisions.* New York: Harper & Row, 1960.

Speer, A. *Inside the third reich.* New York: Macmillan, 1970.

Steers, R. M. *Organizational effectiveness: A behavioral view.* Santa Monica, Calif.: Goodyear, 1977.

Stogdill, R. M. Personal factors associated with leadership: A survey of the literature. *Journal of Psychology*, 1948, *25*.

Stogdill, R. M., & Coons, A. E. (Eds.). *Leader behavior: its description and measurement*. Columbus, Ohio: Ohio State University, 1957.

Stoner, J. A. Risky and cautious shifts in group decisions: The influence of widely held values. *Journal of Experimental Social Psychology*, 1968, 4, 442–459.

Strauss, G. Workers: Attitudes and adjustments. In J. M. Rosow (Ed.), *The worker and the job*. Englewood Cliffs, N.J.: Prentice-Hall, 1974.

Strong, E. K. *Vocational interests of men and women*. Stanford, Calif.: Stanford University Press, 1943.

Super, D. E., & Bohn, M. J. *Occupational psychology*. Belmont, Calif.: Wadsworth, 1970.

Tannenbaum, R., & Schmidt, H. W. How to choose a leadership pattern. *Harvard Business Review*, March–April 1958.

Taylor, D. W., Berry, P. C., & Block, C. H. Does group participation when using brain-storming techniques facilitate or inhibit creative thinking. *Administrative Science Quarterly*, 1958, 3, 23–47.

Terkel, S. *Working*. New York: Random House, 1974.

Thompson, J. D. *Organizations in action*. New York: McGraw-Hill, 1967.

Thompson, J. D., & McEwen, W. J. Organizational goals and environment. *American Sociological Review*, 1958, 23, 23–30.

Trist, E. L., Higgin, G. W., Murray, H. & Pollock, A. B. *Organizational choice*. London: Tavistock Publications, 1963.

Trist, E. L., & Bamforth, K. W. Some social and psychological consequences of the long-wall method of coal getting. *Human Relations*, 1951, 4, 1–38.

Van Beinum, H. J. J., & deBel, P. D. *Improving attitudes toward work especially by participation*. London: Tavistock Publications, No. HRC 101, 1968.

Van Maanen, J. Breaking in: Socialization to work. In R. Dubin, (Ed.), *Handbook of work, organization and society*. Chicago: Rand-McNally, 1976.

Van Maanen, J., & Schein, E. H. Improving the quality of work life: Career development. In J. R. Hackman & J. L. Suttle (Eds.), *Improving life at work*. Santa Monica, Calif.: Goodyear, 1977.

Van Maanen, J., & Schein, E. H. Toward a theory of organizational socialization. In B. Staw (Ed.), *Research in organizational behavior*, Vol. I, Greenwich, Conn.: JAI Press, Inc., 1979.

Van Maanen, J., Schein, E. H., & Bailyn, L. The shape of things to come: A new look at organizational careers. In J. R. Hackman, E. E. Lawler, & L. W. Porter (Eds.), *Perspectives on behavior in organizations*. New York: McGraw-Hill, 1977.

Vroom, V. H. *Some personality determinants of the effects of participation*. Englewood Cliffs, N.J.: Prentice-Hall, 1960.

Vroom, V. H. Leadership revisited. In E. L. Cass & F. G. Zimmer (Eds.), *Man and work in society*. New York: Van Nostrand Reinhold, 1975.

Vroom, V. H. Can leaders learn to lead? *Organizational Dynamics*, Winter 1976, pp. 17–28.

Vroom, V. H., & Yetton, P. W. *Leadership and decision making*. Pittsburgh, Pa.: University of Pittsburgh Press, 1973.

Walker, C. R., & Guest, R. H. *The man on the assembly line*. Cambridge, Mass.: Harvard University Press, 1952.

Walton, R. E. *Interpersonal peacemaking: Confrontations and third party consultation*. Reading, Mass.: Addison-Wesley, 1969.

Walton, R. E. How to counter alienation in the plant. *Harvard Business Review*, November–December 1972, pp. 70–81.

Walton, R. E. Improving the quality of work life. *Harvard Business Review*, May–June 1974, pp. 12ff.

Walton, R. E. The diffusion of new work structures: Explaining why success didn't take. *Organizational Dynamics*, Winter 1975, pp. 3–22. (a)

Walton, R. E. From Hawthorne to Topeka to Kalmar. In E. L. Cass & F. G. Zimmer (Eds.), *Man and work in society*. New York: Van Nostrand Reinhold, 1975.

Weber, M. *The theory of social and economic organization*, edited by T. Parsons. Glencoe, Ill.: The Free Press, 1947.

Whyte, W. F. *The street corner society*. Chicago: University of Chicago Press, 1943.

Whyte, W. F. *Human relations in the restaurant industry*. New York: McGraw-Hill, 1948.

Whyte, W. F. *Money and motivation: An analysis of incentives in industry*. New York: Harper & Row, 1955.

Woodward, J. *Industrial organization: Theory and practice*. London: Oxford University Press, 1965.

Wrightsman, L. S. Measurement of philosophies of human nature. *Psychological Reports*, 1964, *14*, 743–751.

Wrightsman, L. S. *Assumptions about human nature*. Monterey, Calif.: Brooks-Cole, 1974.

Wrightsman, L. S. *Social psychology*. Monterey, Calif.: Brooks-Cole, 1977.

Yankelovich, D. The meaning of work. In J. M. Rosow (Ed.), *The worker and the job*. Englewood Cliffs, N.J.: Prentice-Hall, 1974.

Zaleznik, A., Christensen, C. R., & Roethlisberger, F. J. *The motivation, productivity, and satisfaction of workers: A prediction study*. Boston: Division of Research, Harvard Business School, 1958.

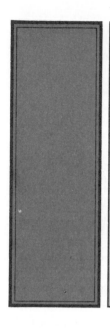

Subject Index

Author
Index

8194